New English First

49p

Poetry Anthologies edited by Rhodri Jones

Themes Series

Men and Beasts
Imagination
Conflict
Generations
Men at Work
Town and Country

Preludes Series

Families
Work and Play
Weathers
Five Senses

New English First

by
Rhodri Jones

Headmaster, John Kelly Boys' High School, Brent

Heinemann Educational Books
LONDON

Heinemann Educational Books

LONDON EDINBURGH MELBOURNE AUCKLAND
TORONTO HONG KONG SINGAPORE KUALA LUMPUR
IBADAN NAIROBI JOHANNESBURG
NEW DELHI LUSAKA KINGSTON

ISBN 0 435 10494 2

First published 1978

Designed and illustrated by Chris Gilbert

Published by
Heinemann Educational Books Ltd
48 Charles Street, London W1X 8AH
Printed and bound in Great Britain by Butler and Tanner Ltd
Frome and London

Contents

Acknowledgements

The author and publishers wish to thank the following for permission to reproduce copyright material:

The Literary Trustees of Walter de la Mare and the Society of Authors as their representative for 'Me' by Walter de la Mare; Jonathan Cape and the Executors of the C. Day Lewis Estate for 'Circus Lion' from *Collected Poems 1954*; Michael Joseph for the extract from *A Kestrel for a Knave* by Barry Hines and for the extract from *There is A Happy Land* by Keith Waterhouse; J. M. Dent & Sons and Trustees for the Copyrights of the late Dylan Thomas for the extract from 'Holiday Memory' from *Quite Early One Morning*; Faber & Faber for the extract from *The Winter of the Birds* by Helen Cresswell and for 'Elephants' from 'Circus' from *The Collected Poems of Louis MacNeice*; Penguin Books Ltd for the extracts from *The School that I'd Like* ed. Edward Blishen, for the extract from *A Dog So Small* by Philippa Pearce and for 'A Dog in the Quarry' by Miroslav Holub from *Selected Poems*; Kestrel Books and Penguin Books Ltd for the extract from *The Night the Water Came* © Clive King 1973; Hamish Hamilton for the extract from *The Fishing Party* by William Mayne, for 'A Snapshot of Rex' from *Thurber Carnival* by James Thurber and Hamish Hamilton and John Christopher for the extract from *The White Mountain* by John Christopher; Macmillan London and Basingstoke for 'The Caged Bird in Springtime' by James Kirkup from *Poetry Back* by Gibson and Wilson and for the extract from *Jennifer, Hecate, Macbeth and Me* by E. L. Konigsburg; James Kirkup for 'Thunder and Lightning' from *The Prodigal Son*; Chatto & Windus for 'Merry-Go-Round' by David Gill from *The Pagoda* and for the extract from *A High Wind in Jamaica* by Richard Hughes; Collins for the extract from *The Weirdstone of Brisingamen* by Alan Garner; Mr S. Selvan for *Man, in England, you've just got to love animals* by Samuel Selvan; Victor Gollancz for the extract from *The Peppermint Pig* by Nina Bawden; Harcourt Brace Jovanovich, Inc. for 'Who do you think you are?' from *The People, Yes* by Carl Sandburg © 1936 by Harcourt Brace Jovanovich, Inc. © 1964 by Carl Sandburg and for 'Arithmetic' from *Complete Poems* © 1950 by Carl Sandburg; Mrs R. C. Ashbee for the extracts from *William—In Trouble* by Richmal Crompton; A. D. Peters & Co. Ltd for the extract from *Sound of Thunder* by Ray Bradbury; Francis Selormy for the extract from *The Narrow Path* (published in the African Writers Series, Heinemann Educational Books); Lutterworth Press and Harper & Row for the extract from *The Tower by the Sea* by Meindert de Jong; Pergamon Press Ltd for the extract from *London Morning* by Valerie Avery; The Bodley Head for the extract from *Beowulf: Dragon Slayer* by Rosemary Sutcliff; Oxford University Press for the extract from *Tom's Midnight Garden* by Philippa Pearce; Andre Deutsch Ltd for the extract 'Cricket in the Road' from *Sandra Street* by Michael Anthony; Doubleday & Co. Inc. for *The Tom-cat* by Don Marquis; Martin Secker & Warburg Ltd for 'Saturday Storm' from *Times Three* by Phyllis McGinley; Mrs A. M. Walsh for 'Last Day of the Summer Term' from *The Truants* by John Walsh; Julian Mitchell for his poem 'Holiday'; Daily Mirror Children's Literary Competition for 'Christmas' by Thomas Royle.

It has not been possible in all cases to trace copyright-holders; the publishers would be glad to hear from any such unacknowledged copyright-holders.

Illustrations

Introduction

For the Pupil

This course is intended to help you to a deeper understanding of what English is about. It should help you to gain pleasure and understanding from reading, and skill and fluency in writing and talking. It is not meant to be easy. If you wish to improve your ability in English, you will have to work hard. There is no getting away from that.

Included in the course are many pieces of writing, some taken from what might be called traditional examples of English literature, some from writing specifically aimed at young readers, and some which have been written by people of your own age. It is hoped that you will enjoy these for their own sake and also find in them a source of inspiration for your own writing.

For the Teacher

This course is designed for use with mixed ability classes. The material is intentionally demanding, and some pupils may find some of it difficult. But no pupil will improve his command of written and spoken English unless he is stretched and comes face to face with the challenge of new ideas, new imaginative adventures, new words and new ways of looking at and understanding words.

If pupils are to meet this challenge successfully, the teacher is, of course, essential. He must encourage and guide and be ready to adapt the material, where necessary, to the particular needs of his class and to the needs of individuals within his class. As well as providing much practice in writing and reading, the course is intended to provide much opportunity for oral work which the teacher can initiate, and to which pupils of all abilities can contribute their ideas and experiences. Since all young people also enjoy being read aloud to, it is hoped that the teacher will use his skill to bring alive the many extracts from novels used in the course and to make them more readily accessible to his pupils whatever their ability.

UNIT 1

All About Me

 ### Reading and Understanding

Why do people read?

Here are some possible answers to that question.

1. People read to obtain information. For example, if you want to know what is on television at five thirty on Saturday evening, you look up the *Radio Times* or the daily newspaper; if you want to know the meaning of the word 'pterodactyl', you look it up in a dictionary. (What *does* it mean?)

2. They read for pleasure. For example, people enjoy adventure stories because they want to know what happens next, what the ending is. They also enjoy reading about people doing things that they themselves would never have the chance of doing.

3. They read to find out about other people's lives. We are all – or nearly all – curious about other people, about our neighbours, about the people in the next street, about the workmen on the building site around the corner, or about the other children playing in the park. It is the same with reading. If our interest is aroused, we want to learn as much as we can about real people who do unusual things, or about characters that writers have invented. They can help us share other worlds or take us into places where we could never actually go ourselves.

4. Reading can also help us to make up our minds about how we should lead our lives. It can help us decide between what is right and what is wrong. It can shape our opinions and influence our views. For instance, some people's lives are guided by what they read in the Bible. But there are less obvious examples too. Perhaps a story about a boy being saved from drowning will encourage the reader to be brave as well, or a story about a fox being hunted will persuade the reader that blood sports are cruel.

What do you enjoy reading?

Has anything you have read influenced your views or opinions?

Find further examples of each of the reasons for reading given above.

Can you think of any other reasons why people read?

Comics

In one sentence, describe what a comic is.

Do you read comics? What do you enjoy about them?

Describe some of the favourite characters you know from comics.

Some adults say comics are bad for you. Can you think of any reasons why this might be?

People Writing about Themselves

In the course of this book, we shall be looking at different kinds of writing. Some will give us factual information; others will be simply for enjoyment. Some will tell us about how people live and what kind of people they are; others will help us make up our minds about important things.

Let's start with some writing about people. It is written by the people themselves, members of a class like yours, about your own age.

Portrait of a Tutor Group

My interests in the subjects at school – English is the best lesson. Though, I could do better at English, because I find poetry comes easy, but in stories and essays, I am not too sure. French I like next because it's a different language, and I like the country France. And one day when I have enough French to succeed in this, I hope to write a French poem. I like science a lot, and often at home I have a discussion with my Dad about say what is beyond space – the answer normally is obviously space. When I was younger I cried when I found out there were no women astronauts.

When I was five I always stroked every dog I saw. One day there was this big bull-dog chained up. It was growling and showing its teeth. I walked near and put out my hand. My Mum pulled me back and started telling me off, etc. At which I replied, No, Mum, look it's laughing.

LORRAINE

There are a great many things I like and I don't, e.g. I like girls, football, athletics, fashion. I like going out, people, travelling and life, and taking clocks apart and motor racing. I don't like winter, fishing, swimming, cross-country, old houses, people who nag and always have the miseries, coppers. I hate to get up in the morning and fighting.

ALAN

My interests are making planes out of wood and scouting and seeing places like Holland and Norway and Germany. I dislike green foods and all that and maths and French. I like sweets. I like getting my own way. I would like to be a pilot. I am a bit nervous. At one time I got stuck in a lift. Then I was nervous. I like drawing.

LESLIE

When I grow up I would like to be a ballerina as I am now training to be. At times I am very stingy with my food and always want a second sharing. At home I am the best at eating food.

AUDRÉ

I like animals, babies and young children. I like summer and swimming. I like going out with my friends. I also like going out at night, but I don't get much of a chance because my Mum and Dad don't like it.

SANDRA

I dislike the age I am because it is a between age. You are too old to play with dolls and too young to stay out late (10 or 11 at night). I would sooner be at school because I have heard that when you are at work you wish you were back at school.

SUSAN

I don't like all these flash clothes. I go around in jeans, T-shirt and polo-neck jumper. When I grow up I would like to be a draughtsman or underwater biologist. I don't like girls much because they get on my nerves.

PAUL

I like football, darts, swimming, travelling and also climbing up to high places, and camping with a tent in my back garden. I don't like sports that are dangerous like cricket, rugby and golf. My interests are keeping pets like cats, dogs, rabbits and many other animals. I don't like being bossed around too much. I like school when there's nothing else to do. My favourite lessons are drama, English and gymnastics, counting football. The only thing that ever happened to me was when I was nearly kidnapped.

I like girls that are usually blond. I don't like people that talk a lot or keep coming to my house every time a big feature film starts.

COSTAS

I eat a lot of sweets. I don't like keeping quiet. I like talkative friends. I'm not lazy but I don't like brushing my teeth. I collect stamps. I dislike vegetables.

ROBBY

I don't like being in a quiet place much. I suppose I have quite a sense of humour but I don't like it when the joke's on me. I don't like people who go on at me because they are better than me.

MICHAEL

I like fishing. I go to the Norfolk Broads. My Mum says I help her a lot. I like watching television. I have lots of friends. When I am in trouble, they help me.

MARTIN

My main interest is football and I play quite a lot. I like mostly any kind of food but I am not keen on chops, parsnips and fish. I don't really have any hobbies, but I have a lot of interest in pop records and collecting football souvenirs. I don't mind reading, but I like to read mostly football things.

JOHN

I stop and look at the reflection on the wall and I wonder if it is me. I am unlike anyone I know and yet I am the same. I have the same values, I am jealous and if people hurt me I hurt them back. I like people who like me and I dislike people who dislike me. I like people to think highly of me.

Certain things irritate me – open doors, sweaty hands. I like to work on my own or with someone on whom I'm not dependent. I dislike all forms of housework and prefer to read or work. People irritate me and I sometimes enjoy hurting them.

I'm not sure what my attitude to life is but I know I have to work to get anywhere. Knowing this I find no patience with people who are slow or just don't care. I may get angry or upset but over the years I have tried not to show it – sometimes not with very good results. I enjoy school and like to do well at it. As a person I prefer not to stand out in a crowd. For this reason I prefer darker coloured clothes and ordinary hairstyles.

Looking at the reflection I realise that it is how I appear to other people not to myself. According to their own nature they can interpret my reflection in other ways.

JUNE

Talk about these people and what they say.
Can you form an idea of what each is like from what they say?
Are any of them like you? Do any of them share your likes and dislikes?
Which of them think more deeply about themselves?
Which of them would you like to meet?

A Class Portrait

Study this photograph of a class.
Can you tell anything about any of the people from the way they look? (Look at their smiles and the way they hold their hands.) Do you think they enjoy being photographed?

 Writing

Who am I?

If you were asked the question, 'Who are you?', you could answer, 'I am Jeremy Spencer or Mary Henderson' or whatever your name is. But that doesn't tell the questioner very much. On the other hand, if you give the questioner a few more details about yourself, he is able to build up a much fuller picture. You could tell him where you were born, about your family, about your likes and dislikes, about your pets, about your opinions, about what you look like, about the kind of friends you have. All of these present a portrait which could only be a portrait of you and no one else. Here is a poem which is saying more or less the same thing.

Me

As long as I live
I shall always be
My Self – and no other,
Just me.

Like a tree –
Willow, elder,
Aspern, thorn,
Or cypress forlorn.

Like a flower,
For its hour –
Primrose, or pink,

Or a violet –
Sunned by the sun,
And with dewdrops wet.

Always just me.
Till the day come on
When I leave this body,
It's all then done.
And the spirit within it
Is gone.

WALTER DE LA MARE

Why does the poet compare himself to different trees and different flowers?

Sum up in a sentence the idea the poet is trying to get across.

What is a Man?

On the other hand, you could take a more down to earth view of who you are as in this poem.

Who do you think you are
and where do you think you came from?
From toenails to the hair of your head you are
  mixed of the earth, of the air,
Of compounds equal to the burning gold and
  amethyst lights of the Mountains of the
  Blood of Christ at Santa Fe.
Listen to the laboratory man tell what you are
  made of, man, listen while he takes you apart.
Weighing 150 pounds you hold 3,500 cubic feet of
  gas – oxygen, hydrogen, nitrogen.
From the 22 pounds and 10 ounces of carbon in
  you is the filling for 9,000 lead pencils.
In your blood are 50 grains of iron and in the rest
  of your frame enough iron to make a spike
  that would hold your weight.
From your 50 ounces of phosphorus could be
  made 800,000 matches and elsewhere in
  your physical premises are hidden 60 lumps
  of sugar, 20 teaspoons of salt, 38 quarts of
  water, two ounces of lime, and scatterings of
  starch, chloride of potash, magnesium, sul-
  phur, hydrochloric acid.
You are a walking drug store and also a cosmos
  and a phantasmagoria treading a lonesome
  valley, one of the people, one of the minions
  and myrmidons who would like an answer to
  the question, 'Who and what are you?'

CARL SANDBURG

(There are some difficult words here. 'Cosmos' means 'the universe'; 'phantasmagoria' means 'imaginary shadowy figure'; 'minions' means 'servants'; 'myrmidons' means 'hired ruffians'.)

The poet is giving the view of 'the laboratory man', the scientist, who sees that all people are the same, made up of the same chemicals, though perhaps in different proportions.

Do you agree with this view, or is there more to man than this?

Is there anything in the poem to suggest that the poet believes there is more to human beings than this?

Hopes for the Future

Another way of writing about yourself is by describing your hopes for the future. Here is Edward Flack writing about what he wants to be when he grows up. In the course of his account he tells us a great deal about himself. (*Beware:* Edward was sometimes careless about his spelling!)

What Edward Flack Wrote In His Exercise Book, Headed 'What I Would Like To Be When I Grow Up'. And Which, After Reading It Through, He Carefully Tore Out And Replaced With a Harmless Piece About Wanting To Be A Footballer, An Almost Exact Replica Of All The Other Essays Sent In By The Boys In His Class

What I would like to be when I grow up, is a hero. I read a lot of books and in all of them my Favourate person is always the hero. But I do not just mean that. I mean, every book has a hero, it has to, but not necessarily what I would call a *real* hero. For instance in this book I have been reading called *Stig of the Dump* there is this boy called Barney that has all the adventures, but this does not mean that he is an actual hero. A real hero is a man who does bold and noble deeds, David in David and Goliath and Perseus and St George and so on to mention a few names.

My favourate hero is Hercules because he did not just stop at doing one or two bold deeds, but kept right on doing them the whole time (and so did Robin Hood for that matter, another of my favourates.) Practicly everything he did was a brave and noble deed and he was as strong as a lion. Even when he was only a baby he strangled a snake in his cradle, so he must have been born a hero I suppose as the average baby would not even think of doing this. Gary Ferrands who lives up our street is around the same age as Hercules was when he strangled the snake which is less than a year old, and all he does is just lie there in his pram and twang these blue plastic ducks he has. Not that I am criticizing as I realise that I was proberly just the same at that age and so are most babies, but it does tend to show that heroes are born and not made and so perhaps I have not got much chance of becoming one.

You might wonder how I have got it into my head to become a hero and I think the real reason is not having a real father. I think boys like to grow up like their fathers but as I do not know who my father was or my mother I do not know what to be like. It is as if I could be *anything* if you see what I mean, and if I really can be, then I choose to be a hero. I like to think that my real father was something like an ace pilot for instance or a mountaineer who was killed performing a feat of daring. And I think my mother proberly died of a broken heart after this.

You may say why not model yourself on your foster father but this really is not the same thing at all and I know I would not really like being a bus conductor. And I expect my foster mother would like me to take over her grocery shop when I grow up but there is no chance of this though I have not told her yet.

My real trouble is that although I would like to be a hero I already know that I was not born one. And of course you cannot go and train as one, like being an engineer or a teacher for instance, and so I realise that I will have to train myself. This means for one thing doing a daily feat of daring if possible. I have already started doing this. I picked a fight with Patrick MacKay only last week and got my lip cut and blood all over my jacket and only just lost. I also climbed up Ma Briggses wall for a dare and pinched that old pair of wheels that have been in her yard for ages and which we're going to make into a go-cart. I have got hold of a book of exercises for training the RAF and am doing some each day before breakfast although in fact I do not show much prowess at press-ups etc. I have also started daring myself things, the main one of which is not to be afraid of the dark, which I am afraid I am rather. I do a kind of test or ordeal every night and am sure I am improving.

So there is a chance that I can train myself for this job in life but there is only one thing that bothers me and that is this. If for instance Hercules was alive today or St George what would they do to *be* heroes? There just do not seem to be the jobs for heroes that there used to be and of course no dragons or nine headed monsters or anything like that or at least not to my knowledge. It is obvious that David would have been no good whatever without Goliath, and I keep on wondering who or what will be my Goliath? I suppose if David had not found his he would have just been an unsung hero and no one would ever have heard of him. And the whole point of heroes is that everyone hears about them and marvels at their great and mighty deeds.

I always go through the newspaper at home to see if there is anything about a hero in them and also watch the television news, but so far there has been no sign of one. In fact all the headlines seem to be about politics and so on, and sometimes I really worry about this and wonder if nowadays we have politicians instead of heroes. I think it is a very bad swap. None of the politicians I ever seen on television are anything like a patch on Perseus or Hercules and in fact many of them seem really silly and even my mother says they are terrible liars. Also I think you can tell a lot from people's faces and I have never yet seen a politician with a face I really like and they are usually rather fat.

There was this boy on *Blue Peter* who had got a special award for saving two other boys in a dingy

which had overturned and that was certainly a very brave deed. But when you actuerly saw the boy you could not actuerly imagine him making a career out of being a hero. He was just an ordinary boy really and rather a let down when you actuerly saw him.

Mike MacKay says he is going into the army when he is old enough and I think he thinks that will be a brave and noble thing to do. But I could not disagree more. I think that all wars are wicked and stupid and when I see all those poor people in Vietnam for instance on the television I feel really sick. What point is there in killing innocent people just for a piece of land which is what most wars are about from what I can gather. And how can the soldiers bring themselves to shoot and bomb other people? Mr Brown's son is a soldier and when he comes home and walks up the Street in his uniform I often look at him and just cannot imagine him wanting to kill anyone or actually firing a gun at somebody. He is perfectly ordinary from what I can see and once even bought me an ice cream. They say it is orders that makes them do it, but what kind of orders are they to tell you to do a thing like that? No soldier is a hero in my view. In fact all soldiers are just like sheep. And there again, I *know* Mike MacKay and anyone less like a hero you could not imagine. I mean he is strong all right I do not deny this, but there is more to being a hero than that.

I have rather gone off the point here but I do feel strongly about war and so on. But to get back to my own problems. At school Mr Fowler is always saying human nature never changes and that history repeats itself and so on, and so I am quite sure that there *is* room for heroes, even nowadays, and shall not give up hope.

I do not suppose for a moment that David for instance knew about Goliath when he was my age or that Robin Hood knew that he was going to grow up to rob the rich to feed the poor. So I shall just get on with the job of training myself and trust that by the time I am old enough to be a real hero something will turn up. Heroes do not get discoraged easily and I do not mean to either.

HELEN CRESSWELL, *The Winter of the Birds*

What, according to Edward, is the difference between a hero in a book and 'a real hero'?

Why was Hercules Edward's favourite hero?

What does Edward mean when he says 'heroes are born and not made'?

Why does Edward put down his wanting to be a hero to the fact that he doesn't have a real father?

How does Edward train to be a hero?

What does he see as the main difficulty today about being a hero?

Why does Edward not regard soldiers as heroes?

What does Mr Fowler mean when he says 'history repeats itself'?

Why do you think Edward tore out this description of his hopes and replaced it by one in which he said he wanted to be a footballer?

Discuss some of the ideas Edward has about heroes, parents, war and the world today.

Who would be your hero?

What would you like to be when you grow up?

The Way People do Things

Another way we can learn about people is by watching the way they do things. The way a person folds a tablecloth or puts down his coat can tell us something about the kind of person he is. The same is true of writing. Read the following extract in which Huckleberry Finn describes how he hopes to escape without trace. (*Beware:* Huckleberry writes very much as he speaks and doesn't bother very much about grammar.)

While we laid off, after breakfast, to sleep up, both of us being about wore out, I got to thinking that if I could fix up some way to keep pap and the widow from trying to follow me, it would be a certainer thing than trusting to luck to get far enough off before they missed me; you see, all kinds of things might happen. Well, I didn't see no way for a while, but by-and-by pap raised up a minute, to drink another barrel of water, and he says:

'Another time a man comes a-prowling round here, you roust me out, you hear? That man warn't here for no good. I'd a shot him. Next time, you roust me out, you hear?'

Then he dropped down and went to sleep again – but what he had been saying give me the very idea I wanted. I says to myself, I can fix it now so nobody won't think of following me.

About twelve o'clock we turned out and went along up the bank. The river was coming up pretty fast, and lots of driftwood going by on the rise. By-and-by along comes part of a log raft – nine logs fast together. We went out with the skiff and towed it ashore. Then we had dinner. Anybody but pap would a waited and seen the day through, so as to

8

catch more stuff; but that warn't pap's style. Nine logs was enough for one time; he must shove right over to town and sell. So he locked me in and took the skiff and started off towing the raft about half-past three. I judged he wouldn't come back that night. I waited till I reckoned he had got a good start, then I out with my saw and went to work on that log again. Before he was t'other side of the river I was out of the hole; him and his raft was just a speck on the water away off yonder.

I took the sack of corn meal and took it to where the canoe was hid, and shoved the vines and branches apart and put it in; then I done the same with the side of bacon; then the whisky jug; I took all the coffee and sugar there was, and all the ammunition; I took the wadding; I took the bucket and gourd, I took a dipper and a tin cup, and my old saw and two blankets, and the skillet and the coffee-pot. I took the fish-lines and matches, and other things – everything that was worth a cent. I cleaned out the place. I wanted an axe, but there wasn't any, only the one out at the wood pile, and I knowed why I was going to leave that. I fetched out the gun, and now I was done.

I had wore the ground a good deal, crawling out of the hole and dragging out so many things. So I fixed that as good as I could from the outside by scattering dust on the place, which covered up the smoothness and the sawdust. Then I fixed the piece of log back into its place, and put two rocks under it and one against it to hold it there – for it was bent up at that place, and didn't quite touch ground. If you stood four or five feet away and didn't know it was sawed, you wouldn't even notice it; and besides, this was the back of the cabin and it warn't likely anybody would go fooling around there.

It was all grass clear to the canoe; so I hadn't left a track. I followed around to see. I stood on the bank and looked out over the river. All safe. So I took the gun and went up a piece into the woods and was hunting around for some birds, when I see a wild pig; hogs soon went wild in them bottoms after they had got away from the prairie farms. I shot this fellow and took him into camp.

I took the axe and smashed in the door. I beat it and hacked it considerably, a-doing it. I fetched the pig in and took him back nearly to the table and hacked into his throat with the axe, and laid him down on the ground to bleed – I say ground, because it *was* ground – hard packed, and no boards. Well, next I took an old sack and put a lot of big rocks in it – all I could drag – and I started it from the pig and dragged it to the door and through the woods down to the river and dumped it in, and down it sunk, out of sight. You could easy see that something had been dragged over the ground. I did wish Tom Sawyer was there, I knowed he would take an interest in this kind of business, and throw in the fancy touches. Nobody could spread himself like Tom Sawyer in such a thing as that.

Well, last I pulled out some of my hair, and bloodied the axe good, and stuck it on the back side, and slung the axe in the corner. Then I took up the pig and held him to my breast with my jacket (so he couldn't drip) till I got a good piece below the house and then dumped him into the river. Now I thought of something else. So I went and got the bag of meal and my old saw out of the canoe and fetched them to the house. I took the bag to where it used to stand, and ripped a hole in the bottom of it with the saw, for there warn't no knives and forks in the place – pap done everything with his clasp-knife, about the cooking. Then I carried the sack about a hundred yards across the grass and through the willows east of the house, to a shallow lake that was five miles wide and full of rushes – and ducks too, you might say, in the season. There was a slough or a creek leading out of it on the other side, that went miles away, I don't know where, but it didn't go to the river. The meal sifted out and made a little track all the way to the lake. I dropped pap's whetstone there too, so as to look like it had been done by accident. Then I tied up the rip in the meal sack with a string, so it wouldn't leak no more, and took it and my saw to the canoe again.

It was about dark, now; so I dropped the canoe down the river under some willows that hung over the bank, and waited for the moon to rise. I made fast to a willow; then I took a bite to eat, and by-and-by laid down in the canoe to smoke a pipe and lay out a plan. I says to myself, they'll follow the track of that sackful of rocks to the shore and then drag the river for me. And they'll follow that meal track to the lake and go browsing down the creek that leads out of it to find the robbers that killed me and took the things. They won't ever hunt the river for anything but my dead carcass. They'll soon get tired of that, and won't bother no more about me. All right; I can stop anywhere I want to. Jackson's Island is good enough for me; I know that island pretty well, and nobody ever comes there. And then I can paddle over to town, nights, and slink around and pick up things I want. Jackson's Island's the place.

MARK TWAIN,

The Adventures of Huckleberry Finn

Instead of leaving it to luck, Huck thought it better to do what?

How do his father's warnings give Huck this idea?

How did Huck's father make a living?

Do you get the impression that Huck's father is hard-working? Give reasons for your answer.

Describe briefly what Huck's plan is and how he goes about it.

What do you think of the plan? Do you think it will work?

What does this account tell us about the kind of person Huck is?

Assignments

Choose one or more of the following to write about:

1. You may be starting life at a new school or you may have a new teacher who doesn't yet know very much about you. Write an account of yourself, remembering the different things that have been discussed so far, so that your teacher can get a clearer view of you as an individual.
2. Make a list of your likes and dislikes. Perhaps you could arrange them in a pattern as a poem.
3. Write down ten sentences about yourself, each of which contains a fact about yourself.
4. If you weren't you, who would you like to be?
5. Describe an incident from your life in which you played a large part.
6. Write about your earliest memories.
7. Look at the picture on the opposite page (of the boy holding two birds). Tell his story as though he himself were speaking.

Language

A. Standard English and Dialect

The language we speak and write is a very complex instrument. It can take many forms depending on such things as where we live, who we are speaking to, what we are trying to communicate. For instance, when you address a friend would you speak differently and use different words from those you would use when you are speaking to the headmaster? Would you expect someone who was born and lives in Scotland to speak differently from someone brought up in London? Would you use words differently in a letter you wrote to your parents while you were on holiday compared with a letter you wrote to the R.S.P.C.A. asking for material for a school project or a letter you wrote to your local newspaper complaining about the lack of playing facilities in your area? Discuss what these differences are and why they exist.

Standard English is the name often given to the more formal English that is found in serious newspapers (such as *The Times*, the *Guardian* or the *Daily Telegraph*) or in radio and television news reports. An understanding of what Standard English is and an ability to employ it are useful in many social and more formal situations, and advice on this is very much part of what this course is about.

Standard English is a kind of universally accepted English. It is not fixed and is changing all the time, but it is generally recognized. Its use enables people from different parts of the country (and, indeed, different parts of the world) to understand each other. Speaking among friends, we might use expressions which people living in another part of the country or another part of the world might not know. If these expressions were very different from Standard English, they could be regarded as part of a dialect.

Dialects can use language in a lively and interesting way. But if you want to be able to communicate with other people (who may come from a different part of the country) then you have to be able to use Standard English. This applies particularly to writing.

Look again at the passage from The Adventures of Huckleberry Finn. *Pick out any words or expressions or ways of saying things that strike you as strange or which you think might not be Standard English.*

Here are some expressions from 'Geordie' or the dialect used in the area of Tyneside. The

spelling emphasizes the pronunciation. Try saying them.

> *Haad yer gobs*: Keep quiet
> *Wordaz on the buroo*: Father is unemployed
> *Hadaway an' get a shyeul o' coal oot the cree*: Put some coal on the fire
> *Aal cloot yer lugs*: I'll clip your ears
> *Wor bairn's hacky mucky*: The baby needs a wash
> *Yer byeuts is clarty*: Your boots are muddy
> *Say taa taa te yor da*: Say goodbye to your father.

If you can't pronounce them, ask your teacher to try.

Does the area you live in have a particular dialect? If so, give examples with translations in Standard English.

Write a story involving a meeting between a local inhabitant and a stranger to the district where a misunderstanding arises through one not knowing what the other is saying.

Make a list in alphabetical order of words which you think might be peculiar to your area. Give their Standard English equivalents. Your teacher may be able to help you.

B. The First Person

Look again at 'The Portrait of a Tutor Group', Edward Flack's story and the extract from *The Adventures of Huckleberry Finn*. You could imagine that the people concerned are all speaking directly to you and someone else has simply written it down. They all use 'I' and 'me' and 'myself'. Any writing or speech from this point of view is said to be in the First Person. 'I', 'me', 'myself' and 'mine' all refer to a single person – there is only one of you. If you are talking about you and your friends, you would use 'we', 'us', 'ourselves' and 'ours'. These are also in the First Person, but they are plural because more than one person is involved. If you worked on any of the suggestions given at the end of the 'Writing' section, you would have used 'I', 'me', 'myself' and 'mine'. You might also have used 'we', 'us', 'ourselves' and 'ours' as well if you were describing something which you share with other people.

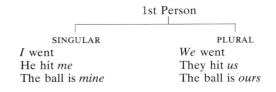

1st Person	
SINGULAR	PLURAL
I went	*We* went
He hit *me*	They hit *us*
The ball is *mine*	The ball is *ours*

All words are divided into different groups o categories according to how they are used i sentences. The name given to the differen categories is Parts of Speech. 'I' belongs to tha group of words known as Pronouns. **A pronou is a word that stands in place of a noun or name** For instance, instead of saying, 'I like fish an chips', you could say, 'Tom or Sandra (or wha ever your name is) likes fish and chips'. Th meaning would be the same, but it would soun more distant and remote as though you wer talking about a stranger. Notice too that th word 'like' becomes 'likes'.

Look at the following sentences and wri them out in your exercise books, changing th word 'I' into your own name or someone else name. Notice that you will have to change som of the other words as well.

1. I watch television every night.
2. I always buy my comic on Fridays on th way home from school.
3. I hope you enjoy playing with my train se
4. I want to do this by myself.
5. Am I right to refuse to give my apple Jennifer?

Look again at the points made in this sectio Don't worry too much if some of them see difficult or if you are not quite clear about the We shall be returning to them in later units, a you will have a chance to try to understa them again then. But it is very important th you remember this rule:

'I' is always a capital letter when it is writt by itself except when it refers to the letter the alphabet.

Vocabulary

A. Autobiography

Do you know what the word 'autobiography' means? You may well have been indulging in it recently without realizing it. That is a clue.

Here is another clue. Write down as many words as you can beginning with 'auto'. Do they have anything in common? Can you work out what 'auto' means?

Here is a third clue. Write down as many words as you can containing the word 'bio'. Do they have anything in common? Can you work out what 'bio' means?

Here is a final clue. Write down as many words as you can containing the word 'graphy'. Do they have anything in common? Can you work out what 'graphy' means?

Don't move on to the next section until you have tried to answer the questions above.

The English language contains many words which originally came from other languages. That is why it is so rich. We shall be looking at further examples in later units, but for the moment we are concerned with the word 'autobiography'. This is made up of three different parts, each of which originally came from a Greek word.

Greek: Auto   bio   graphy
meaning: self   life   writing
autobiography: someone writing about his or her own life
biography: someone else writing about a person's life

See if you can guess from the pictures words containing 'auto', 'bio' or 'graphy'.

Here are some other words to look up in your dictionary:

autotype   bioscope   graphic
              biosphere   lithograph
                            seismograph

Write these words in your notebook together with their meanings.

13

B.   Adjectives

In the 'Language' section, we learned that words could be arranged into different groups according to the kind of work they do. These are called parts of speech. 'I' is a pronoun, and the pronoun is a part of speech. **There are a large number of words which help to describe things, and these are known as adjectives.**

When we are writing about ourselves – writing our autobiographies – we are really trying to describe ourselves and therefore we would expect to use a lot of adjectives. They might be simple ones to describe our physical appearance, such as 'tall', 'short', 'fat', 'red-haired'. Or they may be more difficult words which try to describe the opinions we have or the kind of character we have, words like 'conceited', 'self-opinionated', 'surly' or 'optimistic'. (If you don't know any of these words, look them up in a dictionary and write them in your notebook.)

The easy way to think up adjectives is to begin with the phrase 'I am –' and then fill in the blank with as many words as you can think of. See if you can write down thirty different words. They don't have to be true about yourself. When you have collected thirty words, compare them with the list your neighbour has made. Make one big list containing all the different words thought up by the class.

How many do you think there will be? Fifty? A hundred? Two hundred?

C.   Using your Dictionaries

One of the best ways of extending your vocabulary is through reading. When we are reading, we come across many words whose meaning we half know. There are probably also words whose meanings we don't know. But the sweep of the writing and the context usually help us along, and we can generally understand most of what is being said. Sometimes, however, it is a good idea to stop or go back on what you have read and use a dictionary to check up on words which you have half-understood so that you will know them better next time. Perhaps keep a vocabulary notebook in which you write down these words and their meanings. Try to use them in your own writing. In this way, you will increase the number of words at your disposal. You will be able to understand more fully what you read and be able to use more interesting words when you yourself come to write and talk.

As a start, look again at the passages and poems in this Unit. Can you explain the meanings of these words?

stingy	reflection
premises	enticing
scanning	gooseflesh
souvenirs	compounds
succulent	smouldering
squirm	

Use each of these words in sentences of your own.

NOTE: a dictionary can give several different definitions for a particular word as it can have several different meanings. It is worth noting these different meanings, but if you want to know what the word means in a particular passage, you have to see which definition fits into the context best. For instance, what different meanings can the words 'reflection' and 'compounds' have? Which is the meaning required on p. 3 and on p. 5?

Get into the habit of looking up and making a note of words whose meanings you are unsure of in later passages in this book.

ie   Spelling

A.   Being able to spell correctly is very important. People may be able to understand what you mean if you mis-spell words, but it takes effort on the part of the reader, and why should anyone bother to make the effort to understand what you mean when you yourself don't make the effort to try to get it right in the first place? If something is incorrectly spelled, it creates a bad impression and the reader might not think it worth the bother of reading – even though what you have to say may be very interesting. If you take the trouble to spell correctly, this is merely showing courtesy and consideration for your reader. It is not too difficult. Remember the following points:

1. Make the effort to go over your work looking for spelling mistakes. You may be so involved in what you are writing that you don't want to break the flow by worrying about your spelling too much at the time. That is all right, so long as you remember to check on it later.

2. When you do revise your work for spelling mistakes, make sure you actually look at the words you have written down. Study each word carefully in isolation.

3. Use a dictionary. This is the only way to make sure you have written a particular word correctly. All of us have to use dictionaries at times. Get into the habit. If possible, have a dictionary of your own which you can refer to at any time.

4. Not everyone makes the same spelling mistakes. Each one of us tends to get different words wrong. When you have a piece of written work returned to you, have a look at your spelling mistakes. If possible, keep a notebook in which you write correct versions of the words you get wrong. Keep a different page for each letter of the alphabet so that it is easy to look the words up. Then when you come to use one of the words that you know you have difficulty with, you can check on it in your spelling notebook – and get it right!

B. Look at the extract from *The Winter of the Birds* on p. 6. You were told that Edward Flack had a little trouble with his spelling. Read the passage again and find the words that he has mis-spelled. There are nine words which are incorrect. Some of them are repeated. Write them out correctly in your notebook.

C. Look again at the extract from *The Adventures of Huckleberry Finn*. There you will find words like these:

didn't
hadn't
I'd
o'clock

The full versions of these words would be

did not
had not
I would
of the clock.

A punctuation mark, known as an apostrophe, is used in the shortened versions of these words to show that letters have been left out. Here are some more examples:

don't=do not
isn't=is not
I'll=I will.

Make a list of as many words as you can which use the apostrophe in this way. Make sure you put the apostrophe in the place where the missing letter or letters should be. You should be able to find at least fifty words. Compare your list with that compiled by other people and add any words you find that you didn't think of.

 Activities

A. 1. Earlier we said that you could tell something about a person by the way he put down his jacket. Each one of us would do it in a slightly different way from anyone else. The same is true of other things. For instance, how do you get out of bed in the morning? Do you jump up quick and alert, or do you struggle out bleary-eyed? Show how you do it.

2. Would the weather make any difference? Show how you would get out of bed on a chilly winter morning when it is still half-dark, and how you would do it on a bright summer morning when the sun is shining brightly.

3. Show how you eat your breakfast. Are you wide-awake or are you still half-asleep?

4. What games do you play? In mime (that is with movement only and no words) indicate one of them. Can the rest of the class guess what it is?

5. Do you know what you want to be when you grow up? In mime perform an action connected with this job. See if the rest of the class can name the job.

B. Try having a 'Face to Face'. This was the name of a television programme some years ago when a famous person was asked questions about himself so that the viewers could get an impression of the kind of person he was. In your version, someone could be asked to go out in front of the class, and everyone in the class

15

would have the chance of asking him a question. At the end you would have a fuller idea of the kind of person the 'victim' was. Questions could be about his family, his interests and hobbies, his likes and dislikes, his good points and bad points, his hopes and ambitions. Play fair, though, and don't ask any silly questions. The victim would, of course, have the right to refuse to answer any questions which were rude or too personal!

C. Look at the pieces you wrote in the 'Writing' section. Copy some of them out and put them all on the wall so that others can get an impression of the people who make up your form.

D. Do some research work on your class. First of all, decide what question you are going to ask. Here are some examples:

What is your favourite food?
What do your parents complain of most about you?
What is your favourite television programme?

Make a list of all the members of your class and go around them all asking each one the same question and make a note of the answer. Then study the answers, add up those who said this and those who said that. See if there is any pattern in the answers and come to some conclusion about the general feeling of the class about the question.

Reading List

Do you go to your local library regularly? If not, you should join because reading books is one of the ways in which you can gather ideas for your own writing and improve your skill as a writer. It is to be hoped that you will also gain entertainment and pleasure from reading.

Joining a library is not difficult. All you have to do is go along and ask. When confronted by all those books, you may at first feel bewildered and not know how to begin choosing one to read. Don't worry. You will soon get the idea. Try to get to know some authors whose books you are sure from experience that you will enjoy. If you have read one by an author you

liked, try to read more by the same writer. Listen to what your friends say and take their recommendations. Your teacher will probably suggest books in the course of his teaching: make a note of them and see if they are in the library. The Reading List which follows will also give you some suggestions. Usually, inside the dust cover or at the beginning of the book, there is a synopsis of what the book is about. Read it and see if this captures your interest. Not everyone likes the same books, of course, so don't be put off if you haven't enjoyed a book that was recommended by someone else. Put it down to experience and try again.

(If you look carefully at what has been written above, you will find another reason for reading to add to those given in the 'Reading and Understanding' section. What is it?)

Here are some novels written in the first person. (What does that mean?) Try some of them and see whether you like them.

Daniel Defoe, *Robinson Crusoe*
R. L. Stevenson, *Treasure Island*
R. M. Ballantyne, *The Coral Island*
Leon Garfield, *Devil-in-the-Fog*
Peter Carter, *The Black Lamp*
Gerald Durrell, *My Family and Other Animals*
    A Zoo in my Luggage
E. L. Konigsburg, *Jennifer, Hecate, Macbeth and Me*
John Rowe Townsend, *Gumble's Yard*
    Widdershins Crescent
Mark Twain, *The Adventures of Huckleberry Finn*
Geoffrey Trease, *Cue for Treason*
J. Meade Falkner, *Moonfleet*
Bill Naughton, *The Goalkeeper's Revenge*

Here are some autobiographies:
Richard Church, *Over the Bridge*
Clifford Dyment, *The Railway Game*
Richard Wright, *Black Boy*
Valerie Avery, *London Morning*
Dannie Abse, *Ash on a Young Man's Sleeve*
Laurie Lee, *Cider with Rosie*
James Kirkup, *The Only Child*
Michael Baldwin, *Grandad with Snails*
Jennifer Wayne, *Brown Bread and Butter in the Basement*

UNIT 2

At School

 ## Reading and Understanding

Schools in the Past

In Unit 1 we considered a number of the reasons for people reading. Another one that we didn't think of was that people read about the past so that they can understand and appreciate the present in which they live. As an example, here is an extract from the novel *Jane Eyre*. This novel was first published in 1847 and is to some extent based on Charlotte Brontë's own experiences. The extract describes life at Lowood School, a boarding school that Jane was sent to in order to get her out of the way. (In a later episode, Jane is made to stand on a stool in front of the whole school for several hours because she accidentally broke her slate.)

The next day commenced as before: getting up and dressing by rush-light; but this morning we were obliged to dispense with the ceremony of washing: the water in the pitchers was frozen. A change had taken place in the weather the preceding evening, and a keen north-east wind, whistling through the crevices of our bedroom windows all night long, had made us shiver in our beds, and turned the contents of the ewers to ice.

Before the long hour and a half of prayers and Bible reading was over, I felt ready to perish with cold. Breakfast-time came at last, and this morning the porridge was not burnt; the quality was eatable, the quantity small; how small my portion seemed! I wish it had been doubled.

In the course of the day I was enrolled a member of the fourth class, and regular tasks and occupations were assigned to me: hitherto I had only been a spectator of the proceedings at Lowood. I was now to become an actor therein. At first, being little accustomed to learn by heart, the lessons appeared to me both long and difficult; the frequent change from task to task, too, bewildered me; and I was glad, when about three o'clock in the afternoon, Miss Smith put into my hands a border of muslin two yards long, together with needle, thimble, etc. and sent me to sit in a quiet corner of the schoolroom, with directions to hem the same. At that hour most of the others were sewing likewise; but one class still stood round Miss Scatcherd's chair reading, and as all was quiet, the subject of their lessons could be heard, together with the manner in which each girl acquitted herself, and the animadversions or commendations of Miss Scatcherd on the performance. It was English history; among the readers I observed my acquaintance of the verandah: at the commencement of the lesson her place had been at the top of the class, but for some error of pronunciation, or some inattention to stops, she was suddenly sent to the bottom. Even in that obscure position Miss Scatcherd continued to make her an object of constant notice: she was continually addressing to her such phrases as the following:

'Burns' (such it seems was her name; the girls here were all called by their surnames, as boys are elsewhere) – 'Burns, you are standing on the side of your shoe; turn your toes out immediately.' 'Burns, you poke your chin most unpleasantly; draw it in.' 'Burns, I insist on your holding your head up; I will not have you before me in that attitude,' etc., etc.

A chapter having been read through twice, the books were closed and the girls examined. The lesson had comprised part of the reign of Charles I, and there were sundry questions about tonnage and poundage and ship-money, which most of them appeared unable to answer; still every little difficulty was solved instantly when it reached Burns: her memory seemed to have retained the substance of the whole lesson, and she was ready with answers on every point. I kept expecting that Miss Scatcherd would praise her attention; but, instead of that, she suddenly cried out:

'You dirty, disagreeable girl! you have never cleaned your nails this morning!'

Burns made no answer: I wondered at her silence.

'Why,' I thought, 'does she not explain that she could neither clean her nails nor wash her face, as the water was frozen?'

My attention was now called off by Miss Smith desiring me to hold a skein of thread: while she was winding it, she talked to me from time to time, asking whether I had ever been at school before, whether I could mark, stitch, knit, etc.; till she dismissed me I could not pursue my observations on Miss Scatcherd's movements. When I returned to my seat that lady was just delivering an order, of which I did not catch the import; but Burns immediately left the class, and, going into the small inner room where the books were kept, returned in half a minute, carrying in her hand a bundle of twigs tied together at one end. This ominous tool she presented to Miss Scatcherd with a respectful courtsey; then she quietly, and without being told, unloosed her pinafore, and the teacher instantly and sharply inflicted on her neck a dozen strokes with the bunch of twigs. Not a tear rose to Burns's eyes; and, while I paused from my sewing, because my fingers quivered at this spectacle with a sentiment of unavailing and impotent anger, not a feature of her pensive face altered its ordinary expression.

'Hardened girl!' exclaimed Miss Scatcherd; 'nothing can correct you of your slatternly habits: carry the rod away.'

Burns obeyed: I looked at her narrowly as she emerged from the book-closet; she was just putting back her handkerchief into her pocket, and the trace of a tear glistened on her thin cheek.

CHARLOTTE BRONTË, *Jane Eyre*

Jane says, 'At first, being little accustomed to learn by heart, the lessons appeared to me both long and difficult; the frequent change from task to task, too, bewildered me.' Say in your own words what she means.

If you have recently moved from a junior school to a secondary school, describe your impressions. Do you have any of the feelings Jane had in the sentence quoted above?

Make a list of the hardships that pupils at Lowood School had to endure.

Should girls and boys be called by their first names or their surnames?

What are your views on the kind of activities the pupils are involved in?

What kind of person is Miss Scatcherd?

Do you get any impression that Miss Smith is different?

Why does Miss Scatcherd dislike Helen Burns?

Does Helen deserve her punishment?

Why doesn't Helen cry when she is beaten?

What do we learn about the kind of person Helen is?

Jane is mainly an observer here, but can you deduce anything about her character?

Charlotte Brontë's novel was published in 1847. Look at the way she uses the following words: 'dispense'; 'pitchers'; 'ewers'; 'animadversions'; 'commendations'; 'import'; 'spectacle'; 'sentiment'; 'unavailing'; 'impotent'. Some of these words are unusual or used differently today from how they were used then. (Remember that Standard English is always changing.)

Find out what these words mean.

What are your feelings about corporal punishment? Do you think it should be used in schools?

If we take this as an example of what schools were like in the first half of the last century, how would you say they have changed?

Picturing the Past

Study these two photographs. In one, girls are doing P.E. The photograph was taken at the beginning of this century. The other photograph was also taken at the beginning of this century and shows what was known as an elementary school for pupils under thirteen years of age. Several classes are being taught in the same room.

Describe each of the pictures in your own words.

What conclusions would you draw about the changes in schools that have taken place between then and now?

Schools Today

Of course, nothing is perfect, and even if it were, people would still find things to complain about. Here are three people of your own age writing about the kind of school they would like.

A. *No* Watery cabbage, milk pudding, lakes of custard, compulsory Latin or P.T., art or music exams, teachers' gowns, homework, school hats.

Yes Practical hints on shopping, entertaining, etc. and clothes that suit us, more films and television programmes, more projects and plays in class, more visits to concerts, etc. *Discussion of all types of art and music: pop, jazz, light and serious classical music.* Decent dinners (if possible), earlier dismissals, variety of sports at P.T., French that means something, i.e. commercial, letter-writing, etc. and not (*true*): 'The soldiers are guarding the hotel where the actress is arriving with her niece in their big car.'

ELIZABETH

B. This school would only have people like me who like writing stories and poetry and none of us would laugh at each other for being odd and queer. There would be no handwork and we'd have maths without the problems and we'd have *at least* one lesson a day to make up poetry. There'd be only ten to a class and we would all have nice names like Lalage (Greek for chatterbox), Zoë (Greek for life), and Charlotte because it was the Christian name of Charlotte Brontë, and Imogen from Shakespeare.

Everyone would co-operate with one another and we'd act our own adaptations of novels like *Jane Eyre*. We'd read lots of biographies about famous people like writers and musicians. Composing music for our orchestras would be as important as arithmetic, and famous people would come on unannounced visits to discuss topics of the hour. To have television in our homes would be quite unusual, and we would discuss books instead of television at the dinner table.

Teachers would be there to help and *not* to organize, and they might hint at something to do but not make us do it. They would make sure we had discovered all the important aspects of life and give us gardens to cultivate. We would go on visits to places like Kenwood House, Haworth and Blenheim Palace, and organize ghost hunts in the weekends! The murals on the classroom walls would be of the latest aspect in life we had discovered.

There would be a 'screaming room' where anyone could go and make as much noise as they wanted without anyone hearing and objecting.

When I'm older I'll establish this place for people who feel different. There will be a severe entrance examination to see that you really suit the school, and the fees will be essays, poetry or paintings according to your talents.

LALAGE

C. The school I'd like is what I have: my mother teaches my brother and me at home. We study maths, English, science, history, geography, French and scripture.

This system has many advantages. The most important is that we can learn at our own speed; thus I have recently started A-level maths but am still struggling with O English, while my brother who is three and a half years younger, is advanced in English but only average in arithmetic. Another advantage is that we have much more free time than other children; we don't waste time travelling to and fro and, as we have individual work, the education officer agreed to shorten lesson times for us. I spend a lot of my leisure time reading, bird watching, stamp and coin collecting, doing jigsaws, carpentry, painting, listening to radio, watching T.V., swimming, playing chess, draughts, tennis and table tennis. Another advantage is that we are not hedged in by a lot of silly rules and regulations. We are also free from bullying big boys and from pressure to start bad habits like smoking and drug taking. We dress in comfortable, sensible clothes and do not have to wear some ridiculous uniform, nor do we have to play compulsory games. Again, we have home cooking all the time.

When my mother started, a lot of people told her she was foolish because we would never learn to mix. I don't think this is true because, although I've always liked some time by myself, my brother likes and has lots of friends with whom he goes to play and who come and play with him ... It was also said that we would grow up selfish: I hope we're not. About once a fortnight we have a stall in our front garden to aid Oxfam and have collected £4.12 so far this year. We also do a few odd jobs around the house. People also said Mother would find it too much. I know we get her down at times, but she survives and looks, so people say, much younger than she is ...

The only disadvantage of the system to my mind is the difficulty of doing much advanced practical work in science because of the amount of apparatus required ...

I think it would solve a lot of problems if more people followed our system. Of course, not everyone is qualified to teach older children, but millions of mums could teach juniors. This would reduce the terrible overcrowding in some primary schools. Again, as children would be home for longer, it might help to decrease the birth rate.

FRANK

(*The School that I'd Like*, ed. Edward Blishen)

In the course of describing the school they would like, these writers make or suggest a number of complaints about schools as they exist at the moment. *Make a list of all these complaints. You'll be surprised how many there are. Are they reasonable complaints?*

Talk about your own school. How many of the complaints made by Elizabeth, Lalage and Frank apply to your school?

What are the good things about your school?

Look again at Lalage's account. Can you say anything about the kind of person she might be from the views she expresses?

Read Frank's description of studying at home. Do you agree with his arguments?

What do you think he means by his last sentence?

Writing

An Incident at School

As was implied in 'Writing' Unit 1, a way of helping with your own writing is to look at other people's writing, at the way they describe things and the kind of ideas they have. In this section, we shall be looking at a number of pieces that

may start you thinking about how you yourself could write.

Here, for instance, is an account of an incident from a novel by William Mayne. It is about some children in a junior school.

Miss McGregor rang the bell. Everybody stopped running about and shouting. Tommy Routh was climbing down the gate in and out of the bars. Mary thought he was like a length of wool being woven. He was last in the line, pulling himself together at the waist and dusting his back where it had been on the dusty playground.

The bottom form went into school and the door closed behind them. The voice of Mrs Meadows came out through the open window. The door opened again and Miss McGregor came out with a ball of string. She had put the bell away. Mary could see it inside the window next to a big jar holding the stems of meadowsweet. The meadowsweet looked like heaps of snow. A fly flew through the window to look at it.

Miss McGregor blinked her eyes to get them used to the brightness of the sunshine in the yard.

'It's one o'clock,' she said. 'Is everybody here?'

Carolyn was the eldest, and she had to count them up. Mary counted as well. Carolyn said they were all there, twenty-one. Mary could only count twenty, and she did it again, but it was still twenty.

'Come on, then,' said Miss McGregor. 'Let's start off.'

'Miss McGregor, you'll need your cushion,' said Carolyn.

'No, she won't,' said somebody else, 'she can sit on the grass, we've got to go.'

'I think I would like my cushion,' said Miss McGregor. 'Thank you, Carolyn.'

Carolyn ran in for the cushion, into the empty form room. She caught the others up at the gate. Then they were out in the empty road between the houses of the village. Nobody was about in the sunshine, because they were all having their dinners. Carolyn carried the cushion. Mary took the ball of string, and they walked together beside Miss McGregor, down the lane and into the market place, and then down the road towards the river.

'Caro,' said Mary. 'I could only count twenty people. Why did you count twenty-one?'

'That's what there are,' said Carolyn. 'Perhaps you forgot Tommy Routh.'

'Me?' said Tommy Routh. 'What did you forget about me?'

'I didn't forget him,' said Mary. 'You needn't fuss, Tommy.'

'Count them again,' said Carolyn. 'And I will, too, and we'll see what it is.'

'They're all here,' said Tommy. 'The lot of them.'

'Twenty,' said Mary, pointing at Carolyn, because she was the last to be counted. Carolyn said twenty-one, and she was pointing at herself, too, with her finger on her chest.

'You've done something daft, then,' said Carolyn. 'Do it all again. You say them, and I'll count them.'

They were at the front of everybody, so Mary had to walk backwards to see them all. She said each name, and Carolyn counted them on her fingers, putting the cushion well under her arm to leave her hands empty for the job.

'Tommy Routh, that's nineteen, and you, Caro, twenty,' said Mary. 'I can't make it more.'

'You can,' said Carolyn, 'because I know what you did. You forgot somebody.'

'Kate,' said Mary. 'No, I got her, because I keep counting her and then uncounting her. Tommy Routh, have you got out again?'

'I'm nineteen,' said Tommy Routh. 'What are you?'

'Me?' said Mary. 'I wasn't in. I'm twenty-one. I forgot to count myself.'

'I always count myself, even when I'm alone,' said Carolyn.

WILLIAM MAYNE, *The Fishing Party*

Look carefully at the way William Mayne builds up the atmosphere of a warm country afternoon. Pick out the details which help build up this picture.

Do you remember the episode from The Adventures of Huckleberry Finn *in Unit 1? There we saw that people can tell us about themselves from the way they do things. What can we deduce about Mary, Tommy and Carolyn?*

Carolyn says, 'I always count myself, even if I'm alone'. What do you think she means?

Look again at the way William Mayne describes things, in particular the way he uses comparisons to help us see what he is talking about. He says that Tommy climbing in and out of the bars of the gate was 'like a length of wool being woven', and the meadowsweet 'looked like heaps of snow'. *What does he mean?*

Much of the story is told through the conversation of the children themselves. Does it ring true? Is this how children talk?

Did you guess what was wrong with Mary's counting before she herself did?

William Mayne in this extract is not so much interested in telling a story as in creating the atmosphere of a particular afternoon in a junior school and of how children talk and behave among themselves. Think back to your own days at the junior school. *Do you think this extract is convincing? What details ring true?*

How do junior schools differ in atmosphere from secondary schools?

Talk about your own memories of junior school.

First Day at School

The extract from *The Fishing Party* is fiction. That is, it is an invented story about imaginary characters. It could of course be based on fact or on the author's experience, like *Jane Eyre*. Because it is fiction, it does not mean that it is untrue. It may not actually have happened, but if it is well written we feel that it *could* have happened, that it is true to life.

But let's return to actual experience. We saw in Unit 1 that a way of writing interestingly was to write about yourself and the things that happened to you. Just as we are each individuals and different in many ways from everyone else – as well as sharing many things in common – so when we write about ourselves, the result will be different for each of us.

For instance, can you remember as far back as your first day at your infant school? Here is one boy writing his account. He was fifteen at the time that he wrote it.

My First Day at School

I can remember my first day at the infant school quite well. My mother took me down to the gate of the school, big black iron gates with rust flaking off the bars. There was a huge cedar tree in the grounds, which was propped up by a pair of wooden telegraph-poles. I never went too close to it then because I was never quite sure whether telegraph-poles were very strong. As we went in, we were greeted by a smell of clay, paint and plimsoles, and earlier I had asked my mother what the rubber toe-caps were for. She said that they were to protect your feet. So as I went into school, I kicked the door-frame as hard as I could and discovered to my distaste that they didn't really at all.

Later on, I was taken, with my mother, to see the

Headmistress as were all newcomers. Looking out of the window, I saw what I thought was a walking-stick on the roof. It turned out to be the top end of a fire-escape ladder.

Then my mother went home and I was taken into a classroom with lots of other little boys and girls, all engaged in painting things or doing things in the sand-pit, or knocking down other people's brick buildings. I found a wooden set of farm animals, and broke the donkey. Our classroom had large windows, with strange things outside. These were 'The Apparatus' which we were to climb on during P.E.

The teacher was a friendly person who showed us where things were and where to get milk. I hated milk. Once I was forced to drink it, or rather the teacher left me and the milk with a quarter of an hour to get rid of it. It ended up being poured in the sand-pit.

When it was dinner-time, everyone went home except some of the boys and me. I went off to the dining-hall with the others. We had to go up a sloping corridor called 'The Link' and through a place where there is a notice displayed: 'This is the Quiet Part of the School', and then into the dining-hall. There were rows and rows of trestle-tables and benches. There was a ghastly smell of school-dinner-type stew and cleaning polish.

We all sat down and had our 'food' brought to us. Everyone else dragged the potato off the fork with their upper teeth. I had been used to doing it with my lips, but I thought that this was the right way to do it, so I did.

While I was still about halfway through my 'firsts', the time came to clear away the tables. I was put in a little room to finish my dinner. I watched the other children playing on the grassy banks and my dinner got even colder. In the end I scoffed my pudding and went out, leaving my dinner to its own devices.

In the afternoon, we all sat on the floor and listened to a story about a train or something. At break a boy showed us his clockwork seaplane. It was small, silver and had rubber wheels. He zoomed it down the table and it juddered to a stop at the very edge. He did it again and the same thing happened. To try out his new discovery, he skidded it as hard as he could at the end of the table. The teacher came in just as we were trying to piece it back together.

After break, we did some spelling, and I got my question right which made me most pleased with myself. My mother turned up in the doorway, and I explained to her that plimsoles do not protect your feet, that there was a walking-stick on the roof, and I got about twelve questions right. On the way home I was a dustman because I had my cap on just like dustmen do (back to front). I was proud to be a schoolboy.

PAUL WHITE

What do you think of Paul's experiences? Do they ring true?

What are your memories of your early days at other schools? Talk about them.

Other Aspects of School Life

Finally in this section, here are three poems about other aspects of school life. The first is a rather fanciful description of a standard school subject.

Arithmetic

Arithmetic is where numbers fly like pigeons in
    and out of your head.
Arithmetic tells you how many you lose or win if
    you know how many you had before you lost
    or won.
Arithmetic is seven eleven all good children go to
    heaven – or five six bundle of sticks.
Arithmetic is numbers you squeeze from your
    head to your hand to your pencil to your
    paper till you get the answer.
Arithmetic is where the answer is right and every-
    thing is nice and you can look out of the
    window and see the blue sky – or the answer
    is wrong and you have to start all over again
    and try again and see how it comes out this
    time.
If you take a number and double it and double it
    again and then double it a few more times,
    the number gets bigger and bigger and goes
    higher and higher and only arithmetic can tell
    you what the number is when you decide to
    quit doubling.
Arithmetic is where you have to multiply – and
    carry the multiplication table in your head
    and hope you won't lose it.
If you have two animal crackers, one good and
    one bad, and you eat one and a striped zebra
    with streaks all over him eats the other, how
    many animal crackers will you have if some-
    body offers you five six seven and you say No
    no no and you say Nay nay nay and you say
    Nix nix nix?
If you ask your mother for one fried egg for break-
    fast and she gives you two fried eggs and you
    eat both of them, who is better in arithmetic,
    you or your mother?

                        CARL SANDBURG

The first line of the poem is a comparison. What do you think the poet means?

Do you think the poet is making fun of the subject? How can you tell?

The Sneak

The two boys hid behind the gate.
'Where's the cissy?' said one. 'He's late.'

They were waiting for a boy to walk by,
Waiting to kick him and spit in his eye.

'He's coming. Don't let him get away.'
And they beat him up just like everyday.

The snivelling boy cried as the punches flew,
'You wouldn't like it if it was done to you.'

'No! Nor'd you like it,' one of them said,
'If you'd got told off and sent to bed.

'Telling the teacher and splitting on us,
Then avoiding us by getting the bus.

'Well, you're going to pay, and say sorry too,
Or we'll tell the teacher all the things about you.'

'Well,' said the other, 'say sorry now.
Don't split again, we're gonna make you vow.'

The boy hugged his chest, his eyes turned away.
'All right, but leave me alone everyday.'

'You're a cheat, thief, sneak and mummy's slob.'
'I'm not, I'm not,' the boy gave a sob.

'Go on, get lost,' they gave their last kicks,
And shouted, 'No more of your sneaky tricks.'

                        WENDY ROCKER

What had the victim done?
Do you think he deserved the treatment he received?
Some people say that children can be very cruel to each other. Would you agree?
What kind of things cause quarrels between schoolchildren?

Holiday

When the boys came out of school they threw up
    their caps,
And the air was striped with their spinning.

When the girls came out of school they pulled off
    their stockings,
And the roof-tops streamed with long black ban-
    ners.
When the boys and girls came out of school
All the bells of the town choked with their chim-
    ing.

When the boys walked in the streets their shoes
    purred on the asphalt,
And the corners were bright as butterflies.

When the girls walked in the streets their legs
    shone in shop-windows,
And the cinema-queues trembled with love.

When the boys and girls walked in the streets
It was like a cathedral decked with worshippers.

And when the boys and girls went back to school
All the clocks of the town wrung their rusted
    hands.

JULIAN MITCHELL

Look at the comparisons in this poem: 'the corners were bright as butterflies'; 'It was like a cathedral decked out with worshippers'. What does the poet mean?

Is this how you feel about getting out of school and having to go back?

Assignments

Choose several of the following to write about. If you don't know what to write about, read again the pieces of writing we have studied in this section, and they may give you some ideas. Some of the titles might suggest actual experiences you could describe; others might be fiction, short stories about events and characters that you have made up; others could suggest poems.

1. My First Day at School
2. My Favourite or Least Favourite Subject
3. Things I Like about School
4. Things I Dislike about School
5. The School I Would Like
6. Playing Truant
7. Fight at Break
8. A Portrait of a Teacher
9. Teachers I Have Known
10. Monday Morning
11. School Dinners
12. Morning Assembly
13. Unjustly Punished
14. Late for School

 ## Language

A. The Second Person
Here are some typical school rules:

1. You must use common sense and courtesy at all times.
2. Do not run in the corridors or on the stairs.
3. Do not eat in class.
4. You must not leave the class without permission.
5. Leave your bicycles in the place provided for them.

In the 'Language' section of Unit 1, we saw that if someone is talking about himself and the actual words he uses are written down, he is said to be talking or writing in the first person. For example, read again the account of 'My First Day at School' which is in the first person. The words 'I', 'me', 'my', 'myself', 'mine', 'we', 'us', 'our', 'ourselves', and 'ours' all indicate that something is being said or written in the first person.

Now look again at the school rules given above. If you imagine these words are spoken by a teacher, is he talking about himself? No, he is talking *to* someone, he is addressing *you*. When someone does this, he is said to be using the second person. Words like 'you', 'yourself', 'yourselves' and 'yours' are in the second person.

First Person

SINGULAR	PLURAL
I	we
me	us
my	our
myself	ourselves
mine	ours

Second Person

SINGULAR	PLURAL
you	you
yourself	yourselves
yours	yours

Write five sentences containing these words.
Here are five sentences using the first person.
Write them in your exercise book turning the first

person into the second person. For example, 'I am having sausage and chips for my dinner' becomes 'You are having sausage and chips for your dinner'. Notice that you have to alter not just 'I' and 'my' into 'you' and 'your', but other words may have to be changed as well.

1. I want to ride my new bicycle to school.
2. Our football team is better than theirs.
3. We feel very proud of ourselves.
4. That football is mine.
5. He let us use our new football kit.

B. Statements and Commands

Here are some more school rules:

1. Dismount from your bicycles at the school gates.
2. The area between the Music Block and the Art Block is out of bounds.
3. Ties need not be worn in the summer term.
4. Line up in silence outside classrooms.
5. Sit down quietly and get your books out when you enter classrooms.

Can you see any difference in the way these rules are expressed? Nos. 2 and 3 are statements of conditions that you are expected to conform to. The others speak more directly to you. They tell you what to do. They are orders or commands. If we add the words 'you must' in front of these commands, we can see the full meaning of them. Since we used the word 'you', this means that commands are in the second person.

Say which of the following are statements and which are commands:

1. The playground is crowded with pupils.
2. Don't lose your dinner money.
3. Tell her to stop bothering you.
4. The dinner queue takes a long time to reach the serving hatch.
5. Eat up everything on your plate.

Turn the following statements into commands. For example, 'You should behave yourself in the classroom' becomes 'Behave in the classroom'.

1. You must remember to bring your sports kit on the right day.
2. You need to have a hair-cut.
3. You should wash your hands before eating.
4. Ties are no longer to be worn.
5. The area between the Cycle Sheds and the Main Building is out of bounds.

Write five sentences that are statements and five sentences that are commands.

C. Similes

In the 'Writing' section, we examined some of the comparisons which authors use to make their writing more vivid and to help the reader see more clearly what he is getting at. Let's look at some of them again:

Tommy climbing in and out of the bars of the gate was 'like a length of wool being woven'.
The meadowsweet 'looked like heaps of snow'.
'Arithmetic is where numbers fly like pigeons in and out of your head.'
'The corners were bright as butterflies.'
'When the boys and girls walked in the streets It was like a cathedral decked out with worshippers.'

Do these give you a more vivid idea of what the writer is describing? Work out again the kind of ideas they suggest.

What each of these writers is doing is making a comparison between what he is writing about and some other object or idea with which it has something in common. Exploring the comparison sheds light on the original thing being described. We see it in a completely different way. We understand more fully the way the author sees the original object. Here are some more comparisons for you to examine. *Explore them and say how they help you to see a clearer picture of what is being described.*

1. The car engine sounded as though an angry bee was trying to find his escape from a jam jar.
2. The willow's trailing branches looked like long languid hair.
3. The ball shot through the air like a meteorite.
4. When he stood on the dry twig, the noise was as sharp as a gunshot.

26

5. The surface of the lake was as smooth as a mirror.

The technical name given to this kind of comparison is 'simile'. (Note the spelling.) **A simile is a comparison in which one thing is said to be like another.** The two objects being compared have something in common and by bringing them together in the comparison, a clearer, more vivid picture of the one is given by bringing it close to the other. Watch out for the words 'like' and 'as'. These give the clue that the comparison is probably a simile.

Write similes to create a more vivid impression of the following:

1. a fire
2. the moon
3. the sun
4. waves
5. the wind
6. a knife
7. a tree
8. a dancer
9. a shout
10. a laugh

Try to use similes in your own writing. They will help to make it more interesting and more lively. Here is a poem made up of similes. Some of them are exaggerated and not meant to be taken too seriously. *Examine the similes and say what you think of them.*

Susan

She walks like a duck in a waddly sort of way.
She has eyes like flames and feet like flippers.
She has legs like bean poles and arms like pencils,
Fingers like seaweed shimmering in the sea.
Teeth like ice, ears like fans.
The way she sings makes you scream.
Her hair is like straw that flares in the wind.
Her face is white as snow,
And her cheeks are like hairy peaches.
She pounds down the lane like a giant,
And speaks like an organ.
She pushes you around and bosses you about.
And when she laughs it sounds like a tolling bell.
She whispers like a mouse and hisses like a snake.
She dances like a wizard and lingers like a fox.
She snores like an earthquake and eats like a hog.

JACQUELINE PERRY

Write your own poem in this style describing someone you know. You don't have to be too exact.

Vocabulary

A. -ology

In Unit 1 we saw that the 'bio' part of the word 'autobiography' means 'life'. It is also used in the word 'biology', one of the subjects you may be studying at school. What does the second part of the word 'biology' mean? Look up the following words in the dictionary and try to work it out:

astrology	philology
etymology	phrenology
geology	psychology
ideology	sociology
meteorology	theology
ornithology	zoology

These are difficult words. Write them in your notebook together with their meanings. Try saying them aloud.

B. Words Connected with School Subjects

If you have looked up 'biology' in the dictionary, you will have found that it means 'the science of life and living matter'. Anyone studying biology will come across words that might not be so common in ordinary writing – words such as:

cartilage	gene	plankton
chlorophyll	intestine	pollen
corpuscle	muscle	sepal
		stamen

Some of these words are difficult. Look them up in a dictionary and write them in your notebook together with their meanings.

Can you think of any other words associated with biology?

What about words connected with other school subjects? Write down at least ten words you might use in each of the following: geography, history, mathematics, religious knowledge, chemistry, physics, P.E.

Compare your list with your neighbour's. Add any words that you hadn't thought of to your own list.

C. Nicknames

Can you work out what these names have in common? – Balloon, Barrel, Barrel-Belly, Billy Bunter, Buster, Chubby, Chunky, Diddle-Diddle, Dumpling, Falstaff, Fat Belly, Fatty Harbuckle, Football, Guts, Piggy, Podge, Porky, Steam-Roller, Tank, Tubby, Two Ton Tessy.

They are all nicknames which schoolchildren give to someone who is fat. Have you heard of any of them? Do you use any of them? Do you think they are kind or cruel?

A 'nickname' is 'an additional name'. Sometimes it is a sign of friendliness; sometimes it is meant as an insult. Schoolchildren often call their friends by a nickname or invent nicknames for their teachers. *Do you know of any that are used in your class or in your school?*

Some historical figures are known by their nicknames. Some examples are the Iron Duke, Richard Lionheart, Stonewall Jackson, Capability Brown, the Merry Monarch. To whom do these names refer? Make a list of other historical figures who have nicknames. *Test them out on your neighbour and see if he can give you their real names.*

In some Welsh towns, so many of the inhabitants are called Jones that they are given nicknames to distinguish between them. For example, you might have Jones the Bread, Jones the Electric and Jones the Death. How do you think these three shopkeepers acquired their nicknames? *Can you think of any other examples? If not, invent some.*

Many surnames seem to attract a standard nickname. There must be many people called Miller who are known as Dusty, or Parker who are nicknamed Nosey. Here are some more examples:

Pincher Martin	Sandy Brown
Blacky White	Splinter Wood
Daisy Bell	Reelo Cotton
Ginger Beer	Spud Murphy
Nick Carter	Gipsy Lee
Nobby Clark	

Can you think of any others?

ie Spelling

A. Check through the written work you have done in this Unit. If you have made any spelling mistakes, find out the correct spellings and add the words to your notebook. Learn them.

B. One of the reasons people have difficulty with spelling is because English words are not always spelled the way you would expect from the way they are pronounced. Take, for example, words containing the letters 'ough' such as 'cough', 'borough', 'tough', 'trough', 'bough', 'thorough', 'though', 'furlough', 'through', 'slough', 'rough'. When writing these words you have to remember that they are not spelled the way they are pronounced. *Find another word that they rhyme with.* For instance, 'cough' and 'trough' rhyme with 'off'.

'Bough' and 'slough' rhyme with ...
'Furlough' and 'though' rhyme with ...
'Rough' and 'tough' rhyme with ...
'Through' rhymes with ...
'Borough' rhymes with ...

C. There are other words that have letters which are not pronounced but which have to be written if the words are to be spelled correctly. Here are some examples of silent letters:

Silent 'b', for example 'comb', 'lamb'.
Silent 'g', for example, 'gnaw', 'gnome'.
Silent 'h', for example, 'honest', 'honour'.
Silent 'k', for example 'knave', 'knee'.
Silent 'p', for example 'psychology', 'pterodactyl'.

Find more examples and make lists of them in your notebook. Check also the following words:

mnemonic: find out how to pronounce this word and what it means;
safety: there are many words with 'silent e' too many to discuss here;
salmon: do you pronounce the 'l'?
solemn: what about the word 'solemnity'?

Activities

A. 1. Show how you would walk to school on a wet Monday morning and go home on a sunny Friday afternoon.

2. Show how you would go out on a frosty winter's morning and on a warm sunny morning.

3. Show how you would sit in a favourite lesson and in the lesson that you like least.

4. Demonstrate without using any equipment something you do in one of your lessons. It might be painting or writing or adding up. Try to show whether you enjoy it or not. The others can guess what the activity is.

B. Form a group of four or six. Choose a typical situation that could happen during the school day. Discuss it. What is the main incident? How can you lead into it? How will you finish your scene? Who is going to play the various characters? Rehearse your scene and then play it for the others.

Here are some ideas for you to think about:

1. A new pupil has arrived at the school and is put in your class. Show how the other pupils behave towards him or her. Think about the character of this new pupil. Is he shy or is he a show-off?

2. A teacher is very firm on discipline. Show how the class and the teacher manage to come to terms with each other.

3. The class is having a test and silence is essential. Show how someone disturbs the silence and what happens next.

4. One of the boys in the class is a bully. Show how the others teach him a lesson.

C. Find out what your class's views are on one of the following subjects, using the procedure suggested in Unit 1: homework, uniform, the cane, compulsory games, prefects, morning assembly. Where appropriate, ask each member of the class if he or she is for or against or doesn't know. Add up the numbers expressing each view and draw some conclusion from these figures and the comments made.

D. Discuss some of the subjects suggested in C – or matters such as school rules, the best arrangement of furniture in the classroom, school dinners.

E. Many schools now have pupils who were born in a great number of different countries. For instance, one school has pupils from forty-five different countries. Here is the list:

Aden	Jamaica
Australia	Kenya
Bangladesh	Liberia
Barbados	New Zealand
Britain	Nigeria
Burma	Pakistan
Cameroun	Poland
Canada	Rhodesia
Cyprus	St Kitts
France	St Lucia
Germany	St Vincent
Ghana	Saudi Arabia
Granada	South Africa
Greece	Spain
Guyana	Sri Lanka
Hong Kong	Syria
Hungary	Tanzania
India	Trinidad
Indonesia	Turkey
Iran	Uganda
Ireland	United States of America
Israel	Zambia
Italy	

One boy even claimed to have been born on an aeroplane which had just taken off from Fiji! Ask around and see how many different countries of origin you can find in your school. Put them in alphabetical order. Indicate them on the map of the world. Perhaps you could put an enlarged outline map on the wall with the names of the countries alongside linked up by thread to the countries on the map.

F. Ask your parents and grandparents what school was like when they were young. Perhaps you could use a cassette recorder to capture their comments. Pool the information you obtain with the rest of the class.

Reading List

Here are some novels you may like to read which have a school background.

Meindert deJong, *The Wheel on the School*
Paul Berna, *Flood Warning*
William Mayne, *The Fishing Party*
   No More School
   A Swarm in May
   Cathedral Wednesday
Geoffrey Trease, *No Boats on Bannermere*
C. Day Lewis, *The Otterbury Incident*
Anthony Buckeridge, *Jennings Goes to School*
   Jennings's Diary
Bernard Ashley, *The Trouble with Donovan Croft*
Thomas Hughes, *Tom Brown's Schooldays*
Rudyard Kipling, *Stalky and Co*
Talbot Baines Reed, *The Cock House at Fellsgarth*
   Dominic of the Fifth

There are also some interesting episodes dealing with school life in the following. Your teacher could read you some extracts from them.

Charlotte Brontë, *Jane Eyre*
Charles Dickens, *David Copperfield*
   Nicholas Nickelby
   Great Expectations
   Hard Times

See also the books mentioned at the end of the Reading List in Unit 1.

UNIT 3

Monsters

 Reading and Understanding

Prehistoric Monsters

Monsters: the very sound of the word inspires fear and terror! Throughout time, man has pitted his wits and strength against monsters of various kinds, real and imaginary. It would be interesting to work out what it is about the idea (or the fact) of a monster that makes it so frightening. Obviously, this depends on the particular monster being considered, but some of the following elements may combine to produce the shiver down the spine, the violent heart-beat and the frozen stance – things like size, strangeness, ferocity, loudness, unexpectedness, dangerousness. How many monsters in life and fiction can you think of and which of these qualities do they possess? Can a creature be a monster in one situation and not in another? For instance, is a lion a monster? Think about it in a cage at the zoo and when you are suddenly confronted by it snarling at you in a jungle clearing.

We sometimes call people monsters. Can you think of some examples? What qualities of a monster do they show?

One of the most famous monsters was the dinosaur. You may have seen the skeleton of one in a museum – there is a picture on p. 33. How would you have liked to meet one of them? In the following extract, Ray Bradbury imagines modern man hunting one of the most terrifying dinosaurs, the Tyrannosaurus Rex. The hunters have travelled back in time by means of a time machine to have the excitement of tracking down one of these prehistoric monsters. The encounter is more than they bargained for!

The jungle was wide and full of twitterings, rustlings, murmurs, and sighs.

Suddenly it all ceased, as if someone had shut a door.

Silence.

A sound of thunder.

Out of the mist, one hundred yards away, came *Tyrannosaurus Rex*.

'Jesus God,' whispered Eckels.

'Sh!'

It came on great oiled, resilient, striding legs. It towered thirty feet above half of the trees, a great evil god, folding its delicate watchmaker's claws close to its oily reptilian chest. Each lower leg was a piston, a thousand pounds of white bone, sunk in thick ropes of muscle, sheathed over in a gleam of pebbled skin like the mail of a terrible warrior. Each thigh was a ton of meat, ivory and steel mesh. And from the great breathing cage of the upper body those two delicate arms dangled out in front, arms with hands which might pick up and examine men like toys, while the snake neck coiled. And the head itself, a ton of sculptured stone, lifted easily upon the sky. Its mouth gaped, exposing a fence of teeth like daggers. Its eyes rolled, ostrich eggs, empty of all expression save hunger. It closed its mouth in a death grin. It ran, its pelvic bones crushing aside trees and bushes, its taloned feet clawing damp earth, leaving prints six inches deep wherever it settled its weight. It ran with a gliding ballet step, far too poised and balanced for its ten tons. It moved into the sunlight arena warily, its beautifully reptile hands feeling the air.

'My God!' Eckels twitched his mouth. 'It could reach up and grab the moon.'...

The Thunder Lizard raised itself. Its armoured flesh glittered like a thousand green coins. The coins, crusted with slime, steamed. In the slime, tiny insects wriggled, so that the entire body seemed to

twitch and undulate, even while the monster itself did not move. It exhaled. The stink of raw flesh blew down the wilderness.

'Get me out of here,' said Eckels. 'It was never like this before. I was always sure I'd come through alive. I had good guides, good safaris, and safety. This time, I figured wrong. I've met my match and admit it. This is too much for me to get hold of.'

'Don't run,' said Lesperance. 'Turn around. Hide in the Machine.'

'Yes.' Eckels seemed to be numb. He looked at his feet as if trying to make them move. He gave a grunt of helplessness.

'Eckels!'

He took a few steps, blinking, shuffling.

'Not *that* way!'

The Monster, at the first motion, lunged forward with a terrible scream. It covered one hundred yards in four seconds. The rifles jerked up and blazed fire. A windstorm from the beast's mouth engulfed them in the stench of slime and old blood. The Monster roared, teeth glittering with sun ...

The rifles cracked again. Their sound was lost in shriek and lizard thunder. The great lever of the reptile's tail swung up, lashed sideways. Trees exploded in clouds of leaf and branch. The Monster twitched its jeweller's hands down to fondle the men, to twist them in half, to crush them like berries, to cram them into its teeth and its screaming throat. Its boulder-stone eyes levelled with the men. They saw themselves mirrored. They fired at the metallic eyelids and the blazing black iris.

Like a stone idol, like a mountain avalanche, *Tyrannosaurus* fell. Thundering, it clutched trees, pulled them with it. It wrenched and tore the metal path. The men flung themselves back and away. The body hit, ten tons of cold flesh and stone. The guns fired. The Monster lashed its armoured tail, twitched its snake jaws, and lay still. A fount of blood spurted from its throat. Somewhere inside, a sac of fluids burst. Sickening gushes drenched the hunters. They stood, red and glistening.

The thunder faded.

The jungle was silent. After the avalanche, a green peace. After the nightmare, morning. ...

They wiped the blood from their helmets. They began to curse too. The Monster lay, a hill of solid flesh. Within, you could hear the sighs and murmurs as the furthest chambers of it died, the organs malfunctioning, liquids running a final instant from pocket to sac to spleen, everything shutting off, closing up forever. It was like standing by a wrecked locomotive or a steam shovel at quitting time, all valves being released or levered tight. Bones cracked; the tonnage of its own flesh, off balance, dead weight, snapped the delicate forearms, caught underneath. The meat settled, quivering.

Another cracking sound. Overhead, a gigantic tree branch broke from its heavy mooring, fell. It crashed upon the dead beast with finality.

RAY BRADBURY, *A Sound of Thunder*

The author says the jungle noises stopped 'as if someone had shut a door'. Do you think this is a good comparison? What kind of effect does it create?

Look again at the opening lines. Each statement is written on a separate line. What effect does this have?

In the description of the Tyrannosaurus Rex, the author uses a large number of comparisons, e.g. 'each lower leg was a piston', 'pebbled skin like the mail of a terrible warrior'. Pick out all the comparisons you can and discuss them.

In your own words describe what the monster looked like.

Some features of the monster are surprisingly delicate. Which are they?

Why does Eckels move the wrong way when the monster appears? Look at the way the author uses sounds and silence in the story. Pick out all the instances of their use. How do they help and emphasize what is happening in the story?

Try to go and see a dinosaur like the one above in a museum. How long ago did they live?

33

The Loch Ness Monster

Of course, dinosaurs did exist, but with some monsters there is some doubt about whether they were real or just part of legend. What about the Loch Ness Monster, for instance? Do you think it exists? Look at these pictures. Do they convince you?

Grendel

Here is an account of one of the fights which Beowulf, the Anglo-Saxon hero, had with Grendel. Whether Beowulf or Grendel existed or not is lost in the mists of legend. How true do you think the story is? Could Grendel have been a particularly large bear?

In the darkest hour of the spring night Grendel came to Heorot as he had come so many times before, up from his lair and over the high moors, through the mists that seemed to travel with him under the pale moon: Grendel, the Night-Stalker, the Death-Shadow. He came to the foreporch and snuffed about it, and smelled the man-smell, and found that the door which had stood unlatched for him so long was barred and bolted. Snarling in rage that any man should dare attempt to keep him out, he set the flat of his talon-tipped hands against the timbers and burst them in.

Dark as it was, the hall seemed to fill with a monstrous shadow at his coming; a shadow in which Beowulf, half springing up, then holding himself in frozen stillness, could make out no shape nor clear outline save two eyes filled with a wavering greenish flame.

The ghastly corpse-light of his own eyes showed Grendel the shapes of men as it seemed sleeping, and he did not notice among them one who leaned up on his elbow. Laughing in his throat, he reached out and grabbed young Hondscio who lay nearest to him, and almost before his victim had time to cry out, tore him limb from limb and drank the warm blood. Then, while the young warrior's dying shriek still hung upon the air, he reached for another. But this time his hand was met and seized in a grasp such as he had never felt before; a grasp that had in it the strength of thirty men. And for the first time he who had brought fear to so many caught the taste of it himself, knowing that at last he had met his match and maybe his master.

Beowulf leapt from the sleeping bench and grappled him in the darkness; and terror broke over Grendel in full force, the terror of a wild animal trapped; so that he thought no more of his hunting but only of breaking the terrible hold upon his arm and flying back into the night and the wilderness, and he howled and bellowed as he struggled for his freedom. Beowulf set his teeth and summoned all

his strength and tightened his grip until the sinews cracked; and locked together they reeled and staggered up and down the great hall. Trestles and sleeping benches went over with crash on crash as they strained this way and that, trampling even through the last red embers of the dying fire; and the very walls seemed to groan and shudder as though the stout timbers would burst apart. And all the while Grendel snarled and shrieked and Beowulf fought in silence save for his gasping breaths.

Outside, the Danes listened in horror to the turmoil that seemed as though it must split Heorot asunder; and within, the Geats had sprung from their sleeping benches sword in hand, forgetful of their powerlessness against the Troll-kind, but in the dark, lit only by stray gleams of bale-fire from the monster's eyes, they dared not strike for fear of slaying their leader, and when one or other of them did contrive to get in a blow, the sword blade glanced off Grendel's charmed hide as though he were sheathed in dragon scales.

At last, when the hall was wrecked to the walls, the Night-Stalker gathered himself for one last despairing effort to break free. Beowulf's hold was as fierce as ever; yet none the less the two figures burst apart – and Grendel with a frightful shriek staggered to the doorway and through it, and fled wailing into the night, leaving his arm and shoulder torn from the roots in the hero's still unbroken grasp.

Beowulf sank down sobbing for breath on a shattered bench, and his fellows came crowding round him with torches rekindled at the scattered embers of the fire; and together they looked at the thing he held across his knees. 'Not even the Troll-kind could live half a day with a wound such as that upon them,' one of them said; and Waegmund agreed. 'He is surely dead as though he lay here among the benches.'

'Hondscio is avenged, at all events,' said Beowulf. 'Let us hang up this thing for a trophy, and a proof that we do not boast idly as the wind blows over.'

So in triumph they nailed up the huge scaly arm on one of the roof beams above the High Seat of Hrothgar.

ROSEMARY SUTCLIFF, *Dragon Slayer*

Pick out all the details you can of Grendel's appearance.

What did Grendel realize for the first time when Beowulf seized hold of him?

Sound is important in this story too. Pick out all the references to sounds.

Another factor that helps to create the right atmosphere is the use of darkness and light. Point to all the references to these and say how they affect the telling of the story.

Mechanical Monsters

Many authors writing about the future also imagine monsters, but often these are of a different kind – not animals but machines. The monsters in *The White Mountains* are called Tripods. They consist of a great hemisphere of gleaming metal above three articulated legs and are several times as tall as a house. They have enormous burnished tentacles with which they can pick things up. In this extract from the novel, the narrator and his friends, Henry and Beanpole, who are trying to escape from the Tripods, are tracked down.

Seconds later it was in sight, coming round the base of the hill and, unmistakably, climbing towards us. It was some miles away, but coming on fast – much faster, I thought, than its usual rate of progress.

Henry said: 'The bushes ...'

He did not need to say any more; we were all three running. What he had indicated offered one of the few bits of cover on the hillside, the only one within reasonable reach. It was a small thicket of bushes, growing to about shoulder height. We flung ourselves in amongst them, burrowed into the centre, and crouched down there ...

I felt the ground shiver under me, and again and again with still greater force. Then one of the Tripod's legs plunged across the blue, and I saw the hemisphere, black against the arc of sky, and tried to dig myself down into the earth. At that moment the howling stopped. In the silence I heard a different, whistling sound of something whipping terribly fast through the air and, glancing fearfully, saw two or three bushes uprooted and tossed away.

Beside me, Beanpole said: 'It has us. It knows we are here. It can pull the bushes out till we are plainly seen.'

'Or kill us, pulling them out,' Henry said. 'If that thing hit you ...'

I said: 'If I showed myself ...'

'No use. It knows there are three.'

'We could run different ways,' Henry said. 'One of us might get away.'

I saw more bushes sail through the air, like confetti. You do not get used to fear, I thought; it grips you as firmly every time. Beanpole said:

'We can fight it.'

He said it with a lunatic calm, which made me want to groan. Henry said:

'What with? Our fists?'

'The metal eggs.' He had his pack open already, and was rummaging in it. The Tripod's tentacle whistled down again. It was ripping the bushes up systematically. A few more passes – half a dozen at most – would bring it to us. 'Perhaps these were what our ancestors used, to fight the Tripods. Perhaps that is why they were in the underground Shmand-Fair – they went out from there to fight them.'

I said: 'And they lost! How do you think ...?'

He had got the eggs out. He said: 'What else is there?'

Henry said: 'I threw mine away. They were too much trouble to carry.'

The tentacle sliced into the bushes, and this time we were scattered with earth as it pulled them up. Beanpole said:

'There are four.' He handed one each to Henry and me. 'I will take the others. If we pull out the rings, count three, then stand up and throw. At the leg that is nearest. The hemisphere is too high.'

This time I saw the tentacle *through* the bushes as it scooped up more. Beanpole said:

'Now!'

He pulled the rings from his eggs, and Henry did the same. I had taken mine in my left hand, and I needed to transfer it to my right. As I did so, pain ripped my arm-pit again, and I dropped it. I was fumbling on the ground to pick it up when Beanpole said: 'Now!' again. They scrambled to their feet, and I grabbed the last egg, ignoring the pain of the movement, and got up with them. I ripped out the ring just as they threw.

The nearest foot of the Tripod was planted on the slope, thirty yards or so above us. Beanpole's first throw was wild – he did not get within ten yards of his target. But his second throw, and Henry's, were close to the mark. One of them hit metal, with a clang that we could hear. Almost at once that exploded. There were three nearly simultaneous bangs, and fountains of earth and dust sprouted into the air.

But they did not obscure one plain fact: the eggs had done no damage to the Tripod. It stood as firmly as before, and the tentacle was swishing down, this time directly towards us. We started to run, or rather, in my case, prepared to. Because before I could move, it had me round the waist.

I plucked at it with my left hand, but it was like trying to bend a rock. It held me with amazing precision, tight but not crushing, and lifted me as I might lift a mouse. Except that a mouse could bite, and I could do nothing against the hard gleaming surface that held me. I was lifted up, up. The ground shrank below me, and with it the figures of Beanpole and Henry. I saw them darting away like ants. I was

steeple-high, higher. I looked up, and saw the hole in the side of the hemisphere. And remembered the iron egg still clutched in my right hand.

How long was it since I had pulled the ring out? I had forgotten to count in my fear and confusion. Several seconds – it could not be long before it exploded. The tentacle was swinging me inwards now. The hole was forty feet away, thirty-five, thirty. I braced myself back, straining against the encircling band. Pain leapt in my arm again, but I ignored it. I hurled the egg with all my strength, and what accuracy I could muster. I thought at first that I had missed, but the egg hit the edge of the opening and ricocheted inside. The tentacle continued to carry me forwards. Twenty feet, fifteen, ten ...

Although I was nearer, the explosion was not as loud as the others had been, probably because it happened inside the hemisphere. There was just a dull, rather hollow bang. Despair came back: that was my last chance gone. But at that instant I felt the metal holding me relax and fall away.

I was three times the height of a tall pine; my bones would smash against the ground when I landed. I clutched desperately at the thing against which, a few seconds earlier, I had been struggling. My hands gripped the metal, but I was falling, falling. I looked at the ground, and closed my eyes as it rushed up to meet me. And then there was a jerk which almost tore me from my hold, and the falling stopped. My feet shivered, a few inches from the surface. All I had to do was let go, and step down.

The others came to me. We stared up, in awe, at the Tripod. It stood there, seemingly unharmed. But we knew it was finished, destroyed, lifeless.

JOHN CHRISTOPHER, *The White Mountains*

Beanpole spoke 'with a lunatic calm'. What does that mean?

What are 'the metal eggs'?

What was the 'Shmand-Fair'? If you know any French, that might help.

Henry threw his metal eggs away. What does that suggest about him?

How does the author convey the difference in size between the Tripod and the boys. Look at the comparisons he uses.

What can you deduce about the different characters of the three boys from what they say and do?

Writing

Monsters from the Deep

One of the reasons the Loch Ness Monster holds a strong fascination for people is that it is not possible finally to prove whether it exists or not. Water is much more difficult to explore than land, and it is just possible that there are still strange monsters in the sea that man has not yet discovered. Here is Tennyson's account of the Kraken, a legendary sea-monster.

The Kraken

Below the thunders of the upper deep;
Far, far beneath in the abysmal sea,
His ancient, dreamless, uninvaded sleep
The Kraken sleepeth; faintest sunlights flee
About his shadowy sides; above him swell
Huge sponges of millenial growth and heith;
And far away into the sickly light,
From many a woundrous grot and secret cell
Unnumber'd and enormous polypi
Winnow with giant arms the slumbering green.
There hath he lain for ages and will lie
Battening upon huge seaworms in his sleep
Until the latter fire shall heat the deep;
Then once by man and angels to be seen,
In roaring he shall rise and on the surface die.

ALFRED LORD TENNYSON

What kind of atmosphere does the poem create?

Using Comparisons

Look again at the comparisons Ray Bradbury uses in his description of the Tyrannosaurus Rex. If we pick some of them out and write them down, each on a separate line, they make a kind of poem:

The creature picked up and examined men like toys.
Its mouth gaped in a fence of teeth like daggers.
Its armoured flesh glittered like a thousand green coins.
The skin of its thighs was like the mail of a terrible warrior.

Here is a poem which a pupil wrote using the same kind of idea about her monster.

We went to the hills and there we saw
A monster with skin as green as grass
And teeth as sharp as an axe.
He was bigger than an elephant
Yet walked as daintily as a cat.
He was covered with scales like leaves
And his eyes shone like silver.
His head was the shape of a pear.
He had claws on his feet like railings.
His tail was like a long tree trunk.
He thumped his tail on the ground,
It sounded like an explosion.
He ran as fast as a horse
And made the noise of a jet plane.
He knocked down trees like a bulldozer.
He drank from a pool as if he was dying of thirst.
He grabbed a small animal and tore it apart
Like a cat does a bird.

LYNN SHARPE

Consider each comparison and say how effective you think each is.

For instance, the monster has skin 'as green as grass'. Does this give us a good idea of the colour of the monster's skin? What colour is it exactly? How do we know?

A Comic Monster

Not all monsters are frightening. Sometimes they can be comic or even endearing. Such a monster is the one that Alice encountered in *Alice Through the Looking-Glass.*

There was a book lying near Alice on the table, and while she sat watching the White King (for she was still a little anxious about him, and had the ink all ready to throw over him, in case he fainted again), she turned over the leaves, to find some part that she could read, ' – for it's all in some language I don't know,' she said to herself.

It was like this.

Jabberwocky)

'Twas brillig, and the slithy toves
Did gyre and gimble in the wabe:
All mimsy were the borogoves,
And the mome raths outgrabe.

She puzzled over this for some time, but at last a bright thought struck her. 'Why, it's a Looking-glass book, of course! And, if I hold it up to a glass, the words will all go the right way again.'

This was the poem that Alice read

Jabberwocky

'Twas brillig and the slithy toves
   Did gyre and gimble in the wabe:
All mimsy were the borogoves,
   And the mome raths outgrabe.

'Beware the Jabberwock, my son!
   The jaws that bite, the claws that catch!
Beware the Jubjub bird, and shun
   The frumious Bandersnatch!'

He took his vorpal sword in hand:
   Long time the manxome foe he sought –
So rested he by the Tumtum tree,
   And stood awhile in thought.

And, as in uffish thought he stood,
   The Jabberwock, with eyes of flame,
Came whiffling through the tulgey wood,
   And burbled as it came!

One, two! One, two! And through and through
   The vorpal blade went snicker-snack!
He left it dead, and with its head
   He went galumphing back.

'And hast thou slain the Jabberwock?
   Come to my arms, my beamish boy!
O frabjous day! Callooh! Callay!'
   He chortled in his joy.

'Twas brillig, and the slithy toves
   Did gyre and gimble in the wabe:
All mimsy were the borogoves,
   And the mome raths outgrabe.

'It seems very pretty,' she said when she had finished it, 'but it's *rather* hard to understand!' (You see she didn't like to confess, even to herself, that she couldn't make it out at all.) 'Somehow it seems to fill my head with ideas – only I don't exactly know what they are! However, *somebody* killed *something*: that's clear, at any rate – '
LEWIS CARROLL, *Alice Through the Looking-Glass*

Alice has difficulty in understanding exactly what is happening in the poem. Why?

   How much of the action of the poem can you make out?

 Assignments

Choose several of the following to write about:

1. Write a poem describing a monster made up of comparisons like the one given earlier.
2. Invent the name of a new monster and write a poem about it.
3. Imagine that a scientific experiment goes wrong and some small creature such as a fly or an ant or a wasp grows to a hundred times its normal size. Write about what happens.
4. Write a story about an expedition which sets out to try to find a long-lost monster.
5. Write a story or a description about the world when pre-historic animals were alive.
6. To a small creature like a mouse, a cat would appear as a monster. Write a story about such a monster from the point of view of the small animal.
7. Find out as much as you can about a real or imaginary monster such as a dinosaur, the Loch Ness Monster, the Yeti, and write about it.
8. A live pre-historic monster has been discovered and brought back for display in a zoo. Write a newspaper report of the event or describe the scene when you go to see the monster at the zoo yourself.
9. Write a story or a poem about an unsuccessful monster – one that tries to be terrifying but fails.
10. The Fight to the Finish. Describe a combat between two monsters real or imaginary that ends in death.

 Language

A. Sentences

A sentence is a complete statement that can stand by itself. The first word has a capital letter and the last word is followed by a full stop.

   Here is the opening of the extract from Ray Bradbury's *A Sound of Thunder*.

The jungle was wide and full of twitterings, rustlings, murmurs and sighs.

Suddenly it all ceased, as if someone had shut a door.

Silence.

A sound of thunder.

Consider each statement in turn and say whether it makes sense.

Some people might say that a sentence must have a verb and a subject, but the important thing at this stage is to train your ear and to use your common sense to judge whether a group of words is making a complete statement or not. 'Silence' and 'A sound of thunder' are like stage directions setting the scene. They could be expanded into statements like 'There was silence' and 'There was a sound of thunder'. Which is more effective – 'Silence' or 'There was silence'? Why?

When you are writing, try to break up what you are writing into separate statements, each of which is complete, and each of which begins with a capital letter and ends with a full stop. If possible, read it out loud, coming to an exaggerated stop at the end of each complete statement. Where this break comes, there should be a full stop.

If you have difficulty with this, it might be useful for a while in your writing to take a new line every time you make a new statement – as Ray Bradbury did, though his reasons for doing it were rather different.

Look at each of the following groups of words and say which you would regard as complete understandable statements or sentences:

1. Help!
2. The creature with fiery nostrils.
3. Having pulled back the safety catch.
4. The monster roared furiously.
5. Catch its prey.
6. Its talons were six inches long and sharp as a razor.
7. Its hooded eyes, its matted mane, its pointed ears, its cruel mouth.
8. He felt its hot breath against his face, rasping the flesh, smothering his own breath, blinding his eyes.
9. The monster.
0. Through the forest and over the cliff.

(NOTE: some of these groups of words could make sense in some circumstances but not in others. Can you justify your choice and state when they would make sense and when they wouldn't?)

Write ten sentences on one of the following, taking a new line for each sentence:

1. The dark forest.
2. The monster's lair.
3. Trapped in a cave.
4. Strange noises.
5. The sea monster.

Usually people don't write short enough sentences – or rather, they don't put enough full stops in. *Rewrite the following, putting in full stops as you think necessary. Take a new line for each sentence.*

The monster was horrifying it reared itself high above us its red eyes glared angrily at the intruders who had disturbed its peace beyond it we could see its den a dark hole in the face of the cliff with torn-off branches guarding the entrance we didn't dare move what could we do next I don't know what my companions were feeling but judging from their ash-grey faces they felt the same way I did they were terrified they thought their last hour had come there was no time for thought as the monster was bearing down on us.

(There should be ten sentences.)

It should be clear from this exercise why we need to use full stops and write in sentences. If we don't, the sense is not always clear, and the reader is not able to understand what the writer is saying.

B. The Full Stop

The full stop (.) is a punctuation mark used to show the end of a complete statement or sentence.

It is also used to show that a word has been shortened, e.g.

rev. for reverend

Jan. for January

W. M. Thackeray for William Makepeace Thackeray

It is normal to use the full stop for abbreviations like these which use the first part or the first letter of the word, but not to use the full stop when the abbreviated word contains the last letter of the word. E.g. full stops are not used in

Mr for Mister
St for Saint
Rd for Road.

Some shortened versions of words have become so common that the full stop is no longer required, e.g.

ad for advertisement
pub for public house
tele or TV for television.

Make a list of as many abbreviations as you can where the full stop is required.

Make a list of as many abbreviations as you can where the final letter of the word is used and where there is therefore usually no full stop.

Make a list of as many words as you can like 'ad' and 'pub' which are abbreviations but which are now so commonly used as words in their own right that we leave out the full stop.

C. Nouns

In the 'Language' section of Unit 1, we looked at pronouns and said that they were parts of speech and took the place of nouns, but we didn't really discuss what nouns were. A noun is another kind of part of speech. Words can be divided up into different groups (or parts of speech) according to the kind of job they do, just as tools can be divided up into saws, files, spanners, screwdrivers, etc. according to the different job they do. Just as it is useful to know when making or repairing something that you need a spanner not a saw, so it is sometimes useful when dealing with words to know that you need a noun and not an adjective. (Words are perhaps more complicated. An adjective can sometimes be used as a noun, just as – in an emergency – a spanner can be used as a hammer, but we'll go into that later!)

So that people know what we are talking about, we have to have names for the people and objects we are talking about. These names belong to that part of speech called nouns.

Look around you. Name some of the objects you see, such as windows, desks, chairs, people. All of these words are nouns.

Write down fifty words which are the names of objects and which are therefore nouns.

Vocabulary

A. Nouns

As we saw, nouns are the names we give to people and objects so that we know what is being referred to when we are talking or writing. They help us to distinguish between one person or object and another. For instance, if we use the noun Michael or Mary, we know that we are not referring to David or Diana. The same is true of the names we give to objects or things. We might refer to a particular object as a book, but there are other names or nouns we might use which would define the object more precisely and give a clearer idea of what exactly we are referring to, words like 'volume', 'tome', 'tract', 'textbook', 'pamphlet', 'monograph', 'publication', 'novel', 'play'. *Try to distinguish between the different shades of meaning suggested by these words.*

Similarly, try to explain the difference in meaning between these nouns which all indicate a kind of human or animal noise:

cry, grunt, moan, roar, shout, scream, screech, shriek, squeak, squeal, whine.

Here are a number of nouns which are the names of boats. Find out what precisely each refers to:

packet, liner, whaler, collier, coaster, tanker, freighter, steamer, lighter, trawler, drifter, hulk, yacht, bark, brig, brigantine, schooner, sloop, cutter, corvette, clipper, yawl, ketch, smack, lugger, barge, hoy, wind-jammer, tub, pinnace, launch, dory, skiff, dinghy, wherry, coble, punt, raft, pontoon.

B. Tripods

John Christopher in his novel *The White Mountains* names his monsters 'Tripods'. Can you think why? Remember they consisted of a great hemisphere of gleaming metal above three articulated legs. Do you know what a tripod is in the science laboratory and why it is so called?

'Tri' is a Greek word meaning 'three'. *With that information, work out the meaning of the following words:*

triangle, tricolour, tricorn, trident, triennial, trilogy, trinity, trio, triptych, trireme, trivet.

'Pod' comes from a Greek word meaning 'foot'. In Latin, this word becomes 'ped'. *Can you work out the meaning of the following words?——*

pedal, pedigree, pedestal, pedestrian, pedometer, quadruped.

C. Portmanteau Words

How did you get on with the poem 'Jabberwocky'? Here is Lewis Carroll's own explanation given later in *Alice Through the Looking-Glass*.

'You seem very clever at explaining words, Sir,' said Alice. 'Would you kindly tell me the meaning of the poem called "Jabberwocky"?'

'Let's hear it,' said Humpty Dumpty. 'I can explain all the poems that ever were invented – and a good many that haven't been invented just yet.'

This sounded very hopeful, so Alice repeated the first verse:

'Twas brillig, and the slithy toves
   Did gyre and gimble in the wabe:
All mimsy were the borogoves,
   And the mome raths outgrabe.

'That's enough to begin with,' Humpty Dumpty interrupted: 'there are plenty of hard words there. "Brillig" means four o'clock in the afternoon – the time when you begin *broiling* things for dinner.'

'That'll do very well,' said Alice: 'and "slithy"?'

'Well, "slithy" means "lithe and slimy". "Lithe" is the same as "active". You see it's like a portmanteau – there are two meanings packed into one word.'

'I see it now,' Alice remarked thoughtfully: 'and what are "toves"?'

'Well, "toves" are something like badgers – they're something like lizards – and they're everything like corkscrews.'

'They must be very curious-looking creatures.'

'They are that,' said Humpty Dumpty: 'also they make their nests under sun-dials – also they live on cheese.'

'And what's to "gyre" and to "gimble"?'

'To "gyre" is to go round and round like a gyroscope. To "gimble" is to make holes like a gimlet.'

'And "the wabe" is the grass-plot round a sundial, I suppose?' said Alice, surprised at her own ingenuity.

'Of course it is. It's called "wabe", you know, because it goes a long way before it, and a long way behind it—'

'And a long way beyond it on each side,' Alice added.

'Exactly so. Well then, "mimsy" is "flimsy and miserable" (there's another portmanteau for you). And a "borogove" is a thin shabby-looking bird with its feathers sticking out all round – something like a live mop.'

'And then "mome raths"?' said Alice. 'I'm afraid I'm giving you a great deal of trouble.'

'Well, a "rath" is a sort of green pig: but "mome" I'm not certain about. I think it's short for "from home" – meaning that they'd lost their way, you know.'

'And what does "outgrabe" mean?'

'Well, "outgrabing" is something between bellowing and whistling, with a kind of sneeze in the middle: however, you'll hear it done, maybe – down in the wood yonder – and, when you've once heard it, you'll be *quite* content. Who's been repeating all that hard stuff to you?'

'I read it in a book,' said Alice.

The term 'portmanteau word' has been accepted as a description of a new word which is made by compressing together two or more other words. (What *is* a portmanteau?) Two modern examples in use are 'motel' (which combines the two words 'motorist's hotel') and 'moped' ('motor-assisted pedal bicycle'). Can you think of any others?

 Spelling

A. Monster/Monstrous

The adjective formed from the noun 'monster' is 'monstrous'. Note the spelling. The 'e' of 'monster' is dropped when '-ous' is added.
  Similarly:

disaster becomes disastrous
wonder   wondrous

But:

conifer	becomes	coniferous
danger		dangerous
murder		murderous
thunder		thunderous

Note also the following words which can lead to confusion in spelling:

lustre	lustrous
languor	languorous
traitor	traitorous
vapour	vaporous
humour	humorous
glamour	glamorous
clamour	clamorous
odour	odorous
rigour	rigorous
valour	valorous
vigour	vigorous
rancour	rancorous
pity	piteous
right	righteous
courage	courageous
advantage	advantageous
fury	furious
torture	torturous
rapture	rapturous
adventure	adventurous
ridicule	ridiculous

Learn these spellings. If there are any words whose meanings you are unsure of, look them up in a dictionary. Use some of the words in sentences.

B. Tyrannosaurus Rex

The Tyrannosaurus Rex gets its name from the Greek word 'tyrant' meaning absolute ruler. Note the double 'n' in the forms 'tyranny', 'tyrannical', 'tyrannize'.

Double letters in words can often create problems. When we come to a particular word, we stop and think, 'Is there a double "r" or a double "n"?' The only way to remember is to memorize it. Here are some words for you to learn which sometimes give trouble.

accelerate	intelligent
accommodate	jewellery

account	mattress
appalling	Mediterranean
assassin	necessary
beginning	occurrence
cannibal	parallel
Caribbean	Piccadilly
caterpillar	possess
commemorate	professor
committee	quarrel
different	satellite
disappear	sheriff
disappoint	silhouette
dissatisfy	subterranean
embarrass	stubborn
exaggerate	stubbornness
grammar	success
harass	terrible
inflammable	woollen
innocent	

 Activities

A. 1. You drink a magic drug. Imagine i slowly running down inside your body. Gradu ally, you are transformed into a monster. First the hands, then the arms and shoulders, then th torso and legs, and finally the face and head Now find out how you walk.

2. Transform yourself into a monster again This time, with a group of friends, play handbal or football, as monsters would.

3. You are alone in a forest when you hear a strange sound. You go closer and find a grou of weird half-animal, half-human creature dancing in a clearing. You are drawn into th dance which becomes more and more wild How do you break loose and escape? Or wha happens in the end? (Music would help you t create the right mood here – perhaps 'The Hal of the Mountain King' from Grieg's *Peer Gynt.*

4. You are a monster of some kind. Wha kind of noise do you make when you are angry Or when you are hungry? Or when you ar calling to another monster?

5. You could go on to invent a language you monsters use. It could consist of words begin ning with the same sound – 'k', for instance, o

44

'th'. Or 'Dalek' speech. Or words with no consonants in them. Or the same sound varied in pitch and intonation.

B. 1. Draw a picture of a monster. Make it as strange and unusual, as gruesome and horrifying, as you can. Then write about it.

2. Find out about prehistoric animals from reference books and then write an account of them. Illustrate your account with pictures and drawings.

3. Make a survey of your class to find out how many of them believe that the Loch Ness Monster exists and why.

4. Find out which monster the members of your class would least like to meet on a dark night and ask them to give their reasons.

5. Discuss why horror films are so popular. Give examples you know about or have seen.

Reading List

Try to read one or more of the following books which are largely or partly about monsters:

John Christopher, *The White Mountains*
  The City of Gold and Lead
  The Pool of Fire
H. G. Wells, *The War of the Worlds*
Rosemary Sutcliff, *Dragon Slayer*
C. S. Lewis, *The Last Battle*
Patricia Wrightson, *The Nargun and the Stars*
Nicholas Fisk, *Trillions*
John Wyndham, *The Day of the Triffids*
  The Kraken Wakes
A. Conan Doyle, *The Lost World*
J. R. R. Tolkien, *The Hobbit*
Margery Morris, *About Dinosaurs*
  How Man Began
Robert Silverberg, *Mammoths, Mastodons and Man*

CONSOLIDATION 1

Consolidation means strengthening, and the intention of this section is to enable you to consolidate or strengthen your knowledge of what you have learned in the previous units. You have a chance to go over again some of the points made and to check whether you have understood and remembered them.

A. Parts of Speech

Parts of speech are the names given to the different groups that words can be divided into according to the kind of work they do. There are eight parts of speech: noun, pronoun, adjective, adverb, verb, preposition, conjunction and interjection. We have looked at the first three so far.

PART OF SPEECH	DESCRIPTION	EXAMPLES
noun	the name of something	table, desk, Michael, Susan, carriage
pronoun	a word that can take the place of a noun	I, you, us them, it
adjective	a word that describes a noun or pronoun	brave, red, foolish, large

B. Person

Nouns, pronouns and verbs can be classified according to the person indicated.

PERSON	DESCRIPTION	EXAMPLES
First	the person speaking	I, me, we, us
Second	the person spoken to	you
Third	the person or thing spoken about	he, she, him, her, they, them, sky, sea, tree, river, city, street

C. Mood

The mood of a verb (a part of speech we shall look at in greater detail later) tells us about the action or state of a verb. There are four moods: indicative, imperative, subjunctive and conditional. We studied the first two when we considered statements and commands in Unit 2.

The indicative is the mood used in all ordinary statements and questions and is the mood most commonly found in spoken and written English. The imperative is the mood used to express orders or commands or requests or entreaties.

46

MOOD	DESCRIPTION	EXAMPLES
indicative	used for factual statements and question	The sky is clear tonight. Are you feeling better? The dog picked the bone up in its mouth.
imperative	used for orders, commands, requests, entreaties	Help! Come here. Let's go home. Please find out what has gone wrong.

D. Language

1. What is a dialect?
2. What is Standard English?
3. When must the letter 'i' always be written as a capital 'I'?
4. What is a pronoun?
5. Name ten pronouns.
6. What person are the pronouns in this sentence? – 'I like to fly my kite by myself.'
7. Change the sentence given in 6 into the third person.
8. What is the mood of the verb in this sentence? – 'The birds are searching for worms on the lawn.'
9. Change this statement into the imperative: 'Pupils should not throw stones.'
10. What is a simile?
11. Is this a simile? – 'Jean and Laura, identical twins, were so alike that no one could tell which was which.'
12. Is this a simile? – 'The monster's talons were as sharp as razors.'
13. What is a sentence?
14. How does a sentence begin?
15. How does a sentence finish?
16. Is this a sentence? – 'Failed to appear.'
17. Is this a sentence? – 'Stop.'
18. What is an adjective?
19. Name twenty adjectives.
20. Name two uses of the full stop.
21. Name five abbreviations which need a full stop.
22. Name five abbreviations which do not need a full stop.
23. What is a noun?
24. Name twenty nouns.

E. Vocabulary

1. What is an autobiography?
2. What is a seismograph?
3. What is an autocrat?
4. What does 'self-opinionated' mean?
5. What does 'etymology' mean?
6. What does 'meteorology' mean?
7. What does the Greek work 'bios' mean?
8. What does 'ology' mean?
9. What is a nickname?
10. What is a trident?
11. What does 'tri' in words mean?
12. What is a pedestal?
13. What is a quadruped?
14. What is a portmanteau word?
15. Give an example of a portmanteau word.

F. Spelling

1. Explain the difference between 'whose' and 'who's'.
2. Explain why there is an apostrophe in 'don't'.
3. What is the shortened version of 'cannot'?
4. What is the shortened version of 'shall not'?
5. Are English words spelled the way they are pronounced?
6. Does 'rough' rhyme with 'though'?
7. Name two words that contain a silent 'g'.
8. Name two words that contain a silent 'h'.
9. Spell the word formed by adding 'ous' to 'monster'.

47

10. Spell the word formed by adding 'ous' to 'glamour'.
11. Spell the adjective formed from 'tyrant'.
12. Spell the word which might be used as an alternative to 'rooms' in the notice 'Rooms vacant'. It begins with 'a'.
13. The person in charge of a university department is usually called a p . . . . . .
14. Sicily is an island in the M . . . . . Sea.
15. If at first you don't s . . . . . , try, try and try again.

UNIT 4

Christmas

 Reading and Understanding

Family Christmas

Christmas is traditionally a time when families get together. It is the one time in the year when people travel home, when uncles and aunts congregate, and Christmas dinner sees them all gathered around the same table. It is a time for catching up on the news of what has happened during the previous year, of getting to know each other again and joining in games and festivities that help to unite the family as one. It is a time for children particularly to enjoy themselves, a time for eating and giving presents and going to parties.

The following extract from *A Christmas Carol* by Charles Dickens describes such a family gathering. As you read it, consider what feelings you think the author is trying to convey. How do the different members of the family feel about the Christmas dinner? How is the reader meant to react to them?

Then up rose Mrs Cratchit, Cratchit's wife, dressed out but poorly in a twice-turned gown, but brave in ribbons, which are cheap and made a goodly show for sixpence; and she laid the cloth, assisted by Belinda Cratchit, second of her daughters, also brave in ribbons; while Master Peter Cratchit plunged a fork into the saucepans of potatoes, and getting the corners of his monstrous shirt collar (Bob's private property, conferred upon his son and heir in honour of the day) into his mouth, rejoiced to find himself so gallantly attired, and yearned to show his linen in the fashionable Parks. And now two smaller Cratchits, boy and girl, came tearing in, screaming that outside the baker's they had smelt the goose, and known it for their own; and basking in luxurious thoughts of sage and onion, these young Cratchits danced about the table, and exalted Master Peter Cratchit to the skies, while he (not proud, although his collars nearly choked him) blew the fire, until the slow potatoes bubbling up, knocked loudly at the saucepan lid to be let out and peeled.

'What has ever got your precious father then?' said Mrs Cratchit. 'And your brother, Tiny Tim! And Martha warn't as late last Christmas Day by half-an-hour!'

'Here's Martha, Mother!' cried the two young Cratchits. 'Hurrah! There's *such* a goose, Martha!'

'Why, bless your heart alive, my dear, how late you are!' said Mrs Cratchit, kissing her a dozen times, and taking off her shawl and bonnet for her with officious zeal.

'We'd a deal of work to finish up last night,' replied the girl, 'and had to clear away this morning, Mother!'

'Well! Never mind so long as you are come,' said Mrs Cratchit. 'Sit ye down before the fire, my dear, and have a warm, Lord bless ye!'

'No, no! There's Father coming!' cried the two young Cratchits, who were everywhere at once. 'Hide, Martha, hide!'

So Martha hid herself, and in came little Bob, the father, with at least three feet of comforter exclusive of the fringe, hanging down before him; and his threadbare clothes darned up and brushed, to look seasonable; and Tiny Tim upon his shoulder. Alas for Tiny Tim, he bore a little crutch, and had his limbs supported by an iron frame!

'Why, where's our Martha?' cried Bob Cratchit, looking round.

'Not coming,' said Mrs Cratchit.

'Not coming!' said Bob, with a sudden declension in his high spirits; for he had been Tim's blood horse all the way from church, and had come home rampant. 'Not coming upon Christmas Day!'

'He had been Tim's blood horse all the way from church, and had come home rampant.'

Martha didn't like to see him disappointed, if it were only in joke; so she came out prematurely from behind the closet door, and ran into his arms, while the two young Cratchits hustled Tiny Tim, and bore him off into the wash-house, that he might hear the pudding singing in the copper.

'And how did little Tim behave?' asked Mrs Cratchit, when she had rallied Bob on his credulity, and Bob had hugged his daughter to his heart's content.

'As good as gold,' said Bob, 'and better. Somehow he gets thoughtful, sitting by himself so much, and thinks the strangest things you ever heard. He told me, coming home, that he hoped the people saw him in the church, because he was a cripple, and it might be pleasant to them to remember upon Christmas Day, who made lame beggars walk and blind men see.'

Bob's voice was tremulous when he told them this, and trembled more when he said that Tiny Tim was growing strong and hearty.

His active little crutch was heard upon the floor, and back came Tiny Tim before another word was spoken, escorted by his brother and sister to his stool before the fire; and while Bob, turning up his cuffs – as if, poor fellow, they were capable of being made more shabby – compounded some hot mixture in a jug with gin and lemons, and stirred it round and round and put it on the hob to simmer, Master Peter and the two ubiquitous young Cratchits went to fetch the goose, with which they soon returned in high procession.

Such a bustle ensued that you might have thought a goose the rarest of all birds; a feathered phenomenon, to which a black swan was a matter of course, and in truth it was something very like it in that house. Mrs Cratchit made the gravy (ready beforehand in a little saucepan) hissing hot; Master Peter mashed the potatoes with incredible vigour; Miss Belinda sweetened up the apple sauce; Martha dusted the hot plates; Bob took Tiny Tim beside him in a tiny corner at the table; the two young Cratchits set chairs for everybody, not forgetting themselves, and mounting guard upon their posts, crammed spoons into their mouths, lest they should shriek for goose before their turn came to be helped. At last the dishes were set on, and grace was said. It was succeeded by a breathless pause, as Mrs Cratchit, looking slowly all along the carving-knife, prepared to plunge it in the breast; but when she did, and when the long-expected gush of stuffing issued forth, one murmur of delight arose all round the board, and even Tiny Tim, excited by the two young Cratchits, beat on the table with the handle of his knife, and feebly cried Hurrah!

There never was such a goose. Bob said he didn't believe there ever was such a goose cooked. Its tenderness and flavour, size and cheapness, were the themes of universal admiration. Eked out by the apple sauce and mashed potatoes, it was a sufficient dinner for the whole family; indeed, as Mrs Cratchit said with great delight (surveying one small atom of a bone upon the dish), they hadn't ate it all at last! Yet everyone had had enough, and the youngest Cratchits, in particular, were steeped in sage and onions to the eyebrows! But now, the plates being changed by Miss Belinda, Mrs Cratchit left the room alone – too nervous to bear witnesses – to take the pudding up and bring it in.

Suppose it should not be done enough! Suppose it should break in turning out! Suppose somebody should have got over the wall of the back-yard, and stolen it, while they were merry with the goose – a supposition at which the two young Cratchits became livid! All sorts of horrors were supposed.

Halloa! A great deal of steam! The pudding was out of the copper. A smell like a washing-day! That was the cloth. A smell like an eating-house and a pastry-cook's next door to each other, with a laundress's next door to that! That was the pudding! In half a minute, Mrs Cratchit entered – flushed, but smiling proudly – with the pudding, like a speckled cannon-ball, so hard and firm, blazing in half a quartern of ignited brandy, and bedight with Christmas holly stuck into the top.

Oh, a wonderful pudding! Bob Cratchit said, and calmly too, that he regarded it as the greatest success achieved by Mrs Cratchit since their marriage. Mrs Cratchit said that now the weight was off her mind, she would confess she had had her doubts about the quantity of flour. Everybody had something to say about it, but nobody said or thought it was at all a small pudding for a large family. It would have been flat heresy to do so. Any Cratchit would have blushed to hint at such a thing.

At last the dinner was all done, the cloth was cleared, the hearth swept, and the fire made up. The compound in the jug being tasted, and considered perfect, apples and oranges were put upon the table, and a shovelful of chestnuts on the fire. Then all the Cratchit family drew round the hearth in what Bob Cratchit called a circle, meaning half a one; and at Bob Cratchit's elbow stood the family display of glass. Two thumblers, and a custard-cup without a handle.

These held the hot stuff from the jug, however, as

well as golden goblets would have done; and Bob served it out with beaming looks, while the chestnuts on the fire sputtered and cracked noisily. Then Bob proposed:

'A Merry Christmas to us all, my dears. God bless us!'

Which all the family re-echoed.

'God bless us every one!' said Tiny Tim, the last of all.

CHARLES DICKENS, *A Christmas Carol*

One of the feelings evoked by this account is the excitement of the family at this great annual event. Pick out some of the detail and description which indicates this.

Another very clear feeling that is brought out is the family unity and love that the Cratchits have for each other. Point to details of the story that show this.

What does the teasing of Bob Cratchit when Mrs Cratchit tells him Martha isn't coming tell us about the family and its feeling for each other?

How does the author make vivid Mrs Cratchit's apprehension about the pudding?

How are we meant to feel about Tiny Tim?

The Cratchit family are poor. Pick out the details that tell us this.

Does the fact that they are poor prevent them from being happy?

This story was written over a hundred years ago, and social customs and habits change. For instance, why do the Cratchit children say that 'outside the baker's they had smelt the goose'? What is a 'comforter', 'the copper', 'the hob', 'a custard-cup'? If you don't know, perhaps your teacher can help.

Make a list as on a menu card of the meal the Cratchits ate. How does it compare with what you have for Christmas dinner?

Make a list of all the different foods and drink traditionally associated with Christmas.

Here is a typical Victorian menu for Christmas dinner:

Fine Crayfish Soup
Derby-Style Fat Fowl
Baked Ham
Roast Goose
Goose Liver Mousse in Aspic
Stuffed Artichoke
French Beans in Butter
Plum Pudding & Brandy Sauce
Chestnut Tartlets
Glazed Tangerine
Mincemeat Tartlets

What do you think of that? How does it compare with the meal the Cratchits had?

Another Family Christmas

Some people would say that Charles Dickens's description of the Cratchits' Christmas dinner is sentimental, that is, it is unreal, too full of goodness and tearful emotion to be true, seeing things through rosy coloured spectacles. ('Sentimental' is a difficult word to define. You might get some idea of its meaning by thinking of words like 'gooey', 'soppy', 'soft'.) Would you agree that the story is sentimental? Bear this in mind as you read the next extract which also describes a Christmas dinner, but one that took place more recently.

Nobody minded how much noise we made on Christmas Eve when the house bulged with rich, spicy foods and the tree in Nan's front room bowed under the weight of parcels. Uncle Jack was too drunk to take off his belt, let alone use it across our backsides, and while we pasted together the last of the paper chains, he blew up balloons. As he tied them up, he sang the only song he knew: *What shall we do with the drunken sailor?*

We all joined in the chorus: 'Hooray, and up she rises; hooray, and up she rises!'

Then Grandad, wearing a paper hat, did the sailor's hornpipe, but halfway through he tripped up on the carpet and fell flat on his face just as Nan came in from the kitchen where she had been stuffing the turkey.

'Saints alive!' she exclaimed. 'What's going on in here? Get up you great beery sop. And if you think you're sleeping in my bed tonight, you've another think coming. It's the kennel for you, Dripping Nut, and I mean every word I say.'

'Isn't she (hic) beautiful,' hiccoughed Grandad rising unsteadily to his feet, and then he burst into song: 'K-K-Katie my (hic) beautiful (hic) Katie!'

Grabbing her by the waist he swung her round the room. We clapped and sang as he whirled her faster and faster until he was so dizzy that he collapsed on the sofa with Nan on his lap.

'Well, if you two want to have a little kiss and cuddle,' laughed Uncle Jack, 'we'd better leave the room.'

'That's right,' panted Nan, 'beer in, wits out. When I get my breath back,' she turned to Grandad now lying outstretched on the sofa, 'I'm going to give you a piece of my mind. Why I married you I'll never know. Just look at him. He's got a head like a bladder of lard and he dances like a five-footed bullfrog.'

That night Peter and I were too excited to tell ghost stories and too happy to torment Paul. We lay there listening to the grown-ups singing below and counted the chimes of the grandfather clock in the hall. Would it never be midnight? Would Father never come? I told Peter that I was going to keep awake all night but my eyelids wouldn't let me. Gradually they became heavier and heavier until at last I must have drifted off. But I was awoken by a crash at the foot of the stairs and a woman's voice: 'Watch where you're going, hold on to the banister or you'll never make it.'

The clock chimed the hours. One . . . six . . . eight . . . eleven. Twelve. And then there was another. Thirteen.

A man's gruff voice mumbled: 'Who put (hic) rum in the works (hic)? That's what I'd like (hic) to know.' Footsteps stumbled up the stairs. It was Father Christmas, and as he came into the bedroom he droned:

'Put (hic) in the long boat till (hic) sober!' and a woman's voice whispered: 'Ssh, ssh, you'll wake them.'

'Hooray, and (hic) she rises; hooray, and . . .'

'. . . No, that's not Valerie's stocking. This is.'

I knew that it was morning when I turned over and felt a weight on top of the bedclothes and heard the rustle of paper.

'Peter,' I hissed. 'Are you awake?'

He grunted and turned over.

'Peter,' I hissed louder. 'Wake up. It's Christmas.'

A cold hand pulled me down. 'Valerie, go back to sleep.' I had woken Mum as usual. Peter gave another grunt and a present fell from his bed. He sat up like a bolt.

'Leave me!' he shouted. 'I didn't do it.'

'Oh yes you did, you little liar,' I answered.

He rubbed his eyes. 'Oh, it's morning. Val, are you awake?'

'Been awake all night. And I heard Father Christmas. Guess what? He was drunk. Don't say you heard him because you were snoring your head off all night.'

'Aunt Vi, can we undo our presents?'

'No, it's far too early. Now, be quiet and go back to sleep or you'll wake the whole house.'

'Just one,' I pleaded.

'Go on, Aunt Vi,' Peter echoed. 'Just one.'

'Oh, what's the use?' Mum sighed. 'But one only and then back to sleep.' But before Mum could stop us our new roller skates were strapped on and we were merrily skating round the room when there was a rap on the wall. On the other side were Aunt Rose and Uncle Jack.

'Those damned kids awake already. Gawd give me strength. There's no peace for the wicked.' His voice sounded deeper through the wall while Aunt Rose's seemed higher.

'Be reasonable, Jack. It's only once a year.'

'And a bloody good job, too. Who had the bright idea of giving them skates? That's what I'd like to know.'

'You did, darling.'

'Well, that's the first I've heard of it.' He rapped again. 'Hey, you kids, get back to bed before I come in and fix you, Christmas or no Christmas.'

But by now the whole house was awake and there

were shrieks of delight or groans of disappointment as presents were unwrapped. Soon Aunt Rose appeared in her dressing-gown with a tray full of steaming tea, and Uncle Jack did his best to get the coconuts out of the bottoms of our stockings. 'What goes in must come out, that's common knowledge,' he reasoned, but after a lot of tugging and tearing the stockings were eventually cut.

While the women prepared dinner and Paul hunted through piles of Christmas paper for the key to his new clockwork train Peter and I went with Grandad and Uncle Jack for a walk along the promenade ...

We all had dinner together in Nan's front room and sat squeezed up shoulder to shoulder, plate touching plate. First Aunt Rose found she hadn't a chair, then Mum announced she hadn't a fork. When this had been put right Uncle Jack bellowed: 'Are we ready, folks? Right, let's have a count.' Swaying on his feet, he tried to count us, but came to a different total each time, first there was one too many, then there were three missing. He counted a third time and sure enough there were three missing.

'You're drunk, Uncle.'

'No, you see double when you're drunk.'

'Ugh, fancy seeing two of Paul.'

'Well, let's see who's missing.'

'Nan's not here. Where is she?'

'Suppose she's out in the kitchen, soaking the tins same as usual.'

'Come on, Nan, it's getting cold.'

'You get on without me. I like doing things my way, if you don't mind.'

'That accounts for one. Who else is missing?'

'I know, it's you, Uncle, you forgot to count yourself.'

'So I did. Well, who else is there?'

'Grandad, where's he gone to?'

'He's slid off his chair again.'

'Help him up, someone.'

Our plates were piled high with food and as soon as Nan came in the massacre began.

'Right, folks,' bellowed Uncle Jack. 'Dive in. We don't want anything left this year, because I'm doing the washing up.'

After the meal, the wireless was turned on and we all listened to the King's speech. Grandad tried to stand up to attention while the National Anthem was played, but gradually he slipped under the table and there he remained sleeping soundly till tea time.

Now all the lights were turned out except the fairy lights on the tree and chairs were placed in a semi-circle round it. Our excitement mounted to fever pitch as we waited for the women to change into their best dresses and make up their faces. Just as we thought everybody was there and we could start, we found that Nan was missing again. She kept us waiting on purpose, and when she came in at last, wearing her best blue silk dress and long ear-rings, she pretended that she didn't know what all the fuss was about.

'Hurry up, Nan, hurry.'

'I've got no time for this silly old nonsense,' she said, as she lowered herself into the arm-chair. 'But since you've rushed me, you can do me the honour of giving me the first present. I'll have that one from Ivy because I want to wear them now.' Her blue eyes twinkled as she kicked off her old slippers. 'These have properly gone home.'

'Oh, Nan,' we chorused. 'Don't spoil it.'

We were off. Uncle Jack stood up to cut the presents from the tree, but found he had nothing to cut them with. After all this time he had forgotten the scissors. There was a mad hunt round the house but none could be found, and Nan refused to let us use the meat knife. We children were very nearly bursting when Grandad produced his pen-knife.

'You can borrow this,' he said, 'but mind, I want it back. Last year it ended up in the dustbin.'

Soon presents were being opened all around and paper was strewn over the carpet. Grandad didn't rip his presents open like the rest of us, but untied every single knot in the string, then carefully folded up the sheet of paper before bothering to see what was inside the box.

'Come on, Grandad, come on, see what's inside.'

'Give me a chance. This paper will come in handy for next year. Costs too much to be thrown away.'

'You mean old miser,' said Nan, then seeing what was inside the box: 'That's an insult, that is. They know he's got a head as bald as a skating rink, but I bet every year they buy him bloody hair cream.'

The tree was stripped of presents but at the top the fairy doll still stood in all her glory. This was my moment. When everybody was quiet, Aunt Rose stood up, all eyes were on me and mine were on the doll.

'This is for my favourite niece – Apple Blossom.'

Everybody clapped and cheered as she handed me the doll and kissed me. I burst into tears, then Aunt Rose, then Peter, then Mum. In the end we were all weeping.

'Turn it up, folks,' bellowed Uncle Jack, 'or I'll have to take off my belt.'

VALERIE AVERY, *London Morning*

What touches of harshness prevent this account of Christmas from being too rosy or sentimental?

Pick out some of the things that go wrong.

What words would you use to describe the kind of family life these people lead?

Do you get the impression that they are happy?

Are there any suggestions to tell you that the family are poor or well off?

Pick out some of the things that different people do or say which seem to be typical of them and tell us what kind of person each is?

Why are they all weeping at the end of the story?

Why does Uncle Jack bellow, 'Turn it up, folks, or I'll have to take off my belt.'?

Although written more recently than A Christmas Carol, this account of Christmas took place some years ago. What clues are there in the passage to tell you this? It occurred in the days when television was less common. What part does television play in your Christmas Day? How do you think it has changed the way people spend Christmas? Is this good or bad?

Writing

The Religious Side of Christmas

If you are asked to write about Christmas, it would be difficult to know where to begin. There are so many different aspects you could describe. We have already read about Christmas dinners, opening presents, the Christmas Tree and family gatherings. But there are so many other things associated with Christmas – snow and snowmen, holly and mistletoe, parties and pantomimes, carol-singing, Christmas cards – not to mention the religious side of the festival, the celebration of the birth of Jesus Christ and all the solemn and joyful consequences that that has for many people.

Here is a carol which tells the Christmas story very simply.

Chester Carol

He who made the earth so fair
Slumbers in a stable bare,
Warmed by cattle standing there.

Oxen, lowing, stand all round;
In the stall no other sound
Mars the peace by Mary found.

Joseph piles the soft, sweet hay,
Starlight drives the dark away,
Angels sing a heavenly lay.

Jesus sleeps in Mary's arms;
Sheltered there from harsh alarm,
None can do Him ill or harm.

See His mother o'er Him bend;
Hers the joy to soothe and tend,
Hers the bliss that knows no end.

UNKNOWN

What other Christmas hymns or carols do you know? Make a list of them.

Which aspect of the Christmas story appeals to you?

Have you ever attended a Christmas Eve or Christmas Day service? What were your feelings about it?

Have you ever been carol-singing? Tell the rest of the class what it was like.

Why do we celebrate Christmas?

Do you think Christmas is too commercialized?

Christmas Cards

Here are three greetings from some of the first Christmas cards. Would you say they were religious in feeling? Do you think they are good poems?

Though times and seasons ever change,
    And friends grow scarce and few;
May each succeeding Christmas bring
    Fresh hopes and joys to you.

Peace and love and joy abide
In your home this Christmas tide.

It's an old, old wish
    On a tiny little card,
It's simply 'Merry Christmas',
    But I wish it awfully hard.

55

Christmas
Greetings

Greetings

What a world of magic dwells
In the music of the bells

With every Good Wish
for Christmas
and the New Year

With all good wishes
for Christmas
and the New Year

May the beauty of Christmas
have richer meaning,
And may the joys of the New Year
bring deeper happiness.

Christmas Season

Look at these Christmas cards. Discuss each of them and say why you think each is suitable or not. Which do you like best? Why?

Another View of Christmas

The following poem, written by someone at school, begins by describing the weather he remembers.

Christmas

Christmas to me
was snow
but it never snowed
it always rained
or was sunny.
Once it snowed
and that was Christmas.
But the turkey got burnt
and when you chewed it
mum said 'Do you like it?'
and you said 'Yes'
and that was her Christmas.
Dad's was a cigar
or an ounce of St Bruno or new slippers.

THOMAS ROYLE

How would you describe this poet's view of Christmas?

Are there times when you would agree?

Find out what the words 'cynical' and 'disillusioned' mean. Could they be used to describe the writer of this poem?

57

Father Christmas

Here is an unusual picture of Father Christmas.

What impression of Father Christmas do you get from it? How do we usually think of Father Christmas?

William's Christmas

Finally, let's have a look at some of the attitudes that William, that famous character created by Richmal Crompton, has towards Christmas. When he gives presents, he gives his father 'a bottle of highly-coloured sweets' and his nineteen-year-old sister Ethel a box of chalks. What do you think his motives are? Could this be described as 'cynical'?

And here he is handing over some more presents:

At last she brought out a small pincushion. 'Thank you very much, William,' she said. 'You really oughtn't to have spent your money on me like this.'

'I dint,' said William stonily. 'I hadn't any money, but I'm very glad you like it. It was left over from Mother's stall at the Sale of Work, an' Mother said it was no use keepin' it for nex' year because it had got so faded.'

Again, Mrs Brown coughed loudly but too late.

Aunt Emma said coldly: 'I see. Yes. Your mother was quite right. But thank you all the same William.'

Uncle Frederick had now taken the wrappings from his present and held up a leather purse.

'Ah, this is a really useful present,' he said jovially.

'I'm 'fraid it's not very useful,' said William. 'Uncle Jim sent it to father for his birthday but father said it was no use 'cause the catch wouldn' catch so he gave it to me to give to you.'

Uncle Frederick tried the catch.

'Um … ah … ,' he said. 'Your father was quite right. The catch won't catch. Never mind, I'll send it back to your father as a New Year present … what?'

Should William have revealed where he obtained the presents?
How do his recipients feel?
Is William embarrassed?
Who is embarrassed?

When it comes to the presents William himself and his friends receive, their attitudes are rather different. This is a piece you might like to read simply for enjoyment.

It was only two days before Christmas and the Outlaws stood in Ginger's back garden discussing its prospects, somewhat pessimistically. All except Henry – for Henry, in a spirit of gloomy resignation to fate, had gone to spend the festival season with relations in the North.

'What're *you* goin' to get?' demanded William of Ginger. The Outlaws generally spend the week before Christmas in ascertaining exactly what were the prospects of that day. It was quite an easy task, owing chiefly to the conservative habits of their relatives in concealing their presents in the same place year after year. The Outlaws knew exactly in which drawer or cupboard to pursue their search, and could always tell by some unerring instinct which of the concealed presents was meant for them.

'Nothin' really 'citin',' said Ginger, without enthusiasm, 'but nothin' *awful*, 'cept what Uncle George's giv'n' me.'

'What's that?' said William.

'An ole *book*,' said Ginger with withering contempt; 'an ole book called *Kings an' Queens of England*. Huh! An' I shall have to say I like it an' thank him an' all that. An' I shan't be able to sell it even, 'cept for about sixpence, cause you never can, an' it cost five shillin's. *Five shillin's!* It's got five shillin's on the back. Well, why can't he give me the five shillin's an' let me buy somethin' sensible?'

He spoke with the bitterness of one who airs a grievance of long standing. 'Goin' wastin' their money on things like *Kings an' Queens of England*, 'stead of giv'in it us to buy somethin' sensible. Think of all the sensible things we could buy with five shillin's – 'stead of stupid things like *Kings an' Queens of England*.'

'Well,' burst out Douglas indignantly. ''S not so bad as what my Aunt Jane's got for me. She's gotter ole tie. *A tie!*' He spat the word out with disgust. 'I found it when I went to tea with her las' week. A silly ole green tie. Well, I'd rather pretend to be pleased over any ole book than over a silly green tie. An' I can't even sell it, 'cause they'll keep goin' on at me to wear it – a sick'nin' ole green tie!'

William was not to be outdone.

'Well, you don't know what my Uncle Charles is givin' me. I heard him tellin' mother about it. A silly baby penknife.'

'A penknife!' they echoed. 'Well, there's nothin' wrong with a penknife.'

'I'd rather have a penknife than an old *Kings an' Queens of England*,' said Ginger bitterly.

'An' I'd rather have a penknife *or* a *Kings an' Queens of England*, than a silly ole tie,' said Douglas.

'A *Kings an' Queens of England*'s worse than a tie,' said Ginger fiercely, as though his honour were involved in any suggestion to the contrary.

''Tisn't!' said Douglas equally fiercely.

''Tis!' said Ginger.

''Tisn't!' said Douglas.

The matter would have been settled one way or the other by physical contest between the protagonists had not William thrust his penknife (metaphorically speaking) again into the discussion.

'Yes,' he said, 'but you don't know what *kind* of a penknife, an' I do. I've got three penknives, an' one's almost as big as a nornery knife, an' got four blades an' a thing for taking stones out of horses' hoofs *an'* some things what I haven't found out what they're meant for yet, an' this what he's given me is a baby penknife – it's only got one blade, an' I heard him tellin' mother that I couldn't do any harm with it. Fancy' – his voice quivered with indignation – '*fancy* anyone givin' you a penknife what you can't do any harm with.'

Ginger and Douglas stood equally aghast at this news. The insult of the tie and the *Kings and Queens of England* paled before the deadly insult of a penknife you couldn't do any harm with.

William returned home still burning with fury.

He found his mother in the drawing-room. She looked rather worried.

'William,' she said, 'Mr Solomon's just been here.'

William heard the news without much interest. Mr Solomon was the superintendent of the Sunday School, on which the Outlaws reluctantly shed the light of their presence every Sunday afternoon. Mr Solomon was very young and earnest and well-meaning, and the Outlaws found it generally quite easy to ignore him. He in his official capacity found it less easy to ignore the Outlaws. But he was an ever hopeful man, and never gave up his efforts to reach their better selves, a part of them which had hitherto succeeded in eluding him.

'He's going to take the elder boys out carol singing on Christmas Eve,' went on Mrs Brown uncertainly. 'He came to ask whether I'd rather you didn't go.'

William was silent. The suggestion was entirely unexpected and full of glorious possibilities. But, as he understood well enough the uncertainty in his mother's voice, he received it without any change of expression. The slight disgust, caused by brooding over the ignominy of a penknife he couldn't do any harm with, remained upon his unclassic features.

'Uh-huh?' he said without interest.

'Would you like to go?' said Mrs Brown.

'Wouldn't mind,' said William casually, his expression of disgust giving way to one of mere boredom. Mrs Brown, watching him, thought that Mr Solomon's apprehensions were quite unfounded.

'If you went, William,' she said, 'you'd be quite quiet and orderly, wouldn't you?'

William's expression was one of amazement. He looked as though he could hardly credit his ears.

'*Me?*' he said indignantly. '*Me?* – why, of *course!*'

He seemed so hurt by the question that his mother hastened to reassure him.

'I thought you would, dear. I told Mr Solomon you would. You – you'd like it, wouldn't you, dear?'

'Uh-huh,' said William, careful not to sound too eager.

'What would you like about it, dear?' asked Mrs Brown, priding herself upon her cunning.

William assumed an unctuous expression.

'Singin' hymns an' – an' psalms,' he said piously, 'an – an' that sort of thing.'

His mother looked relieved.

'That's right, dear,' she said, 'I think it would be a very beautiful experience for you. I told Mr Solomon so. He seemed afraid that you might go in the wrong spirit, but I told him that I was sure you wouldn't.'

Mrs Brown's unquenchable faith in her younger son was one of the most beautiful and touching things the world has ever known.

'Oh, no,' said William, looking deeply shocked at the notion. 'I won't go in the wrong spirit, I'll go in, you know – what you said – a beautiful experience an' all that sort of spirit.'

'Yes,' agreed Mrs Brown, 'I'd like you to go. It will be the sort of experience you'll remember all your life.'

As a matter of fact it turned out to be the sort of experience that Mr Solomon rather than William remembered all his life.

William met Ginger and Douglas the next morning.

'I'm goin' waitin' Christmas Eve,' he announced proudly.

'So'm I,' said Ginger.

'So'm I,' said Douglas.

It turned out that Mr Solomon had visited their parents too, yesterday, and to their parents, too had expressed doubts as to the advisability of their sons being allowed to join the party. Though well meaning, he was not a very tactful young man, and had not expressed his doubt in such a way as to placate maternal pride.

'My mother said,' said Ginger, 'why shun't I go same as anyone else, so I'm goin'!'

'So did mine,' said Douglas, 'so so'm I!'

'Yes,' said William indignantly, 'fancy sayin' he thought I'd better not come. Why, I should think I'm 's good at waitin' 's anybody else in the world – why, when I start singin' you c'n hear me at the other end of the village.'

This statement, being unassailable, passed unchallenged.

'Do you know where we're goin'?' continued William.

'He said beginnin' up Well Lane,' said Douglas.

'My Uncle George lives in Well Lane,' said Ginger thoughtfully, 'the one what's givin' me *Kings an' Queens of England*.'

There was a short silence. In that silence the thought came to all three Outlaws that the expedition might have even vaster possibilities than at first they had imagined.

'*Then*, where we goin'?' said William.

'Jus' up the village street,' said Douglas.

'My Uncle Charles,' said William thoughtfully, 'the one what's givin' me the penknife you can't do any harm with, lives right away from the village.'

'So does my Aunt Jane – the one what's givin' me the ole green tie.'

William's face assumed its expression of daring leadership.

'Well,' he said, 'we'll jus' have to do what we can.'

Many, many times before Christmas Eve arrived did Mr Solomon bitterly regret the impulse on which he had suggested his party of waits. He would have liked to cancel the arrangement altogether, but he lacked the courage.

He held several practices in which his party of full-voiced but unmelodious musicians roared 'Good King Wenceslas' and 'The First Noel', making up in volume for what they lacked in tone and technique. During these practices he watched the Outlaws apprehensively. His apprehensions increased as time went on, for the Outlaws were behaving like creatures from another and higher world.

They were docile and obedient and respectful. And this was not normal in the Outlaws. Normally they would by now have tired of the whole thing. Normally they would be clustered in the back row cracking nuts and throwing the shells at friends or foes. But they were not. They were standing in the front row wearing saintly expressions (as far, that is, as the expressions of the Outlaws could convey the idea of saintliness), singing 'Good King Wenceslas Looked Out' with strident conscientiousness.

Mr Solomon would have been relieved to see them cracking nuts or deliberately introducing discords into the melody (they introduced discords, it is true, but unconsciously). He began to have a horrible suspicion that they were forming some secret plan.

RICHMAL CROMPTON, *William – In Trouble*

(In the end, William and his friends get rid of the unwanted presents: they sing carols so dreadfully to Uncle George that he throws *Kings and Queens of England* at them; Aunt Jane is tricked into using the green tie to frighten off wolves; and another subterfuge is used to get rid of Uncle Charles's penknife. To their joy, the boys are given money instead of presents. But if you want to know all the ingenious details about how this was accomplished, you will have to read the rest of the story for yourself.)

 Assignments

Choose several of the following to write about:

1. What I Like and Dislike about Christmas.
2. Shopping for Presents.
3. Opening Presents.
4. How I Spend Christmas Day.
5. Christmas Dinner.
6. The Family Gathering.
7. A Visit to the Pantomine or a Family Outing.
8. Visiting Relations at Christmas.
9. Father Christmas.
10. The Perfect Christmas.
11. Write a story about someone who has to spend Christmas alone.
12. 'Christmas is for Children.' Do you agree?
13. Write a poem suggested by a Christmas card – one you have bought yourself or received, one brought in by your teacher, or one of those on pages 56–7.

 Language

A. Commas

The point of punctuation marks is to enable a reader to understand more easily and more precisely what he is reading. We saw in Unit 3 that full stops indicate the end of a complete statement. **Commas (,) represent a shorter break, a temporary pause in the sense,** while the reader gathers breath before going on to the rest of the statement. For instance,

As soon as I left, the house was plunged into darkness.
Kim received a pair of roller skates, but I much preferred my new football kit.

Rewrite the following sentences, adding commas where you feel they are needed to indicate a temporary pause in the sense:

1. After the clock struck twelve he knew Father Christmas would be on his way.
2. The Christmas tree sparkled with tiny lights and the holly berries glinted bright and red.
3. When we finally reached Oxford Street we found the whole area a mass of Christmas shoppers.
4. Because it was so crowded we couldn't get near the toy counter.
5. Sharon liked the pink dress with scarlet ribbon not the green one with long sleeves.

Commas are also used to divide the items of a list from each other. Without them, the items would be jumbled together, and the meaning would take time to disentangle. For example:

This Christmas, John received a bow and arrow, two model kits, a book, a postal order and a pair of football boots.

(NOTE: a comma is usually not required before the final item in a list like this if the word 'and' is used.)

Rewrite the following sentences, adding commas where they are necessary:

1. Because Mother had overlooked them I had to go out especially to buy paper napkins cocktail sticks candles and a tin of pineapple.
2. For dinner on Christmas Day we are expecting Auntie Molly Uncle Fred cousins Albert and Rose as well as the family next door.

3. I like jelly and custard trifle and cream mince pies and Christmas cake.
4. Now have we got everything – crackers paper hats candles mistletoe holly?
5. On the Christmas tree were lights of every colour – red blue green yellow and orange.

Commas are also used to separate words or phrases like 'of course', 'however', 'nevertheless', 'moreover' from the rest of the sentence. They are words which are added and which could be taken out of the sentence without greatly altering its meaning. For example:

John, of course, was sick after eating too much.
However, he recovered enough to have a hearty tea.

Rewrite the following sentences, adding commas where required:

1. Jennifer as usual wanted to pull the first cracker.
2. It was nevertheless a happy day.
3. Of course we didn't get to bed until very late.
4. We were inevitably very tired.
5. Afterwards there was a great deal to clear up.

A comma is not as strong as a full stop. It should not be used to separate statements from each other which are complete in themselves. A full stop should be used. For example:

NOT   The table was laden down with food, everyone sat gazing at it expectantly.
BUT   The table was laden down with food. Everyone sat gazing at it expectantly.

Rewrite these sentences correctly punctuated, using full stops, not commas:

1. Everyone was ready to eat Uncle Harry began to carve the turkey.
2. Auntie Flo passed round the brussels sprouts the potatoes were crisp and golden.
3. Father poured brandy on the Christmas pudding he struck a match and moved it towards the plate flames licked round the pudding.
4. Mince pies and cream finished the meal everyone was very full.

B. Adverbs

Look again at the extract from *William – In Trouble*. Notice the way the author describes how the characters speak. Here are some examples:

'burst out Douglas indignantly'
'said Ginger bitterly'
'said Ginger fiercely'
'went on Mrs Brown uncertainly'
'said William casually'
'he said piously'.

The words 'indignantly', 'bitterly', 'fiercely', 'uncertainly', 'casually', all give us a clearer idea of how the characters spoke at that particular moment. They are all adverbs. **Adverbs are words which modify (or give us more information about) a verb.** If the author, for instance, used only 'said Ginger', we know that Ginger spoke, but when she uses the phrase 'said Ginger bitterly', we know *how* he spoke as well.

Most adverbs end in '-ly', and are formed by adding '-ly' to the adjective, e.g.

brave	bravely
sad	sadly
strong	strongly
happy	happily

But there are also some common adverbs which exist as independent words, e.g.

soon
there
then
too
off

Rewrite the following sentences, filling in the blanks with appropriate adverbs:

1. He spoke ..... to his enemy.
2. He ran ..... down the street.
3. The train will arrive ......
4. He strolled ..... along the riverside.
5. The wind blew ..... throughout the night.
6. After the storm, the sun shone ......
7. The flames licked ..... at the wood.
8. He rose ..... to his feet.
9. The car moved ..... off.
10. He entered the room ......

Make a list of as many adverbs as you can think of. Put some of them in sentences of your own.

Note that adverbs can also modify adjectives and other adverbs. For instance,

He was driving too fast. ('Too', an adverb, is modifying 'fast', an adverb.)
The sun is very hot. ('Very', an adverb, is modifying 'hot', an adjective.)

Vocabulary

A. What are the meanings of 'sentimental' and 'cynical'?

Describe a sentimental person and a cynical person.

Put the words into sentences of your own.

B. Christmas is the time for games. Playing with words can be fun and can also help to extend your vocabulary. Try some of the following:

1. *Write down as many words as you can, using only the letters contained in one of these words:*

Constantinople
establishment
inexhaustible
hallucination
irreconcilable

You will be surprised how many words you can get.

2. *Here are some tongue twisters. Try saying them aloud as fast as you can.*

Pick a peck of pickled pepper.
Any noisy noise annoys an oyster.
She sells sea shells on the sea shore.

Do you know any more?
Invent some of your own. See if your neighbour can say them without tripping up.

3. *Try to write as long a sentence as you can, all the words of which begin with the same letter.* Here is an example:

Fat flat-footed Freddie Frog flew frantically forward from France for food for freaky fat-headed Frankenstein's family.

4. *Write some riddles like these and see if the rest of the class can guess what they are:*

I'm changing all the time.
Sometimes people like me,
Sometimes they don't.
Only a few men can tell my future.

(Weather)

I can be of anything you like.
It's your choice.
You might like me
Or you could be scared of me.
But you can hardly remember
What I was like.

(A dream)

Many I kill,
Many more will die,
Though many will never admit it was I.

I do not bite,
I cannot hit,
But I strike many down when I am lit.

(A cigarette)

I'm green, then brown,
And then I fall down.

(A leaf)

Room's full, all full,
Can't get a spoonful.

(Smoke)

 Spelling

A. Adverbs

As we saw in the 'Language' section, most adverbs are formed by adding '-ly' to the adjective.

If the adjective already ends in 'l', you still add '-ly', e.g.

usual	usually
casual	casually
cool	coolly
annual	annually
foul	foully
awful	awfully
beautiful	beautifully
boastful	boastfully

If the adjective ends in 'll', just add '-y', e.g.

full	fully
dull	dully

If the adjective ends in 'y', change the 'y' to 'i' and add '-ly', e.g.

happy	happily
merry	merrily
noisy	noisily
cheeky	cheekily

If the adjective ends in 'ue', drop the 'e' before adding '-ly', e.g.

due	duly
true	truly

If the adjective ends in 'ic', add '-ally', e.g.

ironic	ironically
sarcastic	sarcastically
fantastic	fantastically
BUT public	publicly

Learn the spelling of these words.
Write sentences containing the following words: safely, usually, beautifully, fully, dully, noisily, cheekily, duly, truly, fantastically, publicly.

B. Capital Letters

The word 'Christmas' is always spelled with a capital letter; so is the name 'Father Christmas'. It is important for correct spelling to know when capital letters should be used and to remember to use them. Capital letters should be used for proper names and titles, for the first word in a sentence, and for the first word of a quotation. For example:

Michael
Elizabeth
Mr Montgomery
the Duchess of Kent
The Times (note the capital letter in 'The')
the Albery Theatre
The sky is blue. The sun is warm.
He asked, 'What time is it?'

Study these examples and explain the use of the capital letters.

Write down twenty more examples of proper names, titles, etc. where capital letters are required.

Remember the following points:

1. **Days of the week and months require capital letters,** e.g. Monday, January.

2. **The names of the seasons and points of the compass do not require capital letters,** e.g. spring, north. (NOTE, though, that when words like 'north' and 'south' are used to refer to geographical areas or places, they do have capital letters, e.g. the North of England.)

3. **Names of streets and geographical locations should have capital letters for each element of the name,** e.g. Downing Street, Morningside Crescent, the River Thames, the Himalayan Mountains.

4. **Titles such as mayor, headmaster, chairman, duke, etc. have a capital letter when one particular individual is referred to, and when that individual's name could be inserted as an alternative to the title.** When the title is used generally, a small letter is used. Compare

The mayor is elected by the councillors (that is, 'all mayors').
The Mayor opened the new exhibition (that is, one particular mayor, Councillor Somebody).

5. **In titles of novels, plays, etc. only the first and following important words have capital letters,** e.g. 'The Strange Affair of Adelaide Harris', 'Over the Hills and Far Away'.

Rewrite the following sentences, choosing the correct version. Explain the reasons for your choice.

1. Mrs Malony/mrs Malony was elected chairman/Chairman.

2. Turn right and go due north/North if you want to reach North Mymms/north Mymms.

3. In Summer/summer we spend Sundays/sundays at Southend-on-Sea/Southend-on-sea.

4. 'A Midsummer night's Dream'/'A Midsummer Night's Dream' was written by william Shakespeare/William Shakespeare.

5. The Empire Theatre/theatre or Cinema/cinema is in Leicester square/Square.

6. 'The Last of the Mohicans'/'The Last Of The Mohicans' is a novel set in north America/North America.

7. In September/september the sun sinks in the west/West earlier and earlier.

8. The headmaster/Headmaster asked what George/george was doing in the west end/West End when he should have been at school.

 Activities

A. 1. You are expecting a present from your favourite uncle. It arrives. Show how you unpack it and whether it is what you wanted or not.

2. Show how you would decorate a Christmas tree. You may only just be able to reach the top.

3. You are packing a parcel. It is an awkward shape. Show the struggle you have to do the job.

4. You are writing a 'thank you' letter. Show by the way you do it whether you like the present or not.

B. 1. You and your friends have been allowed to make the Christmas pudding. Show how you set about it and what happens. Perhaps your scene could illustrate the saying 'Too many cooks spoil the broth ...'

2. You and your friends are preparing for a party. Try to capture the excitement and confusion. Is everything ready? Have you forgotten anything? Has a guest arrived too soon?

3. Father Christmas arrives to fill the children's stockings while they are asleep. But it is dark, and the children are not asleep. In your scene, show the difficulty Father Christmas has in finding and filling the stockings while trying not to wake the children, and how the children react.

C. 1. Make a collection of Christmas pictures and poems. Put them on the wall as a display or make a little book of them. Some of the poems could be written by yourself or members of your class.

2. Make a Christmas card with a greeting on the inside – it could be a poem.

D. Ask your parents and grandparents what they can remember about Christmas when they were young. Perhaps you could use a cassette recorder to record their comments and stories. Play back your recording to the rest of the class or tell them what you have learned.

E. 1. Find out about Christmas in other countries. How do they celebrate the festival?

2. Find out how some of our Christmas customs originated, for instance, Christmas trees, mistletoe, Santa Claus.

3. Not all races and religions celebrate Christmas. Find out what festivities they have which take the place of Christmas or which are similar to it.

4. If you were allowed to decorate your classroom for Christmas, how would you do it? Draw a plan and indicate the kind of decorations you would have. Or you could make it a room at home.

5. Make a survey of the members of your class, asking each of them what he or she is getting for Christmas or what he or she would like to get for Christmas.

Reading List

Christmas scenes occur in the following novels and collections of stories. Try to read some of them.

Louisa M. Alcott, *Little Women*
Charles Dickens, *A Christmas Carol*
Alison Uttley, *The Country Child*
Janet McNeill, *Try These for Size*
Kenneth Grahame, *The Wind in the Willows*
Arthur Ransome, *Old Peter's Russian Tales*
Michael Bond, *More About Paddington*
Dylan Thomas, *Quite Early One Morning*
Russell Hoban, *The Mouse and his Child*
Geraldine Kaye, *Nowhere to Stop*
Marjorie Lloyd, *Fell Farm at Christmas*
Helen Cresswell, *The Winter of the Birds*
Philippa Pearce, *A Dog So Small*
E. W. Hildick, *Louie's Snowstorm*

See also:

The Christmas Book, ed. James Reeves
Festivals, ed. Ruth Manning-Sanders
Red-Letter Days, ed. Gillian Avery
The Christmas Book, Esme Eve
The Noël Streatfeild Christmas Book

UNIT 5

Pets

 ### Reading and Understanding

Wanting a Pet

At some time or other in his life almost everyone has kept a pet. It could have been a dog or a cat or something less usual such as a parrot or a tortoise or even a crocodile. Even if you have never had a pet, there must have been times when the thought of having a pet has crossed your mind. There might even have been times when you have longed to have a pet, but circumstances may have been such that this was not possible. Why do people keep pets? What circumstances can sometimes make this difficult? These are questions which you may be able to answer more fully after you have read and considered the material in this unit.

Both of these questions are raised in the following extract from *A Dog So Small* by Philippa Pearce. While on holiday with his grandparents, Ben has been promised a dog as a birthday present. Now, his birthday has arrived.

The stream of traffic was much thicker as Ben hurried homewards. He rushed up to his usual crossing at the traffic-lights, and a policeman said warningly, 'Now then, son, not so fast,' thinking he might recklessly try to cross at once. But Ben waited for the red traffic-light as usual. However urgent your business, you simply had to, in London. A cat which did not know about this scudded across the road without waiting. 'Oh!' said Ben, and closed his eyes because he could not bear to look, and opened them again at once because, after all, he had to know. The cat looked neither to right nor to left, but suddenly quickened her pace as a car flew towards her. Cat and car sped on paths that must cross. 'She's done for!' said the policeman. The car passed, and there was the cat, safe on the further pavement. She disappeared at once down some area-steps, and Ben thought that when she reached the bottom she would certainly sit down to get her breath back and to count her nine lives. The policeman was shaking his head.

Ben crossed soberly and safely at the red, and then began running again. When he turned into his home street, he saw that the time was late enough for most of the dustbins to have been put out on to the pavement. His father was just trundling the Blewitt dustbin out to be emptied in its turn. This was the day of his father's late work-shift on the Underground.

As Mr Blewitt was going indoors, he saw Ben at the end of the street and waved to him to hurry. Perhaps it was just for breakfast, but perhaps it was for the post. Ben tore along.

The post had come, and it was all for Ben. His father had piled it all by his place for breakfast. There were also presents from May and Dilys, Paul and Frankie; and his mother and father had given him a sweater of the kind deep-sea fishermen wear (from his mother, really) and a Sheffield steel jack-knife (from his father). They all watched while, politely, he opened their presents first of all, and thanked them.

He was not worrying that there had been no dog standing by his place at the breakfast-table. He was not so green as to think that postmen delivered dogs. But there would be a letter – from his grandfather, he supposed – saying when the dog would be brought, by a proper carrier, or where it could be collected from. Ben turned eagerly from his family's presents to his post.

He turned over the letters first, looking for his grandfather's handwriting; but there was nothing. Then he looked at the writing on the two picture-postcards that had come for him – although you would hardly expect anything so important to be left to a postcard. There was nothing. Then he began to have the feeling that something might have gone wrong after all. He remembered, almost against his will, that his grandfather's promise had been only a whisper and a nod, and that not all promises are kept, anyway.

He turned to the parcels, and at once saw his grandfather's handwriting on the small, flat one. Then he knew for certain that something was wrong. They would hardly send him an ordinary birthday present as well as one so special as a dog. There was only one explanation: they were sending him an ordinary present *instead of* the dog.

'Open it, Ben,' said his mother; and his father reminded him, 'Use your new knife on the string, boy.' Ben never noticed the sharpness of Sheffield steel as he cut the string round the parcel and then unfolded the wrapping-paper.

They had sent him a picture instead of a dog.

And then he realized that they *had* sent him a dog, after all. He almost hated them for it. His dog was worked in woollen cross-stitch, and framed and glazed as a little picture. There was a letter which explained: 'Dear Ben, Your grandpa and I send you hearty good wishes for your birthday. We know you would like a dog, so here is one. . . .'

There was more in the letter, but, with a sweep of his hand, Ben pushed aside letter, packing-paper, string and picture. They fell to the floor, the picture with a sharp sound of breakage. His mother picked it up. 'You've cracked the glass, Ben, and it's a nice little picture – a little old picture that I remember well.'

'I think it's a funny birthday present for Ben, don't you, Paul?' said Frankie; and Paul agreed. May and Dilys both thought it was rather pretty. Mr Blewitt glanced at it and then back to the newspaper he had opened.

Ben said nothing because he could not. His mother looked at him, and he knew that she knew that, if he hadn't been so old, and a boy, he would be crying. 'Your grannie treasured this because it was a present from your Uncle Willy,' said Mrs Blewitt. 'He brought it home as a curio, from his last voyage – the last voyage before he was drowned. So you see, Granny's given you something that was precious to her.'

But what was dead Uncle Willy or a woolwork dog to Ben? He still could not trust himself to speak; and now they were all looking at him, wondering at the silence. Even his father had put the paper down.

'Did you expect a *real* dog?' Frankie asked suddenly.

Everyone else answered for Ben, anyway.

His mother said, 'Of course not. Ben knows perfectly well that Granny and Grandpa could never afford to buy him a real dog.'

His father said, 'And, anyway, you can't expect to keep a dog in London nowadays – the traffic's too dangerous.' Ben remembered the cat scuttering from under the wheels of the car that morning, and he hated his father for being in the right. 'It isn't as if he had any garden to let a dog loose in,' went on Mr Blewitt; 'and we're not even near an open space where you could exercise it properly.'

'There's the park,' said Dilys. But Ben knew that park. It was just a large, flat piece of grass in front of a museum. There was a straight, asphalted path diagonally across it, and seats set in islands of asphalt. There was a notice-board by the gate with forty-two by-laws beginning 'No person shall –' Eight of these said what no person should let a dog do there; and an extra regulation for that park said that dogs must be kept on leads. But you never saw a dog there, anyway.

May was saying, 'What about the River?' She only thought sensibly on her own subject, nowadays. 'Couldn't a dog swim in the River for exercise?'

Then Paul and Frankie and even Dilys laughed at the idea of Ben's exercising the dog he hadn't been given in the only open space, which was the River. They laughed merrily among themselves. Ben's hands, half-hidden by the wrapping-paper that his mother had picked up from the floor, clenched into angry fists. Mrs Blewitt, still watching him anxiously, took the letter again to skim through the rest of it. 'They say they hope you won't be disappointed by their present – well, never mind that – and – why, Ben, just listen! – they ask you to go and stay with them again, as soon as you're able. Isn't that nice? You always like that. Now, let's see when you might go. . . . . Not next week, but perhaps the week after, or perhaps even—'

On this subject Ben had to speak. 'I don't want to go there,' he said. 'I don't ever want to go there again. I shan't.'

PHILIPPA PEARCE, *A Dog So Small*

Having read the whole extract, why do you think the episode at the beginning about the cat is included?

When did Ben first begin to feel worried that he had not been given a dog, and why?

What is there in Ben's reaction to the use of his new jack-knife that shows that there is only one present that he really wants?

The truth is revealed in a single short sentence that forms a complete paragraph on its own. How does this bring the fact home more immediately to the reader?

Comment on the different reactions of the family to the picture of the dog that Ben has been sent.

Do you think that Ben should really have been pleased about this present? Why?

Why did the family feel it unreasonable for Ben to expect a real dog?

Why doesn't Ben want to go and stay with his grandparents again?

Looking After a Pet

Of course, looking after a pet is not something which can be undertaken lightly. It involves responsibility. You have to know how to look after a pet and be prepared to give up your time to cater for its needs. This extract from *A Kestrel for a Knave* describes how Billy looks after his rather unusual pet, a kestrel, and how at least one other person reacts to it.

He unlocked the shed door, slipped inside and closed it quietly behind him. The hawk was perched on a branch which had been wedged between the walls towards the back of the shed. The only other furniture in the shed were two shelves, one fixed behind the bars of the door, the other high up on the wall. The walls and ceiling were whitewashed, and the floor had been sprinkled with a thick layer of dry sand, sprinkled thicker beneath the perch and the shelves. The shelf on the door was marked with two dried mutes, both thick and white, with a central deposit of faeces as crozzled and black as the burnt ends of matches.

Billy approached the hawk slowly, regarding it obliquely, clucking and chanting softly, 'Kes, Kes, Kes.' The hawk bobbed her head and shifted along the perch. Billy held out his gauntlet and offered her a scrap of beef. She reached forward and grasped it with her beak, and tried to pull it from his glove. Billy gripped the beef tightly between forefinger and thumb; and in order to obtain more leverage, the hawk stepped on to his fist. He allowed her to take the beef, then replaced her on the perch, touching the backs of her legs against the wood so that she stepped backwards on to it. He dipped into the leather satchel at his hip and offered her a fresh scrap; this time holding it just out of range of her reaching beak. She bobbed her head and tippled forward slightly, regained balance, then glanced about, uncertain, like someone up on the top board for the first time.

'Come on, Kes. Come on then.'

He stood still. The hawk looked at the meat, then jumped on to the glove and took it. Billy smiled and replaced it with a tough strip of beef, and as the hawk busied herself with it, he attached a swivel to the ends of the jesses dangling from her legs, slipped the jesses between the first and second fingers of his glove, and felt into his bag for the leash. The hawk looked up from her feeding. Billy rubbed his finger and thumb to make the meat move between them, and as the hawk attended to it again, he threaded the leash through the lower ring of the swivel and pulled it all the way through until the knot at the other end snagged on the ring. He completed the security by looping the leash twice round his glove and tying the end to his little finger.

He walked to the door and slowly pushed it open. The hawk looked up, and as he moved out into the full light, her eyes seemed to expand, her body contract as she flattened her feathers. She bobbed her head, once, twice, then bated, throwing herself sideways off his glove and hanging upside down, thrashing her wings and screaming. Billy waited for her to stop, then placed his hand gently under her breast and lifted her back on to the glove. She bated again, and again, and each time Billy lifted her carefully back up, until finally she stayed up, beak half open, panting, glaring round.

'What's up then? What's a matter with you, Kes? Anybody'd think you'd never been out before.'

The hawk roused her feathers and bent to her meat, her misdemeanours apparently forgotten.

Billy walked her round the garden, speaking quietly to her all the time. Then he turned up the path at the side of the house and approached the front gate, watching the hawk for her reactions. A car approached. The hawk tensed, watched it pass, then resumed her meal as it sped away up the avenue. On the opposite pavement a little boy, pedalling a tricycle round in tight circles, looked up and saw them, immediately unwound and drove straight off the pavement, making the tin mudguards clank as the wheels jonked down into the gutter. Billy held the hawk away from him, anticipating a bate, but she scarcely glanced up at the sound, or at the boy as he cycled towards them and hutched his tricycle up on the pavement.

'Oo that's a smasher. What is it?'

'What tha think it is?'

'Is it an owl?'

'It's a kestrel.'

'Where you got it from?'

'Found it.'

'Is it tame?'

'It's trained. I've trained it.'

Billy pointed to himself, and smiled across at the hawk.

'Don't it look fierce?'

'It is.'

'Does it kill things and eat 'em?'

'Course it does. It kills little kids on bikes.'

The boy laughed without smiling.

'It don't.'

'What's tha think that is it's eating now then?'

'It's only a piece of meat.'

'It's a piece o' leg off a kid it caught yesterday. When it catches 'em it sits on their handlebars and rips 'em to pieces. Eyes first.'

The boy looked down at the chrome handlebars and began to swing them from side to side, making the front wheel describe a steady arc like a windscreen wiper.

'I'll bet I dare stroke it.'

'Tha'd better not.'

'I'll bet I dare.'

'It'll have thi hand off if tha tries.'

The boy stood up, straddling the tricycle frame, and slowly lifted one hand towards the hawk. She mantled her wings over the meat, then struck out with her scaly yellow legs, screaming and raking at the hand with her talons. The boy jerked his hand back with such force that its momentum carried his whole body over the tricycle and on to the ground. He scrambled up, as wide-eyed as the hawk, mounted, and pedalled off down the pavement, his legs whirring like bees' wings.

Billy watched him go, then opened the gate and walked up the avenue. He crossed at the top and walked down the other side to the cul-de-sac, round, and back up to his own house. And all the way round people stared, some crossing the avenue for a closer look, others glancing back. And the hawk, alert to every movement, returned their stares until they turned away and passed on.

BARRY HINES, *A Kestrel for a Knave*

What can you deduce from the passage about how to care for and feed a kestrel? (You may have to look up some of the technical terms in a dictionary, e.g. gauntlet, jesses, bate, mantle.)

What details are given about the appearance and behaviour of the kestrel?

How would you describe Billy's attitude towards his pet? Consider how he feels when he is feeding it and when he is showing it to the boy on the tricycle.

The author says, 'The boy laughed without smiling'. What do you think he is trying to tell us about what the boy is thinking?

The author says 'And all the way round people stared, some crossing the avenue for a closer look, others glancing back'. What do you imagine they were thinking?

The novel *A Kestrel for a Knave* has been filmed under the title *Kes*. If you can, see the film and note particularly how Billy looks after his pet and his feelings towards it.

Writing

Meet Our Pets

Talk about your pets. See how many different kinds of pets are owned by your class. Tell of any unusual or comic adventures your pet has had. Which do you think is the best kind of pet to have and why? Talk about the responsibilities of looking after a pet.

Here are some schoolchildren of your own age writing about their pets.

My tortoise is a small one. He has a very strong shell. It has not got very bright colouring. My brother called him Ossie. We usually let him walk around the garden, and he always tried to climb over an eight-inch wooden border, but he has only succeeded once.

Tortoises are very clumsy things and sniff at everything, even toy soldiers. They are also very lazy, and we have some mint in our garden which Ossie is always sleeping in.

They always like you to wet their shell when it is hot. When it does eat, its mouth opens wide and its tongue sticks out. It then drags whatever it is eating into its mouth. They do not drink a lot of water.

KENNETH NEALE

My budgie Jerry is very playful. He likes to sit on my finger and play with my hair. We let him fly around the room and he likes to tap the mirror with his beak. We named him Jerry because he does things like flying upside down, so we named him Jerry after the comedian Jerry Lewis.

Lulu, my other budgie, is not playful. She bites and scratches. Sometimes she just sits on the swing with Jerry. Now Lulu has five eggs and does not play with Jerry very much. Before she had eggs she used to play with Jerry and they would chase each other round the room. Now she just sits there in the nesting box. We named her Lulu because we could not find a name to suit her. They both whistle all day long.

THOMAS THOMA

Sometimes when I'm sitting on the sofa sticking my stamps in, my parrot gives me a hard look like that of a sparrow hawk. When I'm putting its food in, it gives me a good bash. When it eats, it gets its food on one of its feet and cracks its peanuts with its beak. If you're watching her, she drops the peanut because she's shy. But she's a good pet when you teach her how to speak.

MUSA IBRAHIM

My cat is grey with a touch of ginger around his neck. He has dark grey on his tail and his eyes are greeny-yellow. My cat is very friendly and purrs loudly. His name is Smokey and he does not fight and he walks calmly past dogs. He's always hungry.

My other cat's name is Dino and he is black with a few white hairs. He is a fighting cat and comes home with sores on his head and body. One day Dino went out and came home the next day with his tail chopped in half and bleeding a lot and he had to go to the vet to have some injections to kill the pain. His tail is all right now but he still has some nerves in his tail that go wild and make him run across the room. I always make a fuss over him – more than ever now – and I feed him with juicy fish every day. He's a very slim cat and has got bright yellow eyes and in the dark his eyes go emerald green and glisten.

JACKIE HUNTER

My dog Fluff is vicious with small animals. When she kills mice, she grabs its tail and keeps clawing at it until it is dead. She has killed many birds, especially pigeons. She pounces on them, then picks them up in her mouth. Then she throws them away.

Fluff hates men with hats on. She stands and growls at them until they take off their hats and then she's all right.

There is a hole in our garden fence. Fluff has never gone through it but she has been tempted by many cats. Fluff chases many cats up our cherry tree. Someone need only say 'cats' and she rushes to the top of our garden and stands there growling.

TERESA LANE

My mouse is a girl. I keep it in a drawer in my shed. Once I had a boy but a cat got it because my mother forgot to close the door. My mouse started chipping away at the top of the drawer so it could climb into the other drawer. My brother keeps making houses out of boxes for it.

We buy its food from the local pet shop. Every morning I change its milk and give it more food. When I bring its drawer into the room it often climbs on top of the buildings and looks down, but when it senses a long drop it retreats back into its box. For exercise I take it out of its drawer and let it roam around the room, making sure all the doors are shut. It always likes to keep itself clean by licking itself.

I don't know why but sometimes it gets very scared and whenever I try to pick it up it always runs for its house. The thing I like best about it is the way it cleans itself and keeps its fur shiny.

PHILIP PHILIPPOU

My dog Penny doesn't like being on a lead. She likes to run free.

We taught her tricks when she was younger. She can catch things in her mouth. If we put a biscuit or a sweet on her nose, she tosses it in the air and catches it in her mouth. When we put a sweet on the floor for her, she won't take it until you tell her to. When my Mum or Dad comes home from work, she greets them and starts to show her teeth.

My dog every night she knows its time for bed she keeps running in and out, running upstairs barking at my Mum and Dad. She sleeps on my Mum or Dad's bed or in the corner on some blankets. My dog will not eat tinned food. She likes liver, mincemeat, hearts. She goes for all the dear food. If you mention coming out in the van, she runs out the door and sits at the van door.

My dog is like a human being.

VENETIA TOLLITT

Do you think these accounts give you a clear picture of the pets described?

Do you get a good view of their different characters?

Which account do you like best and why?

73

Fred Bassett

The last writer above said her dog was like a human being. Do you think dogs think that human beings are like dogs? What do pets think about their owners? Here are some cartoons about Fred Bassett and his owners. Do you think they are funny? Why?

Portrait of a Dog

Here is a longer description of a dog. It is by the American writer James Thurber.

A Snapshot of Rex

I ran across a dim photograph of him the other day, going through some old things. He's been dead about forty years. His name was Rex (my two brothers and I named him when we were in our early teens), and he was a bull terrier. 'An American bull terrier,' we used to say, proudly; none of your English bulls. He had one brindle eye that sometimes made him look like a clown and sometimes reminded you of a politician with derby hat and cigar. The rest of him was white, except for a brindle saddle that always seemed to be slipping off and a brindle stocking on a hind leg. Nevertheless, there was a nobility about him. He was big and muscular and beautifully made. He never lost his dignity even when trying to accomplish the extravagant tasks my brothers and I used to set for him. One of these was the bringing of a ten-foot wooden rail into the yard through the back gate. We would throw it out into the alley and tell him to go get it. Rex was as powerful as a wrestler, and there were not many things that he couldn't manage somehow to get hold of with his great jaws and lift or drag to wherever he wanted to put them, or wherever we wanted them put. He would catch the rail at the balance and lift it clear of the ground and trot with great confidence towards the gate. Of course, since the gate was only four feet wide or so, he couldn't bring the rail in broad-side. He found that out when he got a few terrific jolts, but he wouldn't give up. He finally figured out how to do it, by dragging the rail, holding on to one end, growling. He got a great, wagging satisfaction out of his work. We used to bet kids who had never seen Rex in action that he could catch a baseball thrown as high as they could throw it. He almost never let us down. Rex could hold a baseball with ease in his mouth, in one cheek, as if it were a chew of tobacco.

He was a tremendous fighter, but he never started fights. I don't believe he liked to get into them, despite the fact that he came from a line of fighters. He never went for another dog's throat, but for one of its ears (that teaches a dog a lesson), and he would get his grip, close his eyes, and hold on. He could hold on for hours. His longest fight lasted from dusk until almost pitch-dark, one Sunday. It was fought in East Main Street in Columbus with a large, snarly nondescript that belonged to a big coloured man. When Rex finally got his ear grip, the brief whirlwind of snarling turned to screeching. It was frightening to listen to and to watch. The Negro boldly picked the dogs up somehow and began swinging them around his head, and finally let them fly like a hammer in a hammer-throw, but although they landed ten feet away with a great plump, Rex still held on.

The two dogs eventually worked their way to the middle of the car-tracks, and after a while two or three street-cars were held up by the fight. A motorman tried to pry Rex's jaws open with a switch rod; somebody lighted a fire and made a torch of a stick and held that to Rex's tail, but he paid no attention. In the end, all the residents and storekeepers in the neighbourhood were on hand, shouting this, suggesting that. Rex's joy of battle, when battle was joined, was almost tranquil. He had a kind of pleasant expression during fights, not a vicious one, his eyes closed in what would have seemed to be sleep had it not been for the turmoil of the struggle. The Oak Street Fire Department finally had to be sent for – I don't know why nobody thought of it sooner. Five or six pieces of apparatus arrived, followed by a battalion chief. A hose was attached and a powerful stream of water was turned on the dogs. Rex held on for several moments more while the torrent buffeted him about like a log in a freshet. He was a hundred yards away from where the fight started when he finally let go.

The story of that Homeric fight got all around town, and some of our relations looked upon the incident as a blot on the family name. They insisted that we get rid of Rex, but we were very happy with him, and nobody could have made us give him up. We would have left town with him first, along any road there was to go. It would have been different, perhaps, if he had ever started fights, or looked for trouble. But he had a gentle disposition. He never bit a person in the ten strenuous years that he lived, nor ever growled at anyone except prowlers. He killed cats, that is true, but quickly and neatly and without special malice, the way men kill certain animals. It was the only thing he did that we could never cure him of doing. He never killed or even chased a squirrel. I don't know why. He had his own philosophy about such things. He never ran barking after wagons or automobiles. He didn't seem to see the idea in pursuing something you couldn't catch, or something you couldn't do anything with, even if you did catch it. A wagon was one of the things he couldn't tug along with his mighty jaws, and he knew it. Wagons, therefore, were not a part of his world.

Swimming was his favourite recreation. The first time he ever saw a body of water (Alum Creek), he trotted nervously along the steep bank for a while, fell to barking wildly, and finally plunged in from a height of eight feet or more. I shall always remember that shining, virgin dive. Then he swam upstream and back just for the pleasure of it, like a man. It was fun to see him battle upstream against a stiff current, struggling and growling every foot of the way. He had as much fun in the water as any person I have known. You didn't have to throw a stick in the water to get him to go in. Of course, he would bring back a stick to you if you did throw one in. He would even have brought back a piano if you had thrown one in.

That reminds me of the night, way after midnight, when he went a-roving in the light of the moon and brought back a small chest of drawers that he had found somewhere – how far from the house nobody ever knew; since it was Rex, it could easily have been half a mile. There were no drawers in the chest when he got it home, and it wasn't a good one – he hadn't taken it out of anybody's house; it was just an old cheap piece that somebody had abandoned on a trash heap. Still, it was something he wanted, probably because it presented a nice problem in transportation. It tested his mettle. We first knew about his achievement when, deep in the night, we heard him trying to get the chest up on to the porch. It sounded as if two or three people were trying to tear the house down. We came downstairs and turned on the porch light. Rex was on the top step trying to pull the thing up, but it had caught somehow and he was just holding his own. I suppose he would have held his own till dawn if we hadn't helped him. The next day we carted the chest miles away and threw it out. If we had thrown it out in a near-by alley he would have brought it home again, as a small token of his integrity in such matters. After all, he had been taught to carry heavy wooden objects about, and he was proud of his prowess.

I am glad Rex never saw a trained police dog jump. He was just an amateur jumper himself, but the most daring and tenacious that I have ever seen. He would take on any fence we pointed out to him. Six feet was easy for him, and he could do eight by making a tremendous leap and hauling himself over finally by his paws, grunting and straining; but he lived and died without knowing that twelve- and sixteen-foot walls were too much for him. Frequently after letting him try to go over one for a while, we would have to carry him home. He would never have given up trying.

There was in his world no such thing as the impossible. Even death couldn't beat him down. He died, it is true, but only, as one of his admirers said,

after 'Straight-arming the death angel' for more than an hour. Late one afternoon he wandered home, too slowly and too uncertainly to be the Rex that had trotted briskly homewards up our avenue for ten years. I think we all knew when he came through the gate that he was dying. He had apparently taken a terrible beating, probably from the owner of some dog that he had got into a fight with. His head and body were scarred. His heavy collar with the teeth-marks of many a battle on it was awry; some of the big brass studs in it were sprung loose from the leather. He licked at our hands and, staggering, fell, but got up again. We could see that he was looking for someone. One of his three masters was not at home. He did not get home for an hour. During that hour the bull terrier fought against death as he had fought against the cold, strong current of Alum Creek, as he had fought to climb twelve-foot walls. When the person he was waiting for did come through the gate, whistling, ceasing to whistle, Rex walked a few wobbly paces towards him, touched his hand with his muzzle, and fell down again. This time he didn't get up.

JAMES THURBER, *Thurber's Dogs*

Describe Rex's appearance.

The author says Rex 'never lost his dignity'. What does he mean?

What two things do we learn about Rex from his exploits with the ten-foot rail?

Rex 'was a tremendous fighter, but he never started fights'. What does that mean?

Rex 'never went for another dog's throat, but for one of its ears'. Why?

Rex 'had a kind of pleasant expression during fights, not a vicious one.' Can you explain why?

Rex 'didn't seem to see the idea in pursuing something you couldn't catch'. What does this tell us about his character?

Rex 'would have brought back a piano if you had thrown one in'. What does this tell us about him?

Rex brought back the chest of drawers 'probably because it presented a nice problem in transportation'. What does this tell us about him?

Why did his owners have to dispose of the chest of drawers a long way from home?

Why does the author say he was glad that Rex never saw a trained police dog jump?

Explain why the author says that 'even death couldn't beat him down'.

Describe one of Rex's activities. Is there anything funny about it? Try to say what.

What do you think the author felt about Rex?

Cats

Probably dogs and cats are the most common and popular pets, and often you will find people who like one and not the other. Are you a 'dog-lover' or a 'cat-person'? In general, do you think dogs and cats have different kinds of characters?

In this poem, Don Marquis shows what he feels to be the real character of the cat.

Look at the way the poet describes the cat's appearance and movement. Pick out the words he uses for these. Do they give you a clear picture of the cat?

Describe the two sides of the cat's nature that the poet is pointing out.

Do you think cats have a 'scorn for man'?

Do you think cats just play at being tame?

The Tom-cat

At midnight in the alley
A Tom-cat comes to wail,
And he chants the hate of a million years
As he swings his snaky tail.

Malevolent, bony, brindled,
Tiger and devil and bard,
His eyes are coals from the middle of Hell
And his heart is black and hard.

He twists and crouches and capers
And bares his curved sharp claws,
And he sings to the stars of the jungle nights,
Ere cities were, or laws.

Beast from a world primeval,
He and his leaping clan,
When the blotched red moon leers over the roofs,
Give voice to their scorn of man.

He will lie on a rug tomorrow
And lick his silky fur,
And veil the brute in his yellow eyes
And play he's tame, and purr.

But at midnight in the alley
He will crouch again and wail,
And beat the time for his demon's song,
With the swing of his demon's tail.

DON MARQUIS

Pets in Trouble

Keeping a pet brings with it great responsibilities for looking after it – feeding it, providing somewhere for it to sleep, training it,
cleaning it. Bringing up an animal in a house or
a town can mean that we have to protect it from
danger too. (Look again at the risks the cat in
the extract from *A Dog So Small* takes in crossing the road.) In this poem a dog has got himself
into difficulties and has to be rescued.

A Dog in the Quarry

The day was so bright
    that even birdcages flew open.
The breasts of lawns
    heaved with joy
and the cars on the highway
    sang the great song of asphalt.
At Lobzy a dog fell in the quarry
    and howled.
Mothers pushed their prams out of the park
        opposite
    because babies cannot sleep
    when a dog howls,
and a fat old pensioner was cursing the
        Municipality:
they let the dog fall in the quarry and then leave
    him there,
and this, if you please, has been going on since
    morning.

Towards evening even the trees
    stopped blossoming
and the water at the bottom of the quarry
    grew green with death.
But still the dog howled.

Then along came some boys
and made a raft out of two logs
and two planks.
And a man left on the bank
a briefcase . . .
he laid aside his briefcase
and sailed with them.

Their way led across a green puddle
to the island where the dog waited.
It was a voyage like
    the discovery of America,
a voyage like
    the quest of Theseus.
The dog fell silent,
    the boys stood like statues
And one of them punted with a stick,
the waves shimmered nervously,
tadpoles swiftly
    flickered out of the wake,
the heavens
    stood still,
and the man stretched out his hand.

It was a hand
    linking
    one world with another,
    life with death,
it was a hand
    joining everything together,
it caught the dog by the scruff of its neck

and then they sailed back
to the music of
an immense fanfare
of the dog's yapping . . .

MIROSLAV HOLUB, translated by George Theiner

*One of the things the poet is doing in this poem
is to show how different people react to the disaster. Describe the various attitudes.*
  What would you have done?
  *Why does the poet describe the voyage 'like
the discovery of America' and 'like the quest of
Theseus'?*
  *How does the way the poet describes the water
and the sky help to increase the tension and sense
of danger?*

78

What is a 'fanfare'? Is this an appropriate word to use?

At the beginning of the poem the dog 'howled'. At the end he is 'yapping'. Are these suitable words?

Is it Fair?

Think again about the reasons Ben's father gives in *A Dog So Small* for not keeping a dog. Are we always fair to animals by having them as pets? Should birds be kept in cages and mice in boxes? Read this poem and see whether it helps you to make up your mind.

The Caged Bird in Springtime

What can it be,
This curious anxiety?
It is as if I wanted
To fly away from here.

But how absurd!
I have never flown in my life,
And I do not know
What flying means, though I have heard,
Of course, something about it.

Why do I peck the wires of this little cage?
It is the only nest I have ever known.
But I want to build my own,
High in the secret branches of the air.

I cannot quite remember how
It is done, but I know
That what I want to do
Cannot be done here.

I have all I need –
Seed and water, air and light.
Why, then, do I weep with anguish,
And beat my head with my wings
Against these sharp wires, while the children
Smile at each other, saying: 'Hark how he sings'?

JAMES KIRKUP

Man, in England, You've Just Got to Love Animals

Read the following complete short story for fun. It is written by a Trinidadian in his own dialect, and this is very appropriate and adds to the fun.

Back home in the West Indies it have a kind of dog we does call them pot-hounds, because the only time they around the place is when a pot on the fire and food cooking. Another kind, we call them hat-racks because they so thin and cadaverous you could hang a hat on any one of the protruding bones.

But you mustn't feel them is the only two canine specimens it have. And you mustn't feel that the people down here don't like animals. The only thing is, dog is dog and man is man, and never the twain shall meet in them islands, as they meet in Brit'n.

You give a dog a bone and that is that, and if food left over after Man eat, Dog get it. None of this fancy steak lark, or taking the dog to a shop where they trim it and manicure the nails and put on a pants to keep it warm in the winter.

The topic is man's best friend, because in Bayswater Jackson landlady had a bitch what make one set of pups, and she come to Jackson room one morning to give him one.

'Mr Jackson,' the landlady say, 'here is a pup for you. I know how fond you are of Bessy, and I'm sure you'll take good care of it.'

Now Jackson had a habit, every time he see Bessy, he patting her on the head and remarking what a wonderful animal. And he even went so far as to take Bessy for a walk in the Park one day when the landlady was busy.

But the reason why Jackson getting on like that is only because he want to keep on good terms with her. You know the old saying 'Love me, love my dog'. It so hard for the boys to get a place to live, that when they do get one, they have to make sure that they keep the landlords and landladies in friendly mood.

So Jackson shake his head sadly, cogitate for a few seconds, and say, 'Mrs Feltin, if Bessy make that pup, he deserve a real good master who could bring him up like a stalwart.'

'It is a bitch,' Mrs Feltin say.

'That make it worse,' Jackson say. 'I mean, she have to be brought up like a lady. I can't keep her here in this one room where I have to live.'

'Nonsense,' Mrs Feltin say. 'She can sleep under the stairs in the basement. You always said you wanted a dog.'

That was true. Knowing that words don't cost nothing, one day Jackson did went so far as to say:

'Mrs Feltin, don't forget, wherever I am, the day that Bessy have young ones you must give one to me.'

Jackson watch the puppy wrap up in a white cloth, and Mrs Feltin holding it like a new-born baby.

'You ain't have a male one?' he asked hopefully.

'No,' the landlady say, 'I have given them all away. Don't you want it?'

Well, Jackson know that in this country dogs and cats does live real high, and the people does treat them as if they believe in reincarnation. And he know, too, that if he say 'No' he might as well start looking for another place to live.

But he still hedging. 'How about if you keep it for me, Mrs Feltin, and give me when it get big?'

'It's big enough now,' Mrs Feltin say, 'and, besides, it won't know you for its master then.'

'Yes, I didn't think about that.' Jackson stay quiet for a minute. 'But how about feeding, and so on?'

'Oh, just a little piece of steak. I'm sure she hasn't a big appetite yet.'

Jackson wince when he heard that: stewing meat is the highest he ever treat himself with, except for an occasional 'boiler' on a Sunday. Then he say quickly, noticing the suspicion of Mrs Feltin face. 'All right, thank you very much.'

And he take the pup from her and close the door.

'Look what hell I put myself in for,' he say to himself. 'What to do now? Give it away? Take a ride on the Tube and leave it by High Barnet or Roding Valley, or one of them far-away places with strange-sounding names?'

In the end he put some milk in a saucer and leave it in the corner for the pup and went to work.

In the evening some of the boys drop around to see him and when they see the pup they start to give Jackson hell.

'You keeping a managery now, old man?'

'You could train it for the tracks, boy, and make a lot of money.'

'What you going to call it?'

'I ain't keeping it long enough to give it a name,' Jackson say. 'Anybody want it?'

This time so the puppy looking at all of them as if they is criminals, and it only going by the door and sniffing as if it want to get away from this evil company.

'Why you don't dump it in the Serpentine?'

'Or send it for vivisection and get a few bob?'

'You fellars too malicious,' Jackson say, though in

truth them is ideas that already occur to him and he dismiss them as being too drastic.

'You really want to get rid of it?' one of the boys asked. 'Put it in a paper bag and give me when I going, and I go dump it somewhere far from here.'

Jackson did that, and the friend take the puppy away and leave it up by Finsbury Park Tube station.

Seven o'clock next morning when Jackson turning to catch a last fifteen minutes' sleep before getting up to dress for work, he hear a yelping and a scratching at the basement door. When he go, he see the puppy.

Jackson haul it inside and put some bread and milk in a saucer, thinking all kinds of ways to get rid of the puppy.

When he was leaving the house to go to work he meet Mrs Feltin.

'Good morning,' she say, 'how is the puppy? What do you call her?'

'Am – er – Flossie,' Jackson say.

'It's a nice name,' Mrs Feltin say. 'If you leave the money with me, I could get some nice steak for her lunch while you're at work.'

Poor Jackson had to fork out three-and-six for steak for Flossie, while he himself was studying to get a piece of neck-of-lamb for his own dinner.

Well, the day he get the puppy was a Monday, and the whole week gone by and Jackson low in pocket buying steak for Flossie, and he getting real tired looking after the bitch.

On the Friday he was moaning at work about the situation, when one of his English mates say:

'My missus is looking for a bitch. I'll take Flossie off you.'

Now that a solution was at hand, Jackson do some rapid thinking. 'That bitch is from good stock,' he say. 'The mother is a pure Alsatian and the father is a full-blooded fox-terrier. I wasn't thinking so much of giving away as selling.'

'Give you ten bob,' the Englisher say.

'What about a pound?' Jackson say, and as soon as he sees the Englisher was about to agree he add: 'Or a guinea. Make it a guinea and call it a deal.'

'That's a lot of money,' the Englisher say.

'Think of the dog that you getting,' Jackson say.

'All right,' the Englisher say, 'I'll come with you after work.'

Jackson make the fellar wait by the station in the evening, and he went home and collect Flossie. But just as he was going out, who should he meet but Mrs Feltin!

'Where are you taking Flossie?' she ask.

'To the vet,' Jackson say, thinking fast. 'It look as

if she ailing, and I want to make sure is nothing serious.'

'Quite right,' Mrs Feltin say.

Jackson hurry off to the Tube station, and hand Flossie over to the Englisher.

'Looks like a mongrel to me,' the Englisher observed.

'No, it is a little Hennessy,' Jackson say.

'Ten bob,' the Englisher say.

'All right,' Jackson say, 'you have a real bargain there.'

The Englisher give Jackson ten bob and went away with Flossie. Jackson had a mild-and-bitter in the pub and start to cogitate on what he would tell Mrs Feltin when he see her.

When he went back home, he knock at her door.

'What is it, Jackson?' Mrs Feltin say, alarmed by the look on his face.

'Mrs Feltin,' Jackson say, shaking his head like a man in a daze, 'fate has struck me a cruel blow. Something terrible happen.'

Mrs Feltin held her breath. 'Not Flossie?' she whisper hoarsely.

'Yes. She pass away during the operation at the vet.'

'What was wrong with her?'

'I not so sure. The vet call a big name for the sickness. And I only had she for a few days.'

'What a tragic thing to happen,' Mrs Feltin say, and it look as if she want to cry.

Jackson began to warm up. 'All my friends admire that little bitch, and she and me was coming good friends. If I had some land in England, I bury her on it myself. I was just thinking how that dog would of gone in the films, like another Lassie. Poor Flossie. She gone to rest in the Happy Hunting Ground, for sure.'

'Don't take it so hard,' Mrs Feltin say.

'I can't tell you how I feel,' Jackson say.

'I wish there was something I could do,' Mrs Feltin say. And then she brighten up. 'Wait a minute. There is something. I am getting back one of the pups from my brother – his landlady doesn't like to have animals in the house. You shall have it. No, no, quite all right, don't thank me! I know an animal-lover when I see one.'

SAMUEL SELVON

Assignments

Choose several of the following to write about:

1. My Pet. Describe its appearance and character, how you look after it and why you like it.
2. Write a guide on how to keep a pet to help someone who has never had a pet before.
3. The Rescue. Write a story about a pet that gets into difficulties and how it is rescued. Or perhaps *you* could be in trouble and the pet comes to your rescue.
4. Pet's Eye View. Imagine you are a pet and write an account of your life and your owner.
5. Which makes the better pet – a cat or a dog? Give your reasons.
6. Write a poem about a cat which brings out the two sides of its nature – wild and tame.
7. Do you know of anyone who has an unusual pet? If so, write about it. Or else make up a story about an unusual pet. Perhaps you could make it a comic story.
8. Write an account as in a newspaper involving an unusual pet. Remember to use headlines, e.g. 'Crocodile Escapes' or 'Lion's Roar Keeps Neighbours Awake'.
9. You see someone ill-treating his pet. Write about it and what you do.
10. Write a poem or a story about a pet that is lost or neglected.
11. Why do people keep pets?

 ## Language

A. Verbs

It is high time we had a look at a part of speech which has been referred to already several times, but which we have not discussed in detail – the verb. **This is the name given to a word which tells us what 'action' someone or something is performing, what 'state' he or it is in, or what 'process of change' he or it is going through.**

Most verbs are verbs of action, that is, they answer the question 'What action is he performing?'

Some examples are:

action: walk run speak say sit stand see hear
state: to be – he is sleepy
            he was tired
process of change: become grow

Make a list of thirty verbs.

Pick out the verbs in the following sentences and say whether they are verbs of action, state, or process of change.

1. The pigeon cooed softly to itself.
2. The dog ran suddenly into the middle of the road ignoring the screech of the car's brakes.
3. The dog's nose felt cold.
4. The cat was intent on stalking its prey.
5. The hawk zoomed through the air to seize the mouse.
6. The puppy was growing disappointingly slowly.
7. The rabbit seemed to be wounded.
8. The man spoke sharply to his dog when it began to chase the bird.
9. The cat was content to lie stretched out in the sun.
10. The horse jumped the barrier at the first attempt.

Rewrite the following sentences, filling in the blanks with appropriate verbs. Underline the verbs.

1. The guinea pig . . . . . at the piece of food that . . . . . to it.
2. The goldfish . . . . . slowly round and round the pond.
3. The dog . . . . . loudly when it . . . . . the cat.
4. The cat . . . . . at the stalk of grass.
5. The cat . . . . . out its head as its mistress . . . . . its fur.
6. When it . . . . . its master's step at the door, the dog . . . . . to him.
7. My dog . . . . . all day . . . . . in front of the fire.
8. The canary . . . . . happily all day.

82

9. The dog . . . . . up its ear when it . . . . . a strange sound.
10. The parrot . . . . . its head on one side and . . . . . the words it had . . . . . .

B. Metaphor

In Unit 2, we learned that a simile is a comparison in which one thing is said to be like another. This is a figure of speech, or a way of saying something, a device writers use to make their writing more vivid and to help the reader to a sharper, clearer picture of what he is writing about. **A metaphor is another figure of speech, another kind of comparison. But this time, instead of saying one thing is like another, we say one thing is another, although we know that this is not literally so.**

For instance, here are some phrases taken from Ray Bradbury's story *A Sound of Thunder*, used in Unit 3:

It towered thirty feet above half of the trees, a great evil god . . .
folding its delicate watchmaker's claws . . .
each lower leg was a piston . . .
sunk in thick ropes of muscle . . .
sheathed over in a gleam of pebbled skin . . .
each thigh was a ton of meat, ivory and steel mesh . . .
from the great breathing cage of the upper body . . .
and the head itself, a ton of sculptured stone . . .

Each of these phrases contains a metaphor. The monster was not literally 'a great evil god', but by comparing it to a god, the author brings out its power and terror. It did not literally have watchmaker's claws, but by suggesting that it did, the author makes us aware of a particular quality that the claws have which we might not have considered. Each lower leg was not literally a piston, but the author says it is so that we can compare the leg and a piston in our minds and get a clearer more vivid impression of the power of the leg and how it moves. And so on. *Comment on the rest of the metaphors in the same way.*

A metaphor is a compressed simile. Each of the metaphors given above could be expanded into similes. For example:

The monster was like a great evil god . . . folding its claws, delicate like a watchmaker's . . .
each lower leg was like a piston . . .

And so on. *Change the rest of the metaphors into similes.*

Since the same idea can usually be expressed as a simile or as a metaphor, what then is the difference in effect between them?

Metaphors are more powerful. There is a much stronger effect in saying one thing *is* something else than in saying one thing is *like* something else. Compare the examples given above, and see whether you agree.

Look at the following sentences and say which contain literal statements, which contain metaphors, and which contain similes:

1. The surface of the lake was smooth as glass.
2. The gloss paint on the door was smooth to the touch.
3. 'Why do you put all that war paint on?' asked the girl's father as she prepared herself to go out.
4. The shock made his heart beat faster.
5. When he saw the unexpected figure, his heart leapt into his mouth.
6. The beating of his heart was loud and powerful like a drum.
7. The horse's breath steamed in the frosty air.
8. The air was crystal clear.
9. The air was so clear you could see right across London.
10. The air was thick with flies and insects.

Rewrite the following sentences, changing the similes into metaphors. For instance, instead of saying, 'You are as slow as a tortoise' (a simile), you could say, 'You are a slow tortoise' (a metaphor).

1. You are as stubborn as a mule.
2. The water was as clear as crystal.
3. The clouds floating in the blue sky were like cotton wool.
4. The cat prowled like a tiger in the long jungle-like grass at the bottom of the garden.

5. The tree rose like a tall tower above the roofs of the houses.
6. The moon gleamed like a silver coin in the sky.
7. His fat podgy fingers were like sausages and he could not pick up the delicate pin.
8. The water of the river reflected the trees on its bank like a mirror.
9. The ground beneath the trees was covered with brown and yellow leaves like a carpet.
10. The edge of the saw like a long row of teeth cut through the log.

Write sentences using each of the following words as metaphors:

1. clown	6. trumpet
2. flame	7. sea
3. cloud	8. burn
4. razor	9. whip
5. nail	10. door

Vocabulary

A. Names

If you are asked to give the name of a dog, what name springs first to mind? Is it Rover or Spot or Rex?

Discuss the names people give to their pets. Can you think of any unusual names and why they are used?

Are the names given to dogs different from those given to cats? Invent names suitable for different pets.

B. Canine

'Canine' comes from a Latin word meaning 'dog' and an ending '-ine' meaning 'pertaining to, of the nature of'. The word 'canine' therefore means 'of dogs', 'to do with dogs', 'dog-like'. The expression 'canine fidelity', for instance, means 'the faithfulness and devotion typical of dogs'. Similarly 'feline' means 'of cats', 'to do with cats'. The expression 'feline cunning' would mean 'the slyness typical of cats'.

Can you think of any other words ending in '-ine' which are similar?
What about words meaning——

of the nature of man
of the nature of woman
of the nature of a horse
of the nature of a lion
of the nature of a god
of the nature of the sea?

Look up the meaning of the following words in your dictionary and use each of them in a sentence:

bovine, supine, canine, feline, masculine feminine, marine, leonine, equine, divine vulpine, submarine, aquiline, alkaline Alpine.

C. Dogs

'Dog' is the name given to a particular type of animal, just as bird is the name given to a particular kind of creature. But there are many different species of dog just as there are many different kinds of birds. For instance, spaniel Labrador, mongrel.

How many more species of dog can you name and describe?
How many species of bird can you name and describe?
How many species of cat can you name and describe?
Write these names down.
Choose two different kinds of dog and describe the difference.
Do the same with two different species of birds and of cats.

D. Onomatopoeia

Think about the words we use to describe the noises animals make. We talk about the bark of a dog and the mew of a cat. What other words could you use to describe the noise a dog and a cat makes? Differentiate between the various words.

Here are some more words describing animal noises. *Say which words are most appropriate for which animals.*

84

ululate, howl, roar, bellow, blare, yelp, bay, yap, growl, snarl, howl, grunt, squeak, neigh, bray, purr, bleat, low, moo, croak, crow, screech, caw, coo, gobble, quack, cackle, cluck, cheep, chirp, chirrup, twitter, wail, hum, buzz, hiss, hoot, whine, whinny, scream

Most of these words have been created by trying to make a word that imitates the noise made. 'Purr', for instance, or 'moo' represents in a word the kind of sound a cat or a cow makes. The name given to the use of a word whose sound suggests the meaning is onomatopoeia.

This is not limited to the sound animals make. The word 'crash', for instance, tries to reproduce in itself the kind of noise it is describing. The same is true of words like 'murmur' and 'sizzle' and many more.

Find ten more words whose sound suggests the meaning. Put them into your own sentences.

 Spelling

A. Onomatopoeia

Note the spelling. Onomato*poei*a is frequently used in *poe*try.

B. SK

The sound 'SK' at the beginning of words sometimes gives rise to difficulty. If you compare 'scream' with 'squeal' you will see what I mean. And there are also words like 'skate' and words like 'school'.

Here is a long list of words beginning with a 'SK' sound. Many of them will be familiar. *Make sure you know how to spell them all by learning them. If there are any words the meaning of which you do not know, look them up in your dictionary and write a sentence for each of them.*

scab, scabbard, scabies, scaffold, scald, scale, scalp, scalpel, scamp, scan, scandal, scant, scapegoat, scar, scarce, scare, scarf, scarlet, scathing, scatter, scavenger, scoff, scold,

sconce, scone, scoop, scoot, scope, scorch, score, scraggy, scramble, scrawny, scrap, scrape, scratch, scrawl, scream, screech, screed, screen, screw, scribble, scribe, scrimp, script, scripture, scroll, scrounge, scrub, scruff, scruple, scrutinize, scrutiny, scud, scuff, scullery, sculpture, scum, scupper, scurry, scurvy, scuttle, scheme, scholar, school, schooner, skate, skein, skeleton, sketch, skew, ski, skid, skilful, skill, skillet, skim, skimp, skin, skip, skipper, skirl, skirmish, skirt, skit, skittish, skittle, skive, skulk, skull, skunk, sky, squabble, squad, squalid, squall, squander, square, squash, squat, squaw, squawk, squeak, squeal, squeamish, squeeze, squelch, squib, squint, squire, squirm, squirrel, squint

 Activities

A. 1. Imagine you are holding a pet in your hands. What is it? Pass it carefully round the class.

2. Imitate the movements and actions of a pet. Which one have you chosen? How does it walk? How does it feed itself? How does it clean itself?

3. You are training a dog. What tone of voice would you use? How would you speak to it when it did something wrong? How would you speak to it when you were pleased with it? Illustrate these.

B. 1. Make a collection of pictures and poems about pets.

2. Cartoonists often use pets to show up the peculiarities of human beings. Make a collection of cartoons using pets in this way.

3. Make a survey of your class to find out how many different pets are kept.

4. Make a survey of your class to find out how many prefer cats and how many prefer dogs. Can you draw any conclusions? For instance, do girls prefer cats and boys prefer dogs?

5. Write a monograph (that is, a detailed guide) on a particular pet. Illustrate it with pictures and drawings.

6. If you are allowed to, bring your pet into the classroom and talk about it.

7. Write to the R.S.P.C.A. and ask for information about the kind of work this body does. Make a display of the material you obtain from the society and from other sources and use this as the basis for a talk or a discussion on cruelty to animals.

Reading List

Try to read one or more of the following novels which are about pets:

Philippa Pearce, *A Dog So Small*
William H. Armstrong, *Sounder*
Catherine Cookson, *The Nipper*
   Joe and the Gladiator
Helen Griffiths, *Leon*
Alison Morgan, *Fish*
Anna Sewell, *Black Beauty*
Dodie Smith, *The Hundred and One Dalmatians*
   The Starlight Barking
Gerald Durrell, *My Family and Other Animals*
Enid Bagnold, *National Velvet*

For further poems about pets, see Themes: *Men and Beasts*, edited by Rhodri Jones.

For books about how to look after pets and other topics dealing with pets, see the lists issued by the R.S.P.C.A.

UNIT 6

Storms and Floods

 Reading and
Understanding

The Cyclone

In Britain, we are always complaining about the weather. It is either too hot or too cold; there is too much rain or not enough. Only rarely do we have storms that cause havoc to trees and property, and the sea and rivers normally know their place and keep to it (though there have been floods in which towns have been eaten up and people and cattle drowned). People in hotter climates have been less fortunate, and their storms really are storms.

In this extract, Apu describes the cyclone which struck the island in the Indian Ocean where he lived.

It was the middle of the night when my uncle woke me up and told me to climb a tree. I thought he was playing a joke on me, though he's not a person who plays jokes. In fact, he's usually a rather gloomy man and he thinks climbing trees is a waste of time, unless it's to pick coconuts or betel-nuts or something useful.

My favourite climbing tree is the big branchy one with the thick trunk that stands near our house. (I mean, it used to stand there. I still can't get used to the idea that it's gone.)

When Uncle woke me it was very dark and I could hear the wind blowing hard and roaring in the branches of the tree. He hurried me outside and I couldn't even see the stars, so the sky must have been covered with clouds. It seemed an odd time to be climbing trees and I started to ask questions, but Uncle told me not to argue and to get climbing.

I knew the best way up with my eyes shut. I felt for the low branch above my head, pulled myself up until I could hook my leg over it and hoisted myself up and on to it. I called to Uncle that I was up, and he shouted, 'Higher! Higher!' I felt for the branches and stumps that I knew and climbed upwards until I was clinging to a thin branch that was tossing and swaying and seemed to be doing its best to throw me off.

The grownups were arguing in the darkness below. My uncle was trying to persuade my aunts and cousins to climb up too. I really thought he'd gone crazy like the man in the village the other side of the island who sometimes sits in the trees like a monkey. (I mean he used to, he's not there any more.) Uncle kept shouting, 'The water's coming! The water's coming!' Of course he was right, it did come. I don't know how he knew.

Above the noise of the wind in the branches I could hear some of the words of the argument going on below me. Uncle was shouting, 'Up the tree!' Other voices were saying, 'Not that one', or 'To the boats! To the boats!' I shouted down, 'Come on, I'll help you!' But of course none of them could climb as well as me: they were either too old or too young. I don't think any of them got into my tree.

The wind tore at me and the branches thrashed about me but I was beginning to see things better. It was still nearly pitch dark but suddenly there was something darker and blacker flying through the air like a huge bat and wrapping itself round the lower branches of my tree. I heard the women's voices wailing, 'The roof! The roof!', and I knew it was the thatch of our house going to pieces. I'd seen this happen before. Roofs blow off quite often in the islands. And quite often the water comes up nearly to the top of the mound on which our house is built. But we'd never climbed trees in the middle of the night before.

When the water came it was different from other times. I could hear a roaring of water approaching even above the noise of the wind in the trees and then suddenly it was rushing around the trunk of the tree and pouring over the lower branches. I mean, it didn't rise slowly like the other floods I'd seen; it was halfway up the trunk all at once and I was wet with spray in the highest branches. And then the whole tree seemed to be moving. Yes, I know the branches had been moving but now I had the feeling that everything was slowly toppling, and then I was in the water though I was still holding the branch. And now it was the water instead of the wind that was trying to tear me off the branch, and the rough bark was hurting the skin on my chest and arms as I clung for my life. I struggled and reached for branches above me, caught one and pulled myself clear of the water. There were great salt waves washing over the tree. I could taste them and my eyes stung as I tried to climb above them. The tree was lying right over on its side, and climbing it was quite different. I reached a branch that was clear of the waves and clung on with my arms and legs.

The water didn't seem to be rushing round the trunk as it had been and in the darkness the tops of the other trees seemed to be moving away. Then I knew I was afloat, and alone in the darkness and the storm.

How should I know how long I floated, or how far? All I knew was that I must hang on. Though the current didn't drag at the tree, now that we were floating along with it, the wind still tugged at me and the spray broke over me. The night seemed without end. I even thought that perhaps the sun had been washed away too and it would never return.

I don't know how I got the feeling that I was always moving through the water, voyaging like a ship through the night. I can only remember the darkness of the sky and the blacker darkness of the waves, but perhaps I did see solid things that stayed still while I moved past them. They must have been the tops of palm trees that were still hanging on to the earth with their roots while the water swirled around them.

Then I think I remember feeling I must be dead or that everything had come to an end, because the wind died down and the waves stopped tearing at me and when I looked up I saw the stars. But all around me was darkness and water and all I could do was lie exhausted on my branch. I was nowhere and there was nothing I could do.

And then it all started again. I thought: *no, there can't be more of it; I can't go on.* But the wind was soon raging again and the waves were once again snatching at me. And somehow I did hold on, though there didn't seem to be any reason why I should. But I must have had enough of my wits about me to notice that I seemed to be going back the way I had come. Perhaps I saw those same palm-tree tops passing the other way – but no, I don't know where I got the feeling that I'd turned round and gone back. Now that I come to think of it, perhaps I never did. But I had this very strong feeling at the time.

By then I suppose I had no hope that the storm would ever stop or that things would ever be different. But now there came a change in the movement of the tree. Instead of drifting smoothly like a boat, it was bumping and lurching, and I remember thinking: *We've gone aground.* We stuck fast, and now the current was rushing past again, though the wind and waves were not so fierce. And it wasn't so dark. There was the glow in the sky you see before sunrise. Perhaps there was a sun after all!

I think the sun rose, the water drained away and the wind dropped all about the same time. And there I was.

Where? I was in the tree. The tree was lying on its side among mud and puddles. I had this feeling I was back where I had started, though nothing I could see as the light got stronger looked like the home I knew.

It was a land of mud and battered trees. There was a mound and a creek. Yet if there *had* been houses on the mound, boats in the creek, more trees here and there and more branches on the trees that were standing, it could have been home.

CLIVE KING, *The Night the Water Came*

Do you think the opening sentence is effective?

Apu has to keep reminding himself that things have changed. What does this suggest?

Describe briefly what actually happened.

What impression do you get of the kind of person Apu is?

How would you have felt if this had happened to you?

This story is told by Apu speaking into a tape-recorder. Are there any signs in the way it is written down that suggest this?

A High Wind

The following extract describes the storm that follows a mild earthquake in Jamaica.

The earthquake had done little to clear the air. It was as hot as ever. In the animal world there seemed some strange commotion, as if they had wind of something. The usual lizards and mosquitoes were still absent: but in their place the earth's most horrid progeny, creatures of darkness, sought the open:

land-crabs wandered about aimlessly, angrily twiddling their claws: and the ground seemed almost alive with red ants and cockroaches. Up on the roof the pigeons were gathered, talking to each other fearfully.

It was the custom that, whenever their father had been to St Anne's, John and Emily should run out to meet him, and ride back with him, one perched on each of his stirrups.

That Sunday evening they ran out as soon as they saw him coming, in spite of the thunderstorm that by now was clattering over their heads – and not only over their heads either, for in the tropics a thunderstorm is not a remote affair up in the sky, as it is in England, but it is all round you: lightning plays ducks and drakes across the water, bounds from tree to tree, bounces about the ground, while the thunder seems to proceed from violent explosions in your own very core.

'Go back! Go back, you damned little fools!' he yelled furiously: 'Get into the house!'

They stopped, aghast: and began to realise that after all it was a storm of more than usual violence. They discovered that they were drenched to the skin – must have been the moment they left the house. The lightning kept up a continuous blaze: it was playing about their father's very stirrup-irons; and all of a sudden they realised that he was afraid. They fled to the house, shocked to the heart: and he was in the house almost as soon as they were. Mrs Thornton rushed out:

'My dear, I'm so glad ...'

'I've never seen such a storm! Why on earth did you let the children come out?'

'I never dreamt they would be so silly! and all the time I was thinking – but thank Heaven you're back!'

'I think the worst is over now.'

Perhaps it was; but all through supper the lightning shone almost without flickering. And John and Emily could hardly eat: the memory of that momentary look on their father's face haunted them.

After supper Mrs Thornton sat heroically in a chair, her brood all grouped round her, saying the Psalms and the poems of Sir Walter Scott over by heart: while Emily tried to keep her mind off the storm by going over in her head all the details of the earthquake. At times the din, the rocketing of the thunder and torrential shriek of the wind, became so loud as almost to impinge on her inner world: she wished this wretched thunderstorm would hurry up and get over. She tried to fix her interest on every least detail of the scene around her – to count the slats in the shutter, any least detail that was *outward*. So it was that for the first time she really began to notice the weather.

The wind by now was more than redoubled. The shutters were bulging as if tired elephants were leaning against them, and Father was trying to tie the fastening with his handkerchief. But to push against this wind was like pushing against rock. The handkerchief, shutters, everything burst: the rain poured in like the sea into a sinking ship, the wind occupied the room, snatching pictures from the wall, sweeping the table bare. Through the gaping frames the lightning-lit scene without was visible. The creepers, which before had looked like cobwebs, now streamed up into the sky like new-combed hair. Bushes were lying flat, laid back on the ground as close as a rabbit lays his ears. Branches were leaping about loose in the sky. The negro huts were clean gone, and the negroes crawling on their stomachs across the compound to gain the shelter of the house. The bouncing rain seemed to cover the ground with a white smoke. One boy began to roll away: his mother, forgetting caution, rose to her feet: and immediately the fat old beldam was blown clean away, bowling along across fields and hedgerows like someone in a funny fairy-story, till she fetched up against a wall and was pinned there unable to move. But the others managed to reach the house, and soon could be heard in the cellar underneath.

Moreover the very floor began to ripple, as a loose carpet will ripple on a gusty day: in opening the cellar door the negroes had let the wind in, and now for some time they could not shut it again. The wind, to push against, was more like a solid block than a current of air.

Mr Thornton went round the house – to see what could be done, he said. He soon realised that the next thing to go would be the roof. So he returned to the group in the dining-room. Mrs Thornton was half-way through *The Lady of the Lake*, the smaller children listening with rapt attention. Exasperated, he told them that they would probably not be alive in half an hour. No one seemed particularly interested in his news: Mrs Thornton continued her recitation with faultless memory.

After another couple of cantos the threatened roof went. Fortunately, the wind taking it from inside, most of it was blown clear of the house: but one of the coupled beams collapsed skew-eyed, and was hung up on what was left of the dining-room door – within an ace of hitting John. Emily, to her intense resentment, suddenly felt cold. All at once, she found she had had enough of the storm: it had become intolerable, instead of a welcome distraction.

Mr Thornton began to look for something to break through the floor. If only he could make a hole in it, he might get his wife and children down into the cellar. Fortunately he did not have to look far: one arm of the fallen beam had already done the work for him. Laura, Rachel, Emily, Edward and John, Mrs Thornton and finally Mr Thornton himself, were passed down into the darkness already thronged with negroes and goats.

With great good sense, Mr Thornton brought with him from the room above a couple of decanters of Madeira, and everyone had a swig, from Laura to the oldest negro. All the children made the most of this unholy chance, but somehow to Emily the bottle got passed twice, and each time she got a good pull. It was enough, at their age; and while what was left of the house was blown away over their heads, through the lull and ensuing aerial return match, John, Emily, Edward, Rachel and Laura, blind drunk, slept in a heap on the cellar floor.

RICHARD HUGHES, *A High Wind in Jamaica*

After the earthquake, what signs were there that things were still uncertain?

Describe what a thunderstorm is like in the tropics.

What was unexpected about the way the children's father greeted them?

What two things did this reveal to the children?

Pick out the words that are used to suggest sounds.

The wind is treated as though it is alive. Pick out the words which suggest this.

'The bouncing rain seemed to cover the ground with a white smoke.' Describe what is meant in your own words.

Why was Mr Thornton exasperated to find the children 'listening with rapt attention' to Mrs Thornton reciting The Lady of the Lake?

What does the author mean when he says that Emily found that the storm 'had become intolerable, instead of a welcome distraction'?

Why is drinking the Madeira described as 'this unholy chance'?

What does the author mean by 'the ensuing aerial return match'?

Say whether you think the ending of this extract is effective.

Look at Emily's reactions to the various events described. Are they what you would expect?

 ## Writing

Rain

Of course, in this country, when we think about storms, we think about strong winds and driving rain, loud thunder and violent lightning. After the wild extremes of storms and floods in India and Jamaica, here is a poem describing a storm that affects an ordinary Saturday morning and the people who have to carry on their ordinary lives regardless of the weather.

Saturday Storm

This flooded morning is no time to be
Abroad on any business of mankind.
The rain has lost its casual charity;
It falls and falls and falls and would not mind
Were all the world washed blind.

No creature out of doors goes weatherproof.
Birds cower in their nests. The beast that can
Has found himself a roof.
This hour's for man
To waken late in, putter by his fire,
Leaf through old books or tear old letters up,
Mend household things with bits of thrifty wire,
Refill his coffee cup,
And, thus enclosed in comfort like a shell,
Give thought to, wish them well
Who must this day
On customary errands take their way:
The glistening policemen in the street,
For instance, blowing their whistles through the
      welter
And stamping their wet feet;
And grocery boys flung in and out of shelter
But faithful to their loads;
And people changing tyres beside the roads;
Doormen with colds and doctors in damp suits;
And milkmen on their routes,
Scuttling like squirrels; and men with cleated
      boots
Aloft on telephone poles in the rough gale;
But chiefly trudging men with sacks of mail
Slung over shoulder,
Who slog from door to door and cannot rest
Till they've delivered the last government folder,
The final scribbled postcard, misaddressed.

Oh, all at ease
Should say a prayer for these –
That they come, healthy, homeward before night,
Safer than beasts or birds,
To no dark welcome but an earned delight
Of pleasant words,
Known walls, accustomed love, fires burning
    steady,
And a good dinner ready.

                PHYLLIS McGINLEY

In the poem, the poet describes people staying indoors as leafing through old books, tearing up old letters, doing household jobs and so on. How would you spend a morning like this?

Which of the people who have to go out on this wet Saturday morning do you feel particularly sorry for?

If you had to go out on a day like this, what would you most look forward to on your return home?

The Wind

If you could imagine the wind as a person, what would he be like? This poem imagines the wind himself speaking and describing what he does.

I am the Wind

I am the wind
Running a reckless race
Through the town and countryside,
Through the air, across the fields,
Over the ocean, beside rivers,
Blowing clouds across the sun's face,
Buffeting birds flying home.
I fight the trees, pulling away their covering of
    leaves,
Stealing hats and filling the sails of a sailing yacht.
I am the wind running a reckless race
Against myself.

                      JULIA PEARSON

What do you understand the last two lines of the poem to mean?
What other deeds can you imagine the wind describing himself as doing?

Thunder and Lightning

The following poem describes the effect of thunder and lightning.

Thunder and Lightning

Blood punches through every vein
As lightning strips the windowpane.

Under its flashing whip, a white
Village leaps to light.

On tubs of thunder, fists of rain
Slog it out of sight again.

Blood punches the heart with fright
As rain belts the village night.

                      JAMES KIRKUP

The poet is trying to get across the violent effect of thunder and lightning. Pick out the words which particularly suggest this violence.

Weather Forecast

Study this weather report and forecast from the Guardian. *How many different kinds of weather can you find? What comparisons can you make between the weather in different countries and cities. What other interesting things can you find out?*

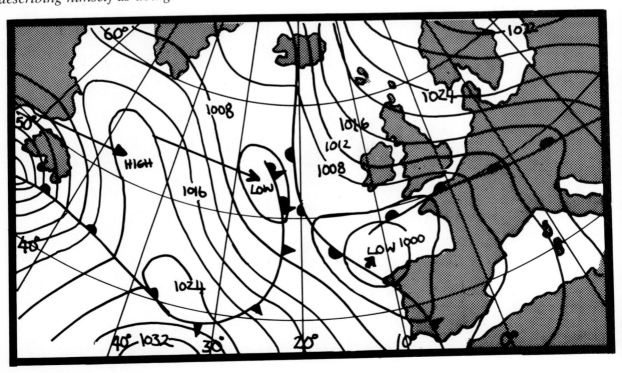

AROUND THE WORLD

Lunch-time reports

		C	F				C	F
Ajaccio	S	16	61		Jersey	C	2	36
Algiers	C	18	64		Las Palmas	F	19	66
Amsterdam	C	2	36		Lisbon	C	12	54
Athens	F	14	57		Locarno	C	2	36
Barbados	C	27	81		London	F	3	37
Barcelona	C	11	52		Luxembourg	C	−3	27
Belfast	R	3	37		Madrid	C	9	48
Belgrade	F	5	41		Majorca	F	14	57
Bermuda	C	23	73		Malaga	F	16	61
Berlin	Sn	−1	30		Malta	F	18	64
Biarritz	C	8	46		Manchester	C	3	37
Birmingham	C	1	34		Miami	C	27	81
Blackpool	Sn	2	36		Milan	C	2	36
Bordeaux	C	6	43		Montreal	C	−6	21
Boulogne	F	2	36		Naples	C	13	55
Bristol	C	2	36		Newcastle	C	3	37
Brussels	F	−1	30		New York	C	8	43
Budapest	C	−4	25		Nice	C	12	54
Cardiff	C	3	37		Oporto	C	14	57
Casablanca	C	16	61		Oslo	Sn	−2	28
Chicago	C	1	34		Ottawa	C		
Cologne	F	−3	27		Paris	S	0	32
Copenhagen	C	1	34		Prague	S	−3	27
Corfu	C	13	55		Reykjavik	R	6	43
Dublin	R	4	39		Rhodes	C	14	57
Dubrovnik	R	4	39		Rome	C	15	59
Edinburgh	C	2	36		Ronaldsway	R	4	39
Faro	C	15	59		Salzburg	S	−7	19
Florence	F	9	48		Stockholm	Sn	−1	30
Frankfurt	C	−3	27		Strasbourg	C	−4	25
Funchal	C	16	61		Tangier	C	17	63
Geneva	C	−2	28		Tel-Aviv	F	19	66
Gibraltar	C	15	59		Tenerife	C	12	54
Glasgow	C	3	37		Toronto	Sn	0	32
Guernsey	C	3	37		Tunis	C	15	59
Helsinki	C	−3	27		Valencia	C	14	57
Innsbruck	F	−11	12		Venice	C	2	36
Inverness	C	1	34		Vienna	C	−4	25
Istanbul	F	11	52		Warsaw	Sn	−3	27

C, cloudy; F, fair; R, rain; S, sunny; Sn, snow.

AROUND BRITAIN

Reports for the 24 hours ended 6 p.m. yesterday:

	Sunshine hrs	Rain in	Max temp C	F	Wthr (day)
EAST COAST					
Scarborough	—	—	3	37	Cloudy
Bridlington	—	.01	3	37	Cloudy
Lowestoft	—	—	5	41	Cloudy
Herne Bay	0.5	—	3	37	Cloudy
SOUTH COAST					
Folkestone	2.8	—	4	39	Sunny
Hastings	3.2	—	4	39	Sunny
Eastbourne	4.4	—	5	41	Sunny
Brighton	3.6	—	5	41	Sunny
Worthing	3.0	—	5	41	Sunny
Littlehampton	4.0	—	5	41	Sunny
Bognor Regis	1.5	—	5	41	Cloudy
Southsea	—	—	6	43	Cloudy
Shanklin	2.8	—	6	43	Sunny
Bournemouth	1.1	—	6	43	Sunny
Poole	0.9	—	6	43	Cloudy
Swanage	0.7	—	6	43	Cloudy
Weymouth	0.8	—	7	45	Cloudy
Exmouth	0.1	—	7	45	Cloudy
Teignmouth	—	—	7	45	Cloudy
Torquay	0.2	—	7	45	Cloudy
Falmouth	—	—	7	45	Cloudy
Penzance	—	.01	7	45	Rain
Jersey	1.4	—	3	37	Cloudy
Guernsey	—	—	5	41	Cloudy
WEST COAST					
Douglas	—	.05	3	37	Sleet
Morecambe	—	.05	3	37	Cloudy
Blackpool	—	.04	2	36	Sleet
Southport	—	.03	2	36	Cloudy
Colwyn Bay	—	—	2	36	Cloudy
Anglesey (Val) ...	—	.16	4	39	Rain
Ilfracombe	—	—	6	43	Cloudy
Newquay	.?	—			Rain
Scilly Isles	—	.04	7	45	Rain
SCOTLAND					
Lerwick	—	.01	6	43	Showers
Wick	—	.20	7	45	Showers
Stornoway	1.3	—	6	43	Sun
Kinloss	—	—	4	39	Cloudy
Dyce	—	.12	3	37	Sleet
Tiree	—	.16	5	41	Rain
Leuchars	0.4	—	3	37	Cloudy
Abbotsinch	—	.24	2	36	Snow
Prestwick	—	.08	1	34	Snow
Eskdalemuir	—	.20	0	32	Snow
N. IRELAND					
Aldergrove	—	.24	3	37	Rain

Cloudy with showers

A SOUTH-EASTERLY airstream covers the country.

London, SE England, Cent S England, the Midlands, Channel Islands, SW England, Wales, NW England, Cent N England: Rather cloudy, scattered outbreaks of sleet or snow; wind SE light or moderate; cold, maximum 2C to 4C (36F to 39F).

E Anglia, E England, NE England, Borders, Edinburgh, Dundee, Aberdeen, Cent Highlands, Moray Firth, NE Scotland, Orkney, Shetland: Rather cloudy; sleet or snow showers; wind SE, moderate; cold, max 2C to 4C (36F to 39F).

Lake District, Isle of Man, SW Scotland, Northern Ireland: Bright intervals, wintry showers; wind SE, moderate; cold, maximum 2C to 4C (36F to 39F).

Glasgow, Argyll, NW Scotland: Bright intervals; mainly dry; wind SE, moderate; cold; maximum 2C to 4C (36F to 39F).

Outlook: Cold or very cold with wintry showers and perhaps longer outbreaks of sleet or snow in the E and S. Night frost.

SCOTTISH SKI REPORT

Cairngorm: Main runs, only one high level run complete. Surface icy. Lower slopes, limited nursery areas, surface icy. Vertical runs 1,000 feet, access roads clear; snow level 2,000 feet.

Glen Shee: Main runs, a few complete. Hard packed snow. Lower slopes, ample nursery areas. Vertical runs 1,000 feet; access roads clear; snow level 2,000 feet.

Glencoe: Main runs, a few complete. Powder snow on hard base. Lower slopes, limited nursery areas. Vertical runs 1,100 feet; access roads clear; snow level 1,000 feet.

Forecast: Cold, rather cloudy, sleet and snow showers.

LONDON READINGS

From 6 p.m. Wednesday to 6 a.m. yesterday: min temp 1C (34F). From 6 a.m. to 6 p.m. yesterday: max temp 4C (39F). Total period: rainfall, 0.05in.; sunshine, nil.

93

Afterwards

One of the pleasant things about storms — perhaps the only pleasant thing? — is when they are over. Then the world can appear fresh and renewed by heavy rain, and plants and trees put on new life. Here is one poet's description of what it is like.

After Rain

The rain of a night and a day and a night
Stops at the light
Of this pale choked day. The peering sun
Sees what has been done.
The road under the trees has a border new
Of purple hue
Inside the border of bright thin grass:
For all that has
Been left by November of leaves is torn
From hazel and thorn
And the greater trees. Throughout the copse
No dead leaf drops
On grey grass, green moss, burnt-orange fern,
At the wind's return:
The leaflets out of the ash-tree shed
Are thinly spread
In the road, like little black fish, inlaid,
As if they played.
What hangs from the myriad branches down there
So hard and bare
Is twelve yellow apples lovely to see
On one crab-tree.
And on each twig of every tree in the dell
Uncountable
Crystals both dark and bright of the rain
That begins again.

EDWARD THOMAS

Why does the poet describe the day as 'pale, choked'?

Why does the poet use the word 'peering' to describe the sun?

What has finally happened to all the leaves?

What makes the 'twelve yellow apples' particularly lovely to see?

What has taken the place of leaves on the trees?

Assignments

Choose several of the following to write about:

1. Write a poem telling the story of Noah.
2. Describe what it is like to be out on a stormy day of strong winds and driving rain.
3. Think about the sounds the wind and the rain make. Can you write a poem about them?
4. You wake up in the middle of the night and hear the sounds of a storm going on around the house. Write about the sounds and your feelings, perhaps as a poem.
5. Imagine you are the wind. Write about what you do, perhaps as a poem.
6. Describe what you would see if you went out on the morning after a violent storm.
7. Write a story about an animal that is trapped by flood water and has to be rescued.
8. The Night the Oak Tree was Struck by Lightning.
9. Caught in the Storm. Write a story about being caught in the open after a sudden storm and having to find shelter.
10. Write about a day in the life of a worker who has to go out in wet weather.
11. The Day It Rained Forever. Imagine it started raining and didn't stop. Tell what happens and what people do.

Language

A. Personification

Personification is another figure of speech like simile and metaphor. In fact, personification is a special kind of metaphor. With a metaphor, we say one thing is another (which literally it is not) for a particular effect. **With personification, we say that an inanimate object or an animal is a human being or has some quality which a human being has (although literally this is not so).** An inanimate object is something like a

95

ship or the sun which does not possess any kind of human or animal life. It is easy to remember what *person*ification is because it is a figure of speech in which we regard an object or an animal as a *person*.

Julia Pearson in her poem 'I am the Wind' uses personification. She treats the wind as though it were a living person. Look at the poem again and see. There are also examples in James Kirkup's poem 'Thunder and Lightning'. A common example of personification is when we call a ship 'she', and treat it as though it were a woman.

Here are some more examples of personification. *Explain why they are personification*.

1. The snow had left its visiting card in the town.
2. The rug had walked along the floor.
3. The leaves whispered to each other in the evening breeze.
4. The rooks gossiped in the tree tops.
5. Hunger cried out from every haggard face.

Say which of the following sentences are metaphors and which are personification. Explain your choice.

1. Fear was alive in every heart.
2. The forest trees made a vault above the glade.
3. The evening sun was meditating over the mellow landscape.
4. The moon was mirrored on the surface of the lake.
5. The cathedral slumbered as dusk fell.

Write sentences, each using personification to illustrate the following:

1. an owl
2. a river
3. a town
4. the stars
5. a room
6. happiness
7. a horse
8. a motor car
9. the wind
10. the moon

B. Conjunctions

A conjunction is another part of speech. It is the name given to those words which join or connect other words or statements. In this sentence, 'The wind and the rain went on without ceas-ing', 'and' is a conjunction because it joins 'wind' and 'rain'. In this sentence, 'Because he was wet through, he changed his clothes', 'because' is a conjunction because it joins (even though it appears at the beginning of the sentence) and shows the relationship between the two statements 'he was wet through' and 'he changed his clothes'.

Here are some conjunctions:

and, but, when, because, until, if, although, while after, before

Make a list of as many others as you can, writing each down as part of a sentence.

Rewrite the following groups of sentences, each as a single sentence, using a conjunction to provide a more precise connection between the two statements.

1. The storm abated in the morning. The tree in the garden had been uprooted.
2. He was glad to reach home. He walked through the driving rain.
3. Visibility was very poor. The rain was lashing down.
4. The wind was blowing wildly. He could hardly move.
5. The first drops of rain appeared. The cat hurried into the house.
6. The wind blew all night. It continued all morning.
7. The garden was flooded. The house was safe.
8. The gusts of wind were so strong. The roof nearly blew off.
9. The first clap of thunder came. He was in the open country.
10. The flash of lightning lit up the sky. He felt afraid.

C. Exclamation Marks

An exclamation mark is a punctuation mark (!) used to show that the words preceding are expressing strong emotion. Look again at the extract from *The Night the Water Came*. The author uses a number of exclamation marks. For instance,

He shouted, 'Higher! Higher!'
Uncle kept shouting, 'The water's coming!'

The water's coming!'
I heard the women's voices wailing, 'The roof! The roof!'

Each of these statements indicates strong emotion, and this is emphasized by using an exclamation mark. Here are some more examples:

My goodness!
What a noise you are making!
You are breaking my arm!
Fire!
What a stupid thing to do!
How dare you!
She felt so happy!

You should be careful in your own writing not to use too many exclamation marks, as the more you use, the less effective they are likely to be. You should also use only one exclamation mark at a time, e.g.

Help! *not* Help!!

Having more than one exclamation mark doesn't really increase the emotion.
When you use an exclamation mark, you don't need to use any other punctuation mark. It can be just as strong at the end of a sentence as a full stop.

Write down ten sentences each using an exclamation mark.

D. Interjections

An interjection is a part of speech. It is the name given to an exclamation which is usually independent from the rest of the sentence. Here are some examples:

Alas! There is no way of escape.
Whew! That was a narrow escape.
Oh! What can we do?
Ah! They have seen us at last.

'Alas', 'whew', 'oh' and 'ah' are interjections. Notice that interjections often have exclamation marks after them because they express emotion.

Can you think of any more interjections? Put them into sentences.

Vocabulary

A. Storms

There are a number of words meaning a storm. In the opening extract in this unit, for instance, we had the word 'cyclone'. What is the difference between a cyclone and a typhoon? Find out what exactly is the difference in meaning between the following words which refer to storms and the wind. Use each of them in a sentence of your own.

gust	typhoon
blast	monsoon
breeze	trade wind
squall	sirocco
gale	mistral
storm	blizzard
tempest	zephyr
hurricane	blustery
whirlwind	cyclone
tornado	

B. Floods

There are also a number of words that can be used to describe the rapid movement of water when it is in a state of flood, words like these:

torrent	gush
bore	sluice
eddy	deluge
vortex	surge
whirlpool	billow
rapids	swell
spate	pour
jet	inundate
spirt	spout

Find out what each of these means exactly and put them into sentences of your own.

C. Weathers

Can you think of any other words which describe states of weather?
Here are some:

drought, snow-storm, drizzle, torrid, torrential, tropical, temperate, bracing, relaxing

Find out from your dictionary what these words mean and what kind of weather or climate they refer to. Add further words of your own. Put them into sentences.

 Spelling

A. Revision

It is time you had another look at the spelling mistakes which you yourself have made in the written work you have done since Unit 2.

Find out what the correct spellings of these words are and copy them into your notebook. Are you keeping them in alphabetical order? Learn them.

B. Lightning/Lightening

There are a large number of words which are spelled almost the same or pronounced practically the same but spelled differently. It is important therefore to look at these words carefully and to make sure you write down the word you want to use and not another one. The words 'lightning' and 'lightening', for instance, could be confused. 'Lightning' is the flash of light during a thunderstorm. 'Lightening' means making or becoming lighter.

Here are some more words where you must get the spelling right if you are to be clearly understood:

accept	except
aerial	Ariel
affect	effect
aisle	isle
alley	ally
allowed	aloud
altar	alter
angel	angle
ascent	assent
aural	oral
bail	bale
ball	bawl
bare	bear
baron	barren
base	bass
beach	beech
bean	been
beer	bier

berth	birth	
blew	blue	
boar	bore	
bough	bow	
brake	break	
bridal	bridle	
broach	brooch	
buoy	boy	
buy	by	bye

Explain the difference in meaning between these words. Learn the spellings. Use some of the words in sentences. More examples of words like these will be given in later units.

 Activities

A. 1. There is a driving wind pushing against you. Show how you would try to get to your destination on foot. Would your clothes be blown about as well as you? Would pieces of paper and leaves be blown against you?

2. There is a sudden flash of lightning. How do you react? You start counting until there is a burst of thunder. Would you react in the same way to the thunder as you did to the lightning?

3. You are walking home in the pouring rain. You are trying to prevent the rain getting into your eyes. It is also trying to run down your neck. Show how you would walk – and how you would react when a trickle of rain eventually succeeds in getting inside your collar.

4. It is windy and raining. Put up your umbrella. Can you manage it? Now use it to protect yourself against the weather. There is a sudden gust of wind. What happens?

B. 1. Form yourselves into groups. In each group, work out what would happen if you were in a small boat on a rough sea. Do you have oars? Is there a sail? Has your outboard motor broken down? Work out the way you would react to the movements of the boat and what happens. Remember that if the wind is strong and the sea is rough you will have to shout to each other – and you will not have much breath to spare to shout very often. Try to create the sound of the wind and the waves as well.

2. You and your friends are in a house as the flood waters begin to enter. What are you going to do about the furniture? How are you going to find somewhere safe from the flood? Make sure that what you do and say makes the situation clear to anyone watching.

3. You and your friends are caught in the open when a violent storm suddenly breaks. What are you going to do? Can you find somewhere to shelter? Can you make a shelter for yourselves? Supposing lightning strikes the tree you are sheltering under?

4. Improvise a play on the story of Noah. What scenes would you divide the story into? Perhaps different groups could choose a different scene.

C. 1. Do some research in the library on famous storms and floods in the past. There may be some which occurred in the area where you live. Give an account of your research to the rest of the class.

2. Find out from your parents or grandparents whether there have been some particularly violent storms or floods in your area that they can remember. If possible, record what they have to say about them on a cassette recorder and play it to the class.

3. Keep an eye open for reports of storms and floods in newspapers. Cut them out and make a display board of them.

D. Do you listen to the weather forecasts on radio or television. Or do you read them in the newspaper? Do you find them reliable as a guide to the weather? Discuss the value of weather forecasts.

Reading List

Try one or more of the following which are about storms or floods or which contain important episodes dealing with them:

Pierre Berna, *Flood Warning*
Hester Burton, *The Great Gale*
Clive King, *The Night the Water Came*
Meindert deJong, *The Wheel on the School*
Elizabeth Enright, *The Four Storey Mistake*
Gerald Raftery, *Snow Cloud, Stallion*
Ivan Southall, *Hills End*
A. Rutgers van der Loeff, *Children on the Oregon Trail*
  Avalanche
Laura Ingalls Wilder, *The Long Winter*
Ian Serraillier, *The Silver Sword*

CONSOLIDATION 2

A. Parts of Speech

What is a part of speech?
What are the names given to the eight parts of speech?
Here are those we have looked at so far.

PART OF SPEECH	DESCRIPTION	EXAMPLES
noun	the name of something	dog, apple, David, mountain, car
pronoun	a word that can take the place of a noun	he, it, them, us, you
adjective	a word that describes a noun or pronoun	bright, dull, pink, large, sleepy
adverb	a word that modifies a verb, an adjective or another adverb	softly, too, quickly, noisily, late
verb	a word that tells us the action someone or something is performing; the state he or it is in; the process of change he or it is going through	jump, sit, speak, listen be, seem become, grow
conjunction	a word that joins other words or statements	and, but, because, when, until, as
interjection	a word that expresses an exclamation	alas, ah, oh, ooh

B. Figures of Speech

A figure of speech is a particular device or way of using words which gives emphasis, variety and vividness to writing or speech. Do not confuse figures of speech with parts of speech.

There are a large number of figures of speech, many of which you need not know. Those we have looked at so far are simile, metaphor, personification and onomatopoeia.

FIGURE OF SPEECH	DESCRIPTION	EXAMPLES
simile	a comparison in which we say one thing is *like* another	The tree is as tall as a steeple. The coffee tasted like mud.
metaphor	a comparison in which we say one thing *is* another (which it literally cannot be)	My head was spinning with tiredness. His voice trumpeted through the hall.
personification	a metaphor in which an inanimate object or animal is given the qualities of a human being	The table groaned. The cows grumbled among themselves.
onomatopoeia	the use of a word or words whose sound suggests the sense	crash; the clash of steel; the buzz of bees.

100

C. Punctuation Marks

Punctuation marks are signs used in writing to help the reader understand more easily and more clearly what he is reading. So far, we have looked at full stops, commas and exclamation marks.

PUNCTUATION MARKS	DESCRIPTION	EXAMPLES
full stop	(i) used to show the end of a sentence (ii) used to show an abbreviation	The bells were ringing loudly. etc., e.g., i.e.
comma	(i) used to separate different statements in a sentence (ii) used to separate the different items of a list (iii) used after words or phrases added to a sentence	Because it was late, we ran all the way to the bus stop. Remember to pack towels, soap, toothbrushes and combs. However, you will not need a clothes brush.
exclamation mark	used to indicate strong feeling	Help! What a nasty thing to do!

D. Language

1. Use the word 'early' in a sentence as an adverb.
2. Write a sentence containing an adverb modifying another adverb.
3. Name twenty verbs. Say whether they are verbs of action, verbs of state, or verbs expressing process of change.
4. Write a sentence using the word 'prison' as a metaphor.
5. Write a sentence in which the word 'tree' is personified.
6. Name twenty conjunctions.
7. Rewrite the following sentences as one using a conjunction:
   The train arrived. He entered the compartment. He sat down thankfully.
8. Write a sentence containing an exclamation mark. Justify the use of the exclamation mark.
9. Do you need a full stop at the end of a sentence if you have an exclamation mark there already?
10. Name five interjections.

E. Vocabulary

1. What does 'cynical' mean?
2. What is a tongue-twister? Give an example.
3. What does 'canine' mean?
4. What does 'marine' mean?
5. Name three different species of cat.
6. What does 'ululate' mean?
7. Distinguish between 'bark', 'growl', 'yap' and 'snarl'.
8. Distinguish between 'typhoon', 'cyclone', 'tornado' and 'hurricane'.
9. What is a drought?
10. What is a blizzard?

F. Spelling

1. How do you spell the adverb formed from 'unusual'?
2. How do you spell the adverb formed from 'annual'?
3. How do you spell the adverb formed from 'public'?
4. How do you spell the adverb formed from 'busy'?
5. When do we need to use a capital letter?

6. What is the difference between 'west' and 'West'?
7. Do the names of the seasons require capital letters?
8. What is the difference between 'the chairman' and 'the Chairman'?
9. Which words in the title of a novel require capital letters? Give an example.
10. Write down the word which means 'the use of a word or words whose sound suggests the sense'.
11. What four different ways are there of spelling the sound SK?
12. Give four examples of each.
13. Write down the word which means 'a flash of light which is followed by thunder'.
14. Distinguish between 'altar' and 'alter'.
15. Distinguish between 'beach' and 'beech'.
16. Distinguish between 'brake' and 'break'.

UNIT 7

Witches and Warlocks

 Reading and Understanding

Superstitions and Suspicions

People have always been superstitious. They won't walk under ladders; if they spill salt, they will throw it over their shoulder; if a black cat crosses their path, they think it will bring them good luck. What other superstitions do you know? Do you pay any attention to them?

It used to be believed that some people had evil powers and could work their magic spells to destroy or harm others. Many a simple old woman, for instance, because she looked old or lived alone or kept a cat as a pet, was informed against, put on trial and suffered a violent death as a witch. If things went wrong, for which there seemed to be no natural explanation, people used to look around for some supernatural reason for it and to see in it the work of the devil carried out by one of his servants – a witch or a warlock. The world was full of fear and suspicion and accusation.

How easy it was for people to see evil in others on the flimsiest of evidence can be seen from this extract from *The Tower by the Sea*. A wise old woman lives by herself in a cottage beside the graveyard. For company, she has a magpie and a cat. It is a white cat with a blue eye.

Spring warmth almost overnight became summer heat. The top halves of the Dutch doors now stood open all day long in Katverloren. The wise old woman, too, left her half-door open for air. With the door open the cat and magpie began to emerge from the house into the strange new world of the churchyard under the tower. No one saw them there in the tall, uncut grass. No one, that is, but the dreamy little girl, who one day crept to the forbidden cemetery to pluck a daisy for a fairy wish. She saw the magpie make its first high flight to the top of the grey tower.

She saw the magpie come tumbling down, half-scared, half-proud. Saw it flutter to a clumsy stop right where the white cat lay on a fallen gravestone. Saw it stand before the cat, screaming loud and long about the great, bold deed it had done. Then the sun glint in the cat's blue eye suddenly caught the magpie's attention. Bold now from its glorious deed of flying to the tip of the tower, it tried right then and there to pluck the cat's blue eye out!

The cat warned the magpie. It chittered its teeth at the chattering bird. The girl in the deep grass could not believe her eyes. The magpie chattered to the cat! The cat talked back to the magpie – she could see its teeth move! No one would believe it, but she had seen it. That cat and that bird talked together – she had seen it!

The saucy magpie, a tremendous fellow to itself now after its high flight, paid no attention to the cat's warnings. Never had the blue eye been so close, so big, so bright. But the cat, done with warning, pulled a paw from somewhere underneath and boxed the magpie on the head. The blow was so sudden it toppled the magpie over. The surprised bird righted itself, flew to a gravestone and screamed angry insults at the cat. Then in a huff it hurled in a straight line from the gravestone through the open door of the little house to sit and sulk in its cage. The cat went back to sleep. Birds sang, birds flitted among the graves – the cat lay sleeping among the birds.

When she was sure the cat was asleep, the awed girl dared crawl out of the graveyard. She trembled with excitement and fear, and once out of the graveyard she flew to tell her grandmother the awesome news. She tore into the house, threw herself at the old woman, and wept with her head buried in her grandmother's lap.

'Child what is it? What is it?' the frightened old woman yammered.

The story came blurting, muffled in the woollen apron and wet sobs and tears.

'I saw that cat with the one blue eye again. He was talking to a magpie. They talked together – and then, and then the magpie flew into the wise old woman's house!'

'Nonsense,' the old woman said sharply, but she half-believed it. 'That's nonsense – a cat and a bird talking! You imagined it. Are you sure you didn't imagine it?' she asked hopefully.

The girl lifted her smeared face. 'They were talking together in the churchyard,' she said solemnly.

'In the graveyard?'

'Come along, Grandmother, I'll show you.'

But when she heard the cat was in the graveyard, the old woman grew firm. 'Nonsense,' she·said. 'I don't believe it. A cat with a blue eye! Why, that's against all nature. You and your broad-daylight dreams!' She pushed the child away, half-afraid of the little girl with her wild imaginings. 'A cat with a blue eye, talking to a magpie!' she snorted. 'I suppose they talked in Dutch.'

The scared girl wanted to be believed, she was insistent. And the superstitious grandmother half-wanted to believe this fearsome, unnatural thing. But there was the awesome graveyard – even though the sun was shining.

'You stay here and mind this baby,' the old crone suddenly decided. 'I'll be right back.'

She bustled next door to tell the old nursemaid there the fearsome news of the cat and the magpie. They called in another, and a third. The old woman told each one over again of the strange, unnatural things going on in the graveyard. She told it as if she had seen it herself. How the old tongues clacked!

Four old women together had courage enough to march on the cemetery in bright sunlight, but they couldn't resist calling to other old women along the street. Thus reinforced, a group of sombre women ventured as far as the hedge around the churchyard. They peered over. Sure enough, there lay a white cat, basking in the sun on a fallen gravestone. At that moment the magpie suddenly flew out of the little house at the edge of the churchyard. It landed on the gravestone, right beside the cat! The cat twitched an ear, opened an eye. The eye was blue! Blue as the sea! The old women behind the hedge stepped back.

The magpie sat beside the cat with its head cocked, listening to the flitting songs of the little birds in the churchyard. It suddenly took it in its head to imitate the little birds in its miserable, raw voice. It sounded silly. The cat paid no attention, but stretched itself along the stone to gather in as much sun as possible. It nudged the magpie. The bird moved over absent-mindedly. For some reason that called its attention to the cat's blue eye. Forgotten were the silly imitations, the magpie bowed and strutted before the cat, tweeting very sweetly to it about the wonderful blue eye. Might it have it, please? The cat chittered its teeth impatiently in warning.

Behind the hedge the old women did not breathe. It was so. It was so! That cat and that bird were talking together! The old women did not dare look at each other, their hands secretly felt for each other for a little safety.

The cat, annoyed by the cheeky magpie, suddenly left the warm gravestone and went sauntering home. The magpie followed, fluttering over the cat at about the height of a man's head. Bird and cat disappeared into the little one-room house. The awed women watched it.

Behind the hedge an old woman found her voice. 'That ... that,' she stammered. 'But that is a witch's cat!'

'They talked,' an old crone whispered in awe.

'That ... that is a witch's cat,' the first old woman shrilled.

'They went into her house. They *live* with her!' another woman pointed out.

'Then she ... then she ...' The shrill old woman did not dare finish. The grandmother of the dreamy girl said it for her:

'Then she is a witch!'

The old heads nodded. The faces were faces of doom.

MEINDERT DEJONG, *The Tower by the Sea*

Why do you think no one knew about the cat and the magpie before?

What evidence is there to suggest from the beginning that the little girl is superstitious?

Why did the cat's blue eye attract the magpie?

Why does the girl's grandmother ask her hopefully 'Are you sure you didn't imagine it?'?

Why does the grandmother try to belittle her grand-daughter's story when she hears it took place in the graveyard?

What evidence is there for the old woman's statement, 'That is a witch's cat'?

Why do the old women think the owner of the cottage is a witch?

The Witches' Sabbat

Graveyards have always been associated with witches and the supernatural. People used to be afraid of graveyards, especially after dark, because of their fear of the unknown. There might be dead spirits about, or the devil, or witches. Would you be afraid of a graveyard today at night? Why?

A graveyard was one of the places where witches would meet and hold their Sabbat or Black Sabbath. Here is an account of such a meeting. Tam o' Shanter, rather the worse for drink, is on his way home on his horse called Meg or Maggie, when he reaches Alloway Church and sees the witches and warlocks at their dance. Tam is saved by his good horse and by the fact that witches or evil spirits have no power to follow their victim any farther than the middle of the next running stream.

(This is a shortened version of the poem by Robert Burns containing many Scots words, some of which are explained in the margins. But don't worry too much about them. Try to get the flow of the story. If your teacher can read it out loud with a broad Scots accent, so much the better. Savour the sound of the words.)

Tam o' Shanter

Weel mounted on his grey mare, Meg,
A better never lifted leg,
rattled   Tam skelpit on thro' dub an' mire,   *puddle*
Despising wind, and rain, and fire;
Whiles glowring round wi' prudent cares,
hobgoblins   Lest bogles catch him unawares:
Kirk-Alloway was drawing nigh,
Whare ghaists and howlets nightly cry.

The lightnings flash from pole to pole;
Near and more near the thunders roll;
When, glimmering thro' the groaning trees,
Kirk-Alloway seem'd in a bleeze;
every cranny   Thro' ilka bore the beams were glancing;
An' loud resounded mirth and dancing.

Inspiring bold John Barleycorn!   *ale*
What dangers thou canst make us scorn!
The swats sae ream'd in Tammie's noddle,   *head*

105

Fair play, he car'd na deils a boddle. *penny*
But Maggie stood right sair astonish'd,
Till, by the heel and hand admonish'd.
She ventured forward on the light:
And vow! Tam saw an unco sight! *strange*

Warlocks and witches in a dance;
Nae cotillion brent-new frae France;
But hornpipes, jigs, strathspeys and reels,
Put life and mettle in their heels.
A winnock-bunker in the east, *window-recess*
There sat auld Nick, in shape o' beast; *shaggy dog*
A towzie tyke, black, grim and large, *give*
To gie them music was his charge:
He screw'd the pipes and gart them skirl, *made*
Till roof and rafters a' did dirl. *vibrate*
Coffins stood round, like open presses,
That shaw'd the dead in their last dresses;
And, by some devilish cantrip slight, *weird trick*
Each in its cauld hand held a light—
By which heroic Tam was able
To note upon the haly table
A murderer's bones in gibbet-airns *irons*
Twa span-lang, wee unchristen'd bairns;
Wi' mair o' horrible and awefu'
Which even to name wad be unlawfu'.

As Tammie glow'rd, amaz'd, and curious,
The mirth and fun grew fast and furious:
The piper loud and louder blew,
The dancers quick and quicker flew:
They reel'd, they set, they cross'd, they cleekit *took hands*
Till ilka carlin sweat and reekit *every person* *smoked*
And coost her duddies to the wark *cast off* *clothes work*
And linket at it in her sark! *set to it* *petticoat*
Now Tam, O Tam! had thae been queans *young women*
A' plump and strapping in their teens!
Their sarks, instead o' creeshie flannen, *greasy flannel*
Been snaw-white seventeen hunder linen! *very fine*
Thir breeks o' mine, my only pair,
That ance were plush, o' gude blue hair,
I wad hae gi'en them off my hurdies *buttocks*
For ae blink o' the bonnie burdies! *one* *girls*

But wither'd beldam, auld and droll,
Rigwoodie hags wad spean a foal, *withered* *wean*
Lowping and flinging on a crummock, *stick*
I wonder didna turn thy stomach.

But Tam kenned what was what fu'
brawlie: *quite well*
There was ae winsome wench and wawlie, *comely*
Her cutty sark, o' Paisley harn, *short vest* *linen*
That while a lassie she had worn,
In longitude tho' sorely scanty,
It was her best, and she was vauntie.— *proud of it*
Ah! little kenned thy reverend grannie,
That sark she coft for her wee Nannie, *bought*
Wi' twa punds Scots ('twas a' her riches),
Would ever grac'd a dance of witches!

But here my Muse her wing maun cour *must fold*
Sic flights are far beyond her pow'r *such*
To sing how Nannie lap and flang
(A supple jade she was and strang)
And how Tam stood like ane bewitch'd
And thought his very e'en enrich'd; *eyes*

Till first ae caper, syne anither, *then*
Tam tint his reason a' the gither *lost*
And roars out, 'Weel done, Cutty-sark!'
And in an instant all was dark;
And scarcely had he Maggie rallied,
When out the hellish legion sallied.

As eager runs the market-crowd,
When 'Catch the thief!' resounds aloud;
So Maggie runs, the witches follow,
Wi' mony an eldritch skreech an' hollow, *frightful*
Ah, Tam! Ah, Tam! thou'll get thy fairin'! *reward*
In hell they'll roast thee like a herrin!
Now, do thy speedy utmost, Meg,
And win the key-stane o' the brig;
There, at them thou thy tail may toss:
A running stream they dare na cross.
But ere the key'stane she could make,
The fient a tail she had to shake!
For Nannie, far before the rest,
Hard upon noble Maggie prest,
And flew at Tam wi' furious ettle: *purpose*
But little wist she Maggie's mettle— *knew* *whole*
Ae spring brought off her master hale,
But left behind her ain grey tail: *witch*
The carlin caught her by the rump,
And left poor Maggie scarce a stump. *every*

Now, wha this tale o' truth shall read,
Ilk man and mother's son, take heed:
Whene'er to drink you are inclined,
Or cutty-sarks run in your mind,
Think! ye may buy the joys o'er dear—
Remember Tam o' Shanter's mare.

ROBERT BURNS

Tell the story in your own words.
(If you can, listen to Malcolm Arnold's Overture Tam o' Shanter, *which gives a graphic account in music of the story.)*

Witch at Work

One of the things traditionally associated with witches is making spells. These usually involve magic powders and magic words, and the following account is no exception. Grimnir has come to Shape-shifter (Selina Place) to get her to use her witchcraft to gain the power of the weirdstone of Brisingamen. But their plotting is being spied on by two children, Susan and Colin.

The room was long, with a high ceiling, painted black. Round the walls and about the windows were draped black velvet tapestries. The bare wooden floor was stained a deep red. There was a table on which lay a rod, forked at the end, and a silver plate containing a mound of red powder. On one side of the table was a reading-stand, which supported an old vellum book of great size, and on the other stood a brazier of glowing coals. There was no other furniture of any kind.

Grimnir looked on with much bad grace as Shape-shifter moved through the ritual of preparation. He did not like witch-magic: it relied too much on clumsy nature spirits and the slow brewing of hate. He preferred the lightning stroke of fear and the dark powers of the mind.

But certainly this crude magic had weight. It piled force on force, like a mounting wave, and overwhelmed its prey with the slow violence of an avalanche. If only it were a quick magic! There could be very little time left now before Nastrond acted on his rising suspicions, and then ... Grimnir's heart quailed at the thought. Oh, let him but bend this stone's power to his will, and Nastrond should see a true Spirit of Darkness arise; one to whom Ragnarok, and all it contained, would be no more than a ditch of noisome creatures to be bestridden and ignored. But how to master the stone? It had parried all his rapier thrusts, and, at one moment, had come near to destroying him. The sole chance now lay in this morthwoman's witchcraft, and she must be watched; it would not do for the stone to become *her* slave. He trusted him no more than could be expected, but the problem of how to rid himself of her when she had played out her part in his schemes was not of immediate importance. The shadow of Nastrond was growing large in his mind, and in swift success alone could he hope to endure.

With black sand, which she poured from a leather bottle, Shape-shifter traced an intricately patterned circle on the floor. Often she would halt, make a sign in the air with her hand, mutter to herself, curtsy, and resume her pouring. She was dressed in a black robe, tied round with scarlet cord, and on her feet were pointed shoes.

So intent on her work was the Morrigan, and so wrapped in his thoughts was Grimnir, that neither of them saw the two pairs of eyes that inched round the side of the window.

The circle was complete. Shape-shifter went to the table and picked up the rod.

'It is not the hour proper for summoning the aid we need,' she said, 'but if what you have heard contains even a grain of truth, then we see that we must act at once, though we could have wished for a more discreet approach on your part.' She indicated the grey cloud that pressed against the glass, now empty of watching eyes. 'You may well attract unwanted attention.'

At that moment, as if in answer to her fears, a distant clamour arose on the far side of the house. It was the eerie baying of hounds.

'Ah, you see! They are restless: there *is* something on the wind. Perhaps it would be wise to let them seek it out; they will soon let us know if it is aught beyond their powers – as well it may be! For if we do not have Ragnarok and Fundindelve upon our heads before the day is out, it will be no thanks to you.'

She stumped round the corner of the house to the out-building from which the noise came. Selina Place was uneasy, and out of temper. For all his art, what a fool Grimnir could be! And what risks he took! Who, in their senses, would come so obviously on such an errand? Like his magic, he was no match for the weirdstone of Brisingamen. She smiled; yes, it would take the old sorcery to tame *that* one, *and* he knew it, for all his fussing in Llyn-dhu. 'All right, all right! We're coming. Don't tear the door down!'

Behind her, two shadows moved out of the mists, slid along the wall, and through the open door.

'Which way now?' whispered Susan.

They were standing in a cramped hall, and there was a choice of three doors leading from it. One of these was ajar, and seemed to be a cloakroom.

'In here, then we'll see which door she goes through.'

Nor did they delay, for the masculine tread of Selina Place came to them out of the mist.

'Now let us do what we can in haste,' she said as she rejoined Grimnir. 'There may be nothing threatening, but we shall not feel safe until we are master of the stone. Give it to us now.'

Grimnir unfastened a pouch at his waist, and from it drew Susan's bracelet. Firefrost hung there, its bright depths hidden beneath a milky veil.

The Morrigan took the bracelet and placed it in the middle of the circle on the floor. She pulled the curtains over the windows and doors, and went to stand by the brazier, whose faint glow could hardly push back the darkness. She took a handful of powder from the silver plate and, sprinkling it over the coals, cried in a loud voice:

'*Demoriel, Carnefiel, Caspiel, Amenadiel!!*'

A flame hissed upwards, filling the room with ruby light. Shape-shifter opened the book and began to read.

'*Vos omnes it ministri odey et destruciones et seratores discorde. ...*'

'What's she up to?' said Susan.

'I don't know, but it's giving me gooseflesh.'

'... eo quod est noce vose coniurase idea vos conniro et deprecur....'

'Colin, I ...'

'Sh! Keep still!'

'... et odid fiat mier alve....'

Shadows began to gather about the folds of velvet tapestry in the farthest corners of the room.

ALAN GARNER, The Weirdstone of Brisingamen

How does the description of the room help to create the right atmosphere?

Why does Grimnir want the power of the stone?

What was the danger Grimnir saw in employing Shape-shifter?

Why was Shape-shifter annoyed with Grimnir?

How did Susan and Colin get into the house?

Describe exactly how Shape-shifter performs the spell?

Look at the way Shape-shifter speaks. How would you describe it?

 ## Writing

Spells

For the magic to work, a witch had to collect all sorts of peculiar and gruesome ingredients and stew them all together before she could announce her spells with some hope of them taking effect. Here are the three witches from Shakespeare's *Macbeth* working out their spell.

> Round about the cauldron go:
> In the poisoned entrails throw.
> Toad, that under cold stone
> Days and nights has thirty-one
> Sweltered venom sleeping got,
> Boil thou first in the charmed pot.
>
> *Double, double, toil and trouble;*
> *Fire burn and cauldron bubble.*

> Fillet of a fenny snake,
> In the cauldron boil and bake;
> Eye of newt and toe of frog,
> Wool of bat and tongue of dog,
> Adder's fork and blind-worm's sting,
> Lizard's leg and howlet's wing,
> For a charm of powerful trouble,
> Like a hell-broth boil and bubble.
>
> *Double, double, toil and trouble;*
> *Fire burn and cauldron bubble.*

WILLIAM SHAKESPEARE, *Macbeth*

And here is an equally nasty version made up by a schoolgirl.

Witches' Brew

> Take one claw of a bat,
> Two ears of a mouse,
> Two cloves of garlic,
> A tiny dried louse,
> A small nip of blood,
> A leg of a rat,
> A tail of a pheasant,
> An old mouldy cat,
> Four dozen fleas,
> A hand off a clock,
> A tip of an arrow,
> A dusty old sock,
> A teaspoon of frogs' legs,
> For flavour a fly,
> Take a small worm,
> But first let it die,
> Mix it with water,
> A small pinch of salt,
> The milk from a cow,
> A basin of malt,
> Keep it stirring for long
> In an old copper pot,
> Serve up with pigs' eyes,
> And make sure it's hot.

JANET SMITH

A Curse

It is difficult to say whether there is any difference between spells, curses and charms – though charms are probably meant to bring about pleasant things. Here is an anonymous Australian curse. Obviously something about the town of Tallarook annoyed the writer.

May good St Peter overlook
The good deeds done in Tallarook;
May each Don Juan who forsook
His sweetheart live in Tallarook;
May all who Matthew's pledges took
Get rolling drunk in Tallarook;
May every pigeon breed a rook
To spoil the crops in Tallarook;
May I get ague, gout and fluke
If I drink rum in Tallarook.

UNKNOWN

Which section of the curse do you think is the least pleasant?
What impression do you get of Tallarook from the poem?

The Witch

What does a witch look like? There is the stereo-type of an old woman with a long pointed nose and a long chin which practically meet. In the extract from *The Weirdstone of Brisingamen*, the author talks about Selina Place's 'masculine tread'. Do you think all witches would be heavy and mannish? Here is a more fanciful and exaggerated portrait of a witch by a schoolgirl.

The Witch

The witch is an ugly creature.
Her clothes are tattered and torn.
She has hair as stiff as wire.
And teeth as black as liquorice.
Her face has wrinkles like cracks in mountains.
Her lips are cold as stone.
Her eyes are like pebbles washed in a stream.
Her nose is sharp as a nail,
Her chin crooked as a twig.
Her fingers are like a spindly tree.
She laughs as she sails about on her broomstick
Because her feet are as big as boats.

GILLIAN PURSEY

Look at the comparisons. Do you think they make sense?

McQuade's Curse

May Satan, with a rusty crook,
Catch every goat in Tallarook;
May Mrs Melton's latest spook
Haunt all old maids in Tallarook;
May China's oldest pig-tailed cook
Spoil chops and steaks in Tallarook;
May all the frogs in Doogalook
Sing every night in Tallarook;
May Reedy Creek create a brook
To swamp the flats in Tallarook;
May rabbits ever find a nook
To breed apace in Tallarook;
May Sin Ye Sun and Sam Ah Fook
Steal all the fowls in Tallarook;
May Ikey Moses make a book
To stiffen sport in Tallarook;
May sirens fair as Lalla Rook
Tempt all old men in Tallarook;
May every paddock yield a stook
Of smutty wheat in Tallarook;

Witches and Demons

Give your impressions of this picture by Breughel the Elder of witches, goblins, demons, devils, imps and familiars. Do you find it frightening? What particular part of it do you find gruesome?

Learning to be a Witch

The whole idea of witches and spells and magic can give rise to all kinds of eerie games and make-believe. In the following extract, the narrator thinks Jennifer, the girl she has just made friends with, is a witch, and she agrees to become her apprentice.

She closed the atlas and looked at me for what seemed like a very long time. Leaning way over and in such a quiet voice that it was almost zero, she said, 'I've decided to make you an apprentice witch.'

'What do I have to do?' I asked.

'Answer "yes" or "no".' I must have looked worried. She didn't let me waste time; she came across soft but fast. 'If you really want to be a witch, nothing you have to do will seem like too much. If you don't really want to be a witch, everything will seem like too much. Answer "yes" or "no".'

I answered, 'Yes.'

'We'll start today,' she said and got down from her chair. She replaced the huge book of maps on its proper shelf before pulling the wagon toward the check-out table. The wagon was loaded with seven heavy, large books. She handed these up to the librarian one at a time and then replaced each one in the wagon after it had been checked out.

The librarian said to Jennifer, 'Did you finish last week's supply?' I guessed that Jennifer was well known at the library.

Jennifer sighed and said, 'Of course.' She grabbed

110

the handle of the wagon and pulled it out the door and down the steps to the street. Those steps are steep. But not a single book fell out of Jennifer's wagon on the bumpity way down.

That Saturday Jennifer was dressed as she was usually dressed for school. That is, she wore a skirt. I later learned that she never wore jeans or shorts. She always wore a skirt. It was always an ordinary skirt. There was one thing about the way she was dressed that Saturday that was unordinary. Around her neck she had a gigantic key. She had it hanging from an old yo-yo string. The wagon was heavy with her books. Jennifer had to pull it with both hands behind her, and she had to lean way over to make the wagon move. That made the key hang very low; it would clung the sidewalk every now and then.

We headed for Samellson Park. We didn't talk much on the way. I didn't ask Jennifer where she lived and whether she had any brothers and sisters and where her father worked. She didn't ask me either. I suspected she knew everything about me anyway. There wasn't too much to know. I am an only child.

When we got to the park, we walked towards the fountain. First, Jennifer took a drink. I'd never seen anyone love water the way Jennifer did. Then we sat down on one of the benches nearby. The water fountain was in the centre of a cement circle. There were paths leading to it from four different sides of the park. I'd guess that the circle was about nine feet across. I soon learned that much as she loved water, Jennifer was more interested in the cement circle than she was in the fountain.

'Now, if you're ready,' she said, 'we'll begin.'

I would have been more ready if Jennifer had not seemed so serious. She was as serious as a doctor ready to give me a DPT booster shot. A witch doctor, I thought. When I answered, I tried to sound firm and a little bit annoyed, the way Jennifer did with the librarian. I said, 'Of course.' Jennifer could not be imitated. My voice came out loud Elizabeth instead of cool Jennifer.

Jennifer took a piece of chalk out of her pocket and made a chalk mark all around the edge of the concrete circle. That crazy key kept scraping along the concrete as she bent over. I hoped that after I became a witch's apprentice, I wouldn't get goose pimples from that noise any more. After the whole circle was completed, Jennifer took a candle from her pocket. She lit it and stuck the candle onto the concrete near the bottom of the fountain by dripping some of the wax first. After standing there with her eyes wide open, staring at the big sky, she marched out of the circle straight over to me.

'Watch me,' she said. 'When I'm ready, I'll point to you. When I point to you, you may enter the magic circle. But be quiet. Don't sneeze, burp, or breathe loud. Also, don't talk.'

Then Jennifer walked back to as near centre as she could get without actually standing inside the fountain. She closed her eyes and spun around three times, holding her hands straight down at her sides. As she spun around, she chanted:

> Xilka, Xilka, Besa, Besa;
> Xilka, Xilka, Besa, Besa;
> Xilka, Xilka, Besa, Besa.

On the third spin, and with her eyes still closed, she pointed right at me. I walked into the magic circle, scared, shaking and certainly not talking.

Jennifer took the big key from around her neck, twirled it over her head, and laid it on the ground near the centre of the circle. Next she took a pin out of her pocket. She pricked her finger; and without even asking permission, she pricked mine, too. Holding her hand over mine, she placed both our hands on the key. Each of our fingers dripped a drop of blood onto it. Jennifer picked it up, spit on it, and handed it to me. So I spit on it, too. She held the key over the candle to dry the spit and the blood. The candle made cackle sounds as she did this. When the key was dry she put it back down on the concrete and blew out the candle. Then she took her forefinger that had been pricked and hooked it to my forefinger that had been pricked. We marched around the key three times before she stopped and picked it up. Holding it out by the yo-yo string, she chanted:

> So thee and me shall never part,
> Wear this key around thy heart.

Jennifer put the key around my neck. The yo-yo was so long that the key hung not around 'thy heart' but around 'thy knees'. Looking me hard in the eyes she stuck out her pricked forefinger. I stuck out mine. We hooked our fingers together and shook them up and down three times and did another march around the magic circle.

I was so impressed with the ceremony that I still didn't want to say anything to break the magic spell. The big key kept clunging me on the knees. I waited until we walked out of the magic circle and were standing back at the bench before I said, 'Don't you think this string is a little long? Unless now that I'm an apprentice my heart has slipped down to my knees.' I laughed at my little joke. Jennifer didn't laugh.

She said, 'I got it from a very tall witch.'

'May I shorten it some?' I asked.

She replied, 'You can tie it up, but don't cut it.'

I lost no time tying it up so that it hung over my heart. My knees already felt black and blue.

Then Jennifer said, 'For the first week of your apprenticeship you must eat a raw egg every day. And you must bring me an egg every day. Make mine hard boiled. And you must read this book about witchcraft; it tells about some of my famous relatives. They were hanged in Salem, Massachusetts.'

I said, 'A *raw* egg?'

She said, 'I knew you'd ask that. R-A-W. Leave my egg by the tree. See you next week.'

And that's the way Jennifer and I parted that first Saturday. We walked in opposite directions. I looked back after I had taken only a few steps. I couldn't see either Jennifer or her wagon. They had disappeared.

All the way home I thought about my friend, Jennifer, the witch. I also thought that I had gone out an ordinary girl and had come back a witch's apprentice. I didn't feel different except that I felt like throwing up every time I thought of eating a raw egg. Every day! *For a week!*

E. L. KÖNIGSBURG,
Jennifer, Hecate, Macbeth and Me

Learning to be a Witch

From the opening section, what impression do we get of Jennifer?

Why does the narrator think it is significant that no books fell out of Jennifer's wagon as it went down the steps?

Describe the initiation Elizabeth has to go through.

Do you think there is anything strange in the fact that Elizabeth has to eat a raw egg every day whereas Jennifer's is hard boiled?

Point out some of the things that are amusing about the story.

Expulsion of a Witch

Of course, we should not forget that belief in witches and witchcraft is still very strong in many parts of the world. This story takes place in Ghana. The spirits of witches are believed to inhabit witch-birds which suck the blood out of their victims. The narrator's friend Tona has died, and the villagers believe it is the work of a witch:

It was several days later that the gong-gong was beaten in the late afternoon and the whole town called to assemble outside the chief's house. The crowd was large when I got there and I could see nothing, but I climbed up a very high tree and, seated in the swaying branches, I watched the whole scene.

After all were assembled the door opened and the chief emerged. He was a middle-aged man dressed in a glowing kente cloth, wearing a gold crown on his head and sandals on his feet. He was preceded by his horn-blower and accompanied by his linguist, bearing his staff of office, and the elders of the town. A small boy of my own age carried the royal stool, and another walked in front of the chief, acknowledging on his behalf the greetings of the crowd. The chief himself did not change expression from one of stern gravity. The stool was set down outside the house and the chief and his party sat.

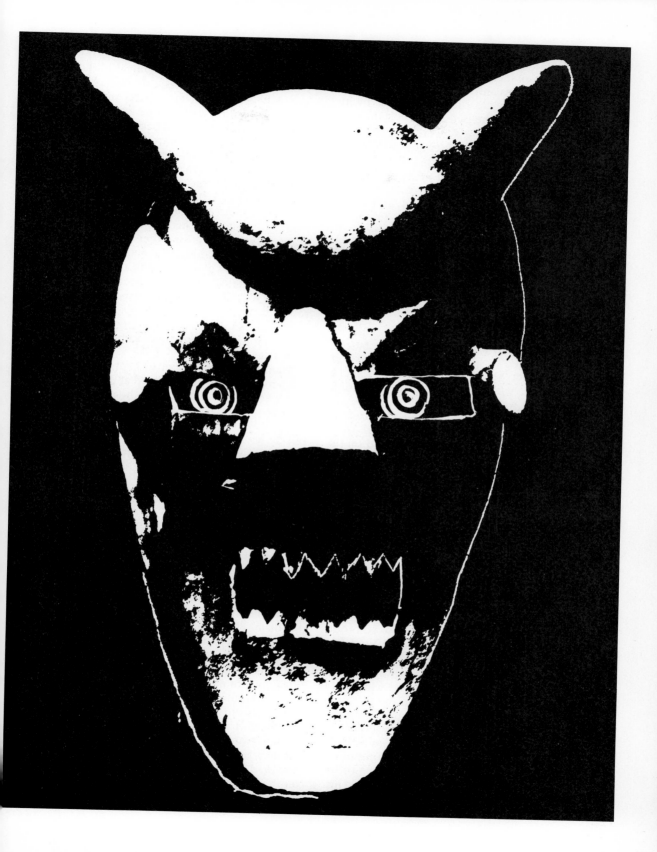

Then came the fetish priest, a tall old man, naked to the waist, and his assistants. Some of these, too, were children no older than myself – little girls in white skirts, their arms and the upper parts of their bodies smeared with white clay, and covered with strings of white cowrie-shells.

The priest stationed himself by an altar that had been set up in the compound, and poured a libation to the god asking that the truth might be revealed.

Another group then came from the chief's house and in the centre of it were three women. Their clothes were torn and they stumbled and wept. Obviously they had been roughly treated. Two were old and ugly. The other was about my mother's age and plump and comely. They were the occupants of the house that Tona's coffin had entered, and they all denied that they had killed the girl. The crowd began to jeer at them and threaten them. A few stones were thrown. But the chief ordered the people to be still.

Three cocks were brought and given to the priest's assistants. The first old woman was brought before the altar and warned to speak the truth or the god would surely kill her. She threw herself on her knees and swore that she was not a witch. The priest took the first cock and with a sharp knife cut its throat half-way across. Then he threw it on the ground. Amid a breathless silence the cock struggled to its feet, ran a few steps and collapsed and died on its back, its breast uppermost. The crowd roared. The god had accepted the woman's answer. She had spoken the truth. She was innocent and free. She fell sobbing to the ground, till her friends came and helped her to her feet.

The second old woman was brought forward. She too denied that she was a witch and the same ritual was followed. Her cock too died on its back and the god acknowledged her innocence.

Now they brought the third woman before the altar. The crowd grew restless and an angry muttering prevented me from hearing what the woman answered. But she stood upright and looked proud and defiant. The priest took the cock in his hand, but then he paused and in a loud and stern voice which silenced the crowd he cried, 'Take care, woman, what you do. If you are guilty the god will surely reveal it. And if you have not spoken the truth the god will surely kill you.' He took up his knife but before he had time to use it the woman fell to the ground, her limbs twitching and foam coming from her mouth. The crowd roared. The priest put down the knife and let the cock flutter away. Two of his assistants raised the woman to her feet and held her

till her strength returned. Then, trembling, she confessed that she was a witch. She was exhorted by the priest and his assistants to confess all her crimes.

Somewhere a drum began to beat, low and insistent. I began to feel faint from the heat and my cramped position. The scene on which I looked seemed to go far away and become small and unreal although I still saw and heard it clearly. I was looking on the witch who had flown over my house and gone on to murder Tona. In a few moments I should hear it from her own lips. More drums began to beat, their different rhythms inter-weaving. The woman said that she had exchanged the life of her own child long ago for her witchcraft power, and had had no more children. Tona's mother had taunted her and jeered at her, speaking of Tona's health and beauty and her success at school, and reviling her for her childless state. Witnesses were called to confirm that this was true. Tona's mother was called and sternly rebuked.

Then again the woman was urged to confess that she had murdered Tona by witchcraft and she said, 'It is true.'

Then the drums began to beat more loudly and the people jeered and shouted abuse at the woman. She was stripped naked and then covered roughly with a torn mat. A few broken pots and old pieces of cloth and a bottle of water were tied in a bundle and put on her head. With shouts and songs and blows she was driven to the edge of the town. I went too. I wanted to see her killed. I was filled with hatred and the desire to see her die.

But when the crowd halted at the end of the town they did not kill her. They told her that if ever she entered Ho again she would be beaten to death, and then they drove her into the bush.

Where would she go? Her nakedness would proclaim that she was a fugitive from justice. Anyone who saw her would know she was a witch. No one would give her food or shelter. The snakes and scorpions and driver ants would endanger her life in the bush. The ghosts and spirits would drive her mad with fear. Probably she would not live long. But she had a chance, and Tona had had no chance.

I walked home quickly for it was almost dark and it was one of my father's strictest rules that we must never be out after dark. This thought brought my mind back to everyday life and turned it from the hatred that was consuming me. Then I thought of Tona's grandfather and how he had cautioned my mother. 'Kofi shines at school. Be careful.' So Tona had died because she came top of her class and her mother had boasted. Suddenly I felt very small and lost. What could I make of a world where to do well at school endangered one's life? My father would not accept anything second-best from me, my mother would boast as Tona's mother had done. And anyway, Tona was gone. All my great plans had been hers too. Now I was alone and afraid, bewildered in a lonely and dangerous world.

I reached home and sat on the ground and wept. But I did not know if I was weeping for myself or for Tona, or even for the lost witch alone in the bush.

FRANCIS SELORMEY, *The Narrow Path*

Who do you think the narrator, Kofi, is weeping for at the end?

What are your feelings about the witch and her punishment?

Assignments

Choose several of the following to write about:

1. Write a poem about a witch which describes her appearance as grotesquely as possible.
2. Write a spell. Make it as gruesome as possible.
3. Write a curse. Make the victim's fate as nasty as possible.
4. Write a story about a witch making a spell that goes wrong.
5. You are passing a graveyard at night when something unexpected happens. Describe your feelings and what happens next.
6. Make a list of as many superstitions as you can. Which do you believe in?
7. Not all witches are wicked. Write a story about a good witch.
8. You suspect that someone is a witch. Describe how you find out whether it is true or not.
9. The Witch Hunt. Write a story about villagers ganging up on and hunting down a suspected witch. Try to make the witch sympathetic.
10. Find out what happened to witches in the sixteenth and seventeenth centuries, and then write a story entitled 'The Trial of a Witch'.
11. Describe a witch's house or workshop.

Language

A. Subjunctive and Conditional

Look again at 'McQuade's Curse'.

> May Satan, with a rusty crook,
> Catch every goat in Tallarook;
> May Mrs Melton's latest spook
> Haunt all old maids in Tallarook . . .

In Unit 2, we looked at two of the moods of the verb, that is, the action or state of the verb – the indicative and the imperative. **The indicative is used for factual statements and questions. The imperative is used for orders, commands, requests and entreaties.** Do the verbs in 'McQuade's Curse' belong to either of these moods?

At first sight, it might appear that they are expressing a request or an entreaty. But, in fact, if this were so, they would be expressed simply as 'Catch every goat . . .', 'Haunt all old maids . . .', etc. **The use of the word 'may' indicates that the verbs are in the subjunctive mood which is used to express a wish.** For instance,

> May you live long.
> May all your troubles be little ones.
> God save the queen.

The subjunctive mood is also used to express uncertainty, hesitation and possibility. For example:

> I am not certain, but he *may* be in the other room.
> If I *were* king, I should free all prisoners.

The fourth mood of the verb is the conditional. This mood expresses actions which are conditional (that is, depend upon) something else. For instance,

> I *should be* grateful if you would send me the information.
> If the weather is fine, we *should be able* to go out.

The words 'should', 'would' and 'could' usually indicate the conditional.

The subjunctive and conditional moods are sometimes rather tricky to identify, and it is not too important if you cannot distinguish between them. In fact, the use of the subjunctive is decreasing in modern everyday English.

State the mood of the verb in italics in the following sentences:

1. If I *were* you, I *should leave* for school now.
2. The old woman *stirred* the pot secretively.
3. *May* you *come* first in the race.
4. *Let*'s *hurry* or we *shall be* late.
5. God *bless* us everyone.
6. If you *should be* in the neighbourhood, *drop* in.
7. *May* you *rot* in hell!
8. *Leave* that alone or you *may be* sorry.
9. *Are* you *going* to the shops?
10. If you *are* tired, you *should go* to bed.

B. Paragraphs

Any extended piece of writing should be divided into paragraphs, that is, sections into which the subject of the writing can be broken up, each dealing with a separate aspect of the subject.

If you were to write page after page without dividing your writing up into separate paragraphs, it would be very boring for the reader, and it would make it more difficult for the reader to follow. Paragraphs give the reader a chance to rest and digest what he has just read before going on to the next paragraph, knowing that the action has shifted or that a slightly different point is about to be discussed. By using paragraphs, a writer is able to indicate and organize his ideas. What he has to say about one aspect of the subject should be included in one paragraph. The fact that he moves on and begins a new paragraph should mean that he has finished with that aspect and is moving on to another.

Look at one or more of the prose extracts in this unit and study the way the passage is divided into paragraphs.

In your own writing, try to keep your paragraphs to a reasonable length. It is not possible to say how long they should be – that depends on what you are writing about – but four or five sentences is usually quite long enough for one paragraph. A series of very short paragraphs can be as tiring as very long ones. Try to avoid single-sentence paragraphs except where there is a particular reason for using them and they produce a particular effect. (A good example of the use of single-sentence paragraphs can be seen in Ray Bradbury's *A Sound of Thunder* in Unit 3.)

Remember to indent a new paragraph well in from the edge of the page so that the reader can see clearly that a new paragraph has in fact begun.

Write a paragraph (four or five sentences) on one or more of the following:

The old woman
The strange cat
The graveyard
Superstitions
Horoscopes
The witch's house

Write about one of the following, making each heading into a separate paragraph:

1. Night – the graveyard – strange noises and shadows – a figure appears – what do you do?
2. A storm – an old house – you seek shelter – no one answers – you go in – what do you find?
3. Neighbours describe an old woman – you see her yourself – you do her a kindness – something good happens.

Vocabulary

A. Awful

In the extract from Meindert deJong's *The Tower by the Sea*, the following expressions are used:

the awesome news
the awed girl
an old crone whispered in awe.

'Awe' means 'fear and wonder'. 'Awesome' means 'inspiring fear and wonder'. The word 'awful' once meant the same, but now it is most commonly used to mean 'great', 'outstanding', 'notable of its kind', 'dreadful' as in these examples:

What an awful nuisance!
How awful!

The word is used loosely and too much. It is probably better to try to avoid it in your own writing.

There are a number of words like 'awful' which once had strong meanings but which through overuse have lost much of their original force. Here are some examples. *Find out what their original meanings were and say what they usually mean today.*

appalling	great
colossal	horrible
dreadful	mammoth
epic	nice
esquire	sensational
fabulous	terrible
fantastic	tragedy
frightful	tremendous
ghastly	

B. Witches and Warlocks

The word 'witch' normally refers to a feminine creature, and the word 'warlock' to a masculine. The name given to the 'sex' of a noun or pronoun is gender. 'Witch' is a noun of feminine gender, and 'warlock' is a noun of masculine gender. If the person or animal referred to is feminine or female (e.g. woman, girl, hen) then the noun is said to be of feminine gender. If the person or animal referred to is masculine or male (e.g. man, boy, cock) then the noun is said to be of masculine gender. Most inanimate objects (e.g. sky, table, music, chimney) do not have a sex, and they are said to be of neuter gender. If a noun can refer either to masculine or feminine (e.g. child, cousin, puppy) it is said to be of common gender.

State the gender of the nouns or pronouns in italics in the following sentences:

1. *She* fed the *kitten* with *milk*.
2. The *children* crossed the *road* while the *traffic* was held up by the *policeman*.
3. The *cows* looked guardedly at the *herdsman* when *he* came to drive *them* to the *cow-shed*.

4. The *cook* was very proud of the *cake he* had made.
5. The *cook* removed *her scones* from the *oven*.

Many words have feminine and masculine equivalents like witch and warlock. *Write out the following lists, filling in the blanks with suitable words:*

FEMININE	MASCULINE
lady	—
mistress	—
—	beau
—	husband
—	mister
hen	—
—	drake
—	boar
—	horse
—	ram
cow	—
—	bachelor
—	lion
—	tiger
vixen	—
—	author
—	waiter
—	god

Find more examples of words which have masculine and feminine equivalents and add them to your lists.

One common way of changing a masculine noun into a feminine noun is by adding '-ess'. For instance, actor, actress. There are some examples of this in the list above. *Can you think of any more?* (Make sure you spell them correctly.)

 Spelling

A. Awful

Note that the 'e' of 'awe' is dropped in the words 'awful' and 'overawing', but retained in 'aweing', 'awesome' and 'awestruck'. *Use each of these words in sentences.*

B. Weird

The word 'Weirdstone' in the title of the novel *The Weirdstone of Brisingamen* is a compound word made up of 'weird' and 'stone'. Note the spelling of 'weird'.

There are not many spelling rules in English to help you. Most of the time you just have to get down and learn the word by heart. But there is one rule that is very well known and that is the rule for 'i' before 'e'. The full rule is as follows:

'i' before 'e' except after 'c' when the sound is 'ee'.

Here are some words which follow this rule:

brief	ceiling
fierce	conceit
grief	conceive
mischief	deceive
pier	perceive
siege	receipt
shriek	receive
yield	

But even this rule has exceptions that you must remember:

seize	weir
seizure	weird

There are also a number of words which are spelled 'ei' where the sound is not 'ee'. For example:

beige	leisure
counterfeit	reign
feint	rein
foreign	reveille
forfeit	skein

The only way to remember these is to memorize them!

C. Cast/Caste

Here are some more words where you have to be sure you get the correct spelling for the word you mean. Explain the difference between them. Learn the spellings. Use some of the words in sentences.

cast	caste		
caster	castor		
censer	censor	censure	
check	cheque		
choir	quire		
choose	chose		
chord	cord		
clothes	cloths		
coarse	course	corse	
coma	comma		
copse	corps	corpse	corse
creak	creek		
cue	queue		
curb	kerb		
currant	current		
dear	deer		
descant	descent		
desert	dessert		
dew	due		
die	dye		
dinghy	dingy		
disc	disk		
discus	discuss		
dose	doze		
draft	draught		
dual	duel		
dully	duly		

 Activities

A. 1. You are preparing a spell. What things are going into the cauldron? Are they slimy and slippery? Are they alive or dead? What words would you speak? What would you do when the spell is complete?

2. Work in pairs, one of you as the witch and the other as the victim. When the witch casts the spell, the victim takes up a twisted shape which is only changed when the witch casts another spell. What feelings does the witch have? What does the victim feel?

3. You are passing a graveyard late at night. How do you respond? How do you move? You hear a strange noise. What do you do?

B. 1. Use the extract from *Jennifer, Hecate, Macbeth and Me* as the basis for an improvised scene.

2. The trial of a witch. Work out who is going to be the witch, who is going to be the judge, and who are going to be the accusers. What is the witch accused of? What is her defence? What is the attitude of the rest of the court?

3. You come upon some witches moving round a magic circle in a forest clearing late at night. You disguise yourself and join the ceremony. One of the witches becomes suspicious. What happens next?

4. Work out the most effective way of saying Shakespeare's 'The Witches' Song' – singly, as a group, or as a class.

C. 1. Make a survey of the class to find out which superstitions most people observe.

2. Find out from reference books or history books accounts of historical cases of witchcraft or famous witches. Make notes on them and report back to the rest of the class.

3. Make a survey of the class to find out how many people read their horoscopes regularly and why.

4. Find out the signs and dates of the zodiac and write a horoscope which you think would be appropriate for each sign.

Reading List

Try to read some of the following books which are about witches, real or imagined:

Meindert deJong, *The Tower by the Sea*
Alan Garner, *The Weirdstone of Brisingamen*
T. H. White, *The Sword in the Stone*
Mollie Hunter, *Thomas and the Warlock*
Mary Norton, *The Magic Bedknob*
  Bedknob and Broomstick
Elizabeth George Speare, *The Witch of Black-bird Pond*
Rosemary Sutcliff, *The Witch's Brat*
C. S. Lewis, *The Silver Chair*
John Masefield, *The Midnight Folk*
E. L. Konigsburg, *Jennifer, Hecate, Macbeth and Me*
Eric Linklater, *The Wind on the Moon*
Nina Bawden, *The Witch's Daughter*
The Hamish Hamilton Book of Witches, ed. by Jacynth Hope-Simpson

Witches, Witches, Witches, ed. Helen Hoke
Journey by Broomstick, ed. G. Palmer and N. Lloyd

UNIT 8

Fairs and Circuses

 Reading and
Understanding

At the Fair

Fairs and circuses suggest crowds of people, lots of noise, fun and excitement. They provide the opportunity for families and children to have a night out, to spend their money and enjoy themselves. Or at least that is the idea. A number of the passages presented here, however, suggest that there are also disappointments, and everything is not necessarily as jolly as it seems. The first extract describes the excitement of visiting the fair: the fact that the children's pet pig Johnnie has also come to the fair and creates chaos merely adds to the excitement.

'Walk up, walk up, ladies and gentlemen, chance of a lifetime to see the World's Fattest Lady. Satisfaction guaranteed, only sixpence.' The booths had raised platforms in front with pictures of what was on show inside and men shouting their wares. 'Roll up, roll up, see the Marvel of Nature, the Elephant Man with a Genuine Trunk.' The men were called barkers, Aunt Harriet said, and you couldn't believe all they said: she had seen the Elephant Man the year before last and there was nothing marvellous about him at all, he only had an extra long nose.

Naphtha flames roared and shivered and flared yellow ribbons of flame on the wind, lighting up gingerbread stalls where gingerbread houses they sold spread with white icing; hoop-la and coconut shies; the booth where you could have a tooth pulled for sixpence or watch it being done to someone else for a penny; and best and most beautiful, the big merry-go-round with its sailing horses and peacocks and unicorns, and its sweet, grinding tune that played on and on . . .

The moon shines tonight on Pretty Redwing,
My Pretty Redwing,
The breeze is dying,
The night birds crying . . .

Theo went to see the Fire Eater and Poll paid threepence to see the tiniest woman in England. There was a toy house in the tent and the Tiniest Woman peeped out of one of the windows. Poll paid her money and went round the back to shake hands with her. She had been bending down to look out of the window but she was still much smaller than Poll even when she stood up; a merry midget whose little hand was hard and horny as an old man's. She squeezed Poll's fingers and said, 'God bless you, my darling.'

They went on the merry-go-round. Theo on a prancing horse with flaring red nostrils and Poll on an ostrich. The seat was slippery and she clutched at its neck while she swooped and soared and the music played *Pretty Redwing* and the coloured world flew round faster and faster. She saw her mother and shouted, 'Look at me, look at me,' and drummed her feet on the side of the ostrich, but the next time round, Mother had vanished. Theo cried out, 'Look, Poll, look . . .' craning round so he almost fell off his horse. He was red-faced and crowing with laughter. 'Look, *Johnnie*,' he screamed, and as the merry-go-round began to slow down, Poll saw their pig galloping past, Mother and George running after him. He was twisting and turning, a great, lumbering, lolloping pig, going mad with excitement as other people shouted and joined in the chase. 'How'd he get out?' Theo said, as he dropped from his horse to the still moving platform, then to the ground. Poll was slower. By the time she was off the ostrich, she had lost sight of them all. She ran round the merry-go-round, crashed into someone who

120

said, 'Watch where you're going,' and when she looked up she saw Noah Bugg's pale eyes gleaming down at her. He held her by the shoulders but she kicked his shin to make him let go and ran wildly on, shouting, 'Johnnie, oh Johnnie . . .'

He came charging towards her like a live cannon ball, his pursuers behind him. Poll held out her arms to stop him and he swerved, grunting, and shot through the open flap of a tent. There was a horrendous crescendo of squealing and shouting, the canvas sides of the tent shook and bulged and then a huge woman with a straggling grey beard sprouting out of her face came thundering out, Johnnie apparently chasing her.

George hurled himself on top of the pig. Johnnie thrashed about, trumpeting, but George hung on to his ears like grim death and he stopped at last, exhausted and trembling.

'Bloody pig,' George gasped, but everyone standing round was roaring with laughter. Even the Bearded Lady.

'Gracious Heavens, what a fright he did give me,' she said in a high-pitched, ladylike voice so much at odds with her appearance that Poll gazed at her wonderingly.

'I'm so sorry, my dear,' Mother said. 'It's our pet pig, he wouldn't have hurt you, though you couldn't have known that, of course. I thought he was safely shut up, I'd no idea he'd followed us to the Fair.'

'Poor Johnnie,' Poll said. 'I expect he was lonely all by himself in the hen house and came looking for us.'

She squatted down and fondled his ears. Noah Bugg said, 'That your famous pet pig?' He didn't seem angry because she had kicked him but grinned at her in a friendly way when she looked at him. Then his grin faded and Poll saw he had seen Theo who had pushed through the laughing crowd and was standing beside her.

Theo gazed back at him steadily. Noah started grinning again. His gooseberry eyes roamed the circle of onlookers and rested on Mother.

Poll said, loudly and quickly, 'I saw Johnnie from the merry-go-round. Did you see me? I was on the ostrich. It was lovely, like flying. Shall we take him home, Mother? I will, if you like, but you'd better come too. He pays more attention to you.'

'No, I'll take him, unless you've had enough of the Fair already! Come along, you bad pig!' Johnnie hung his head as if he knew he'd done wrong and the Bearded Lady gave a light, tinkling laugh and patted his head. 'He looks a bit hang-dog, poor fellow. Or should it be hang-pig?' Poll saw that her hands were big and strong like a man's but looked away at once: it seemed impolite to stare when she hadn't paid for it.

Mother apologised again. The Bearded Lady bowed her head graciously, said no harm had been done, lucky he hadn't knocked over a china stall, that would have been a fine how-do-you-do, and retired to her tent. The crowd began to drift away, now that the excitement was over, but Noah Bugg was still there, watching Mother intently through his pale lashes. She said, in a kindly voice, 'How are you, Noah? Enjoying the Fair?'

Noah wriggled his shoulders and licked his lips nervously as if gathering courage to speak. Poll was sure he was going to say something dreadful, give Theo away, and the full horror of what this would mean suddenly struck her: if Mother knew one of her children had been telling wicked lies about Father something would be broken that could never be mended. She pushed roughly in front of Noah and said, 'Wasn't she *funny*, Mother? That voice – she sounded like Lady March! D'you think she's a woman with a beard or a man with a lady's voice? She's fat in the chest but that could be stuffing.'

'Be quiet, Poll!' Mother was frowning. She took Poll by the wrist and drew her away from the tent. 'It's sad either way, the poor soul. I'm ashamed of you, she might have heard what you said. I've half a mind to make you come home with me to teach you good manners!'

'I'm sorry,' Poll said. 'I didn't think.'

'Then you should! People like that have feelings just like the rest of us. It's bad enough that they should have to earn their livings this way, without rudeness from ignorant children.'

'Yes, Mother.'

'All right, then.' Mother gave Poll a doubtful look as if wondering what lay behind this unusual meekness but Poll kept her face fixed in a look of penitent sadness and Mother said, finally, 'Just remember in future,' and produced an extra threepence out of her purse and told her not to buy too many sweets or she would make herself ill.

When she had gone, a docile Johnnie trotting behind her, Poll giggled to herself and looked round for Theo. She wanted to tell him how clever she'd been, distracting Mother's attention from Noah, but there was no sign of him. No sign of Noah, either, though Poll looked for them both for some time. She bought a toffee apple and watched herself eat it in front of a distorting mirror that made her look thin at the top with a long neck like a swan's, and fat and spread out with little short legs at the bottom. Then she paid a penny and went in the tooth-pulling booth to watch a boy have a tooth out. He sat in a chair on the platform with a sheet round his neck but when the man bent over him with the pincers he turned his back on the audience and another man played a loud tune on a trumpet so Poll couldn't hear if the boy cried or not. When he got out of the chair he looked pale and there was blood on his chin, but he smiled bravely and everyone cheered him.

George was outside the booth with a friend, looking at the notice that said, PAINLESS EXTRACTIONS BY SKILLED OPERATOR. He said, 'Hallo, you bloodthirsty child. Was that gruesome enough for you?'

Poll was annoyed by his superior tone. She said, 'I was just looking for Theo, I thought he might be there,' and George laughed again as if she had said something enormously funny.

He said, to his friend, 'If someone was having their legs amputated my young brother and sister would be sure to be in the front row!'

Poll tossed her head and stalked off. George ran after her and tugged her hair gently. 'Sorry, Poll, just a silly tease. If you really want Theo, he went up the church path while you were watching that painless extraction.'

NINA BAWDEN, *The Peppermint Pig*

How would you describe Aunt Harriet's attitude towards the exhibits at fairs?

What do you think Poll felt when she went round the back to shake hands with the tiniest woman in England?

Describe the effect Johnnie had when he arrived at the fair.

What does Poll find puzzling about the Bearded Lady?

What did Poll not like about the Bearded Lady?

What were Poll's mother's feelings about the Bearded Lady?

What does George think about his younger brother and sister?

What impression do you get of Noah from this extract?

Describe the tricks Poll uses to prevent Noah talking to her mother.

Make a list of all the attractions of the fair mentioned in this extract.

Another View of the Fair

On the whole, Poll seemed to enjoy her visit to the fair, but would you say the same is true of the young narrator of the following account?

Every summer they used to have this big Feast on Church Moor, down past Wharfedale Avenue. Turn right near Holy Cross church and it was down there.

We had about three feasts a year, but this was the biggest of the lot. They had everything you could think of – steam swings, roller coaster, dodgems, ghost train, caterpillar. Everything. It was smashing.

Sometimes the Feast was so big it used to boil over on to the other side of the road, near the allotments.

I liked it down that way. It was the only part of our estate that was anything like. Church Moor, well it wasn't really a moor, it was just a big cinder track. When it was windy the dust used to blow up in big clouds and we used to put goggles on and ride bikes through it, like a sandstorm. On hot Sundays we would trudge through it until there was a film of dust on the toecaps of our best shoes and we could draw faces on it with our fingers.

It was best when there was a feast on, though, all bright and noisy with big cables half-buried in the cinders, leading from the Moon Rocket and the Wall of Death, and ending up in big vans whose motors hummed in the dark corners of the moor . . .

I only had threepence, but I thought I could get some more at the Feast. They had these roll-em-down stalls, where you roll a penny down and it falls on these squares. I always used to win on them. Some of the stalls had like mesh all round them and instead of just squares marked 4d, 3d, 2d, there were ten shilling notes all taped down, with six-pences on them. You had to get your penny over the sixpence to win the ten shilling note. I never won at that though.

Sometimes I would win as much as ninepence on the stalls and then blinking lose it all again. Then I would hang around the Feast, hoping that my Auntie Betty might come and give me some money. She was always trying to win a dinner service at that stall where you get tickets and a light flashes on all these different names and if it finishes up on the name that's on your ticket, well you win. I used to wait round that stall looking for my Auntie Betty.

I walked down Coronation Grove, along Royal Park Crescent and into Carnegie Road. At the bottom of Carnegie Road I could hear the first sounds of the Feast, the steam swings and the music from half a dozen round-abouts all mixed up so that it sounded like the air raid siren that they were always trying out near our school. I began to forget about Ted and sniffed for the cinder-dust smell of the Feast. I turned the corner of Carnegie Road and walked, happy, into the back-wash of the Feast, the candy-floss sticks and bits of coconut shell and brandy-snap bags that had been stamped into the street by all the people coming home. I felt sorry for them as I passed them because they had been and I was just going. Some of them carried prizes, coconuts, teddy bears, lemon squeezers, and one woman had an eiderdown. I thought it would be nice if I could win an eiderdown for my Auntie Betty, and I thought up this dream where I always won something every time I went to the Feast, and always brought home silver tea sets, eiderdowns ('Oo, you haven't brought any more eiderdowns, have you?' said my Auntie Betty), baskets of groceries from Chicken Jim's, until the stall-owners knew me and pretended to be frightened when I went near their stalls . . .

There was a stall called Bingo: large prizes. All the people were putting little counters on little coloured squares, and a man was shouting in a language I didn't understand: 'Clickety-click, sixty six, key of the door, twenty-one. Legs eleven. Sixty-five, old age pension, Kelly's eye, number one. . . .' At one of the stalls I stopped and got one of my pennies out. I started looking at the wooden chutes where you roll your money down. Some of them were curved at the end and some of them straight. The straight ones were best. I rolled my penny down and it went on a line. A fat woman in a white overall scooped it up.

I told myself: 'I'll just have one more go and then if I don't win anything I'll go on another stall.'

I rolled a penny down again. It circled over the stall and came nearly all the way back to me. Then it fell just inside a twopence square in the last line. The fat woman had her back to me, serving someone at the other side of the stall. She turned round and saw my penny in the twopence square.

'You put that there!' she said.

'I didn't!' I cried. 'Did I, missus?'

'I don't know, love, I wasn't watching,' said the woman beside me. She had a new basket with a dinner plate and a Mickey Mouse in.

The fat woman flung two pennies across the stall and said: 'You don't come here again!'

I went away biting my lip to stop from crying.

I walked right through the next avenue of stalls, past the moon rocket and the bumper cars, before I had another go on another roll-em-down stall. I thought the fat woman had someone following me. I found one of those stalls with the mesh in front where you roll the pennies on to the rich black cloth and try to win ten shillings.

First go my penny covered a sixpence. The man – it was a man this time – threw me three pennies and it turned out it wasn't a sixpence, just a three-penny bit. One of the pennies landed just on his side of the mesh when he threw them, and I had to scrabble under the wire with my fingers to get at it.

I had fivepence now. I held the pennies tight until they were hot in my hand. I put my hand to my face and it smelled of copper. I was going to lick it, and then I remembered Marion telling me that if you do, you get cancer. I looked through the noise to see if Ted was near but I couldn't see him.

Behind me was the helter-skelter, like a lighthouse. I had never been on the helter-skelter because it cost sixpence; it was always something unreal and far away. In Film Fun, Laurel and Hardy always went down the helter-skelter when they got £50 given for catching a burglar, but none of the kids I knew went down it.

I went back to one of the stalls and rolled a penny down the chute and it was fourpence straight off, so then I had eightpence. I went up to the helter-skelter and looked at it for a bit, then I walked on again knowing all the time that I was going to have a go on it, and then I walked back. I went up to the pay-box. It was like a picture house pay-box with a big notice, shaped like a shield: 'Oh U Kid!' and 'O.K. Let's Go!' I gave the girl sixpence and a man gave me a doormat. I climbed the stairs inside the helter-skelter. It was all wooden bars and bare canvas. No one else was having a go. I stood up at the top of the slide and looked out over the Feast.

I looked over the patched canvas roofs, and the strings of coloured light bulbs, waiting for someone I knew so that I could wave to them and maybe dive down the slide head first.

There was no one. I sat on the mat at the top of the helter-skelter and gripped both sides with my hands. Then below me, just at the pay-box, I saw Uncle Mad with Raymond Garnett.

Uncle Mad was leaning back on his bicycle. He looked as though he was paying for a go on the helter-skelter. Raymond Garnett was standing with him.

I shouted: 'Garno! Garno! Wa-atch!' and let go. The helter-skelter wasn't much really. Not much better than the slide down in the park. All the way down I was thinking: 'That's blinking sixpence gone west.'

I slid to the bottom, sprung up on my feet as though I was used to it and went over to Raymond Garnett.

'Caw, it's smashing, man! Are you going on?'

KEITH WATERHOUSE, *There is a Happy Land*

What impression do we get of the narrator's feelings about the fair from the opening of this account?

Why did he hang around hoping to see his Auntie Betty?

What does he feel about the people he meets who are coming away from the fair?

What does he wish could happen?

What do you think about the attitude of the fat woman on the roll-a-penny stall?

What was the attraction of the helter-skelter?

When he gets to the top of the helter-skelter, why does the narrator wait?

What does he think of the helter-skelter when he goes down it? Why?

Why does he say what he does say to Raymond Garnett?

Writing

Attractions at the Fair

In the extracts you have read many different kinds of side-shows at the fair have been mentioned and described. Here are two poems which are about two particular attractions you might expect to find at a fair.

The Big Wheel

Waiting to go on the big wheel,
I've paid my money, sixpence a go.
Soon the big wheel stops
And the seat sways to and fro.

Let's jump on quickly
Before it goes up.
Soon everyone's on it.
We all shout, 'We're off!'

First down on the ground,
Now up in the air,
Now people look big,
Now people look small.

We're up in the air,
We can see all around.
The big wheel stops turning,
We jump to the ground.

CAROL FITCHETT

Merry-Go-Round

Between the turning two antipodes
of makeshift sky and lately bolted boards
the golden horses spitted in their threes
sweep round on their predestined tracks.
The children cling like fruit to autumn trees,
taut-faced, a quick tangential smile thrown out
as round they come in threes, in leaping threes,
on snow-bound mounts caparisoned in gold,
and all the while the golden horses come,
the organ chews the cardboard melodies
and carved rococo bandgirls beat their drums.

But at the static centre of this fun,
glimpsed between flying tails and driving heads,
observe the engineer, a mournful rag
suspended from a loose forgotten hand,
a convict in the thrilling world he runs.

DAVID GILL

The first poem is straight-forward: a more or less factual account of what it is like to be on the big wheel. The second poem is more complicated. Study the words carefully. A contrast is made between the children on the round-about and the engineer who is running it. *Why is he called a convict?*

At the Circus

Look at this playbill. Are there any acts omitted that you would expect to see at a circus? Describe what you would expect to see in the acts given here and which you would most like to see.

125

Circus Animals

Many people feel that it is permissible for human beings to risk their lives in circus acts. After all, they can choose; they are not forced to. But what about the animals? How are they trained? Do they enjoy what they are forced to do? Is it really dignified to make them perform acts that are not natural to them? Here are three poems which may raise some doubts in your mind.

Poor Joey

Joey is a performing dog.
He does lots of tricks.
He leads the dogs around the ring
And his trainer's face he licks.

Whenever he enters the sawdust ring
All the children cheer.
Hooray! Hooray! Hooray! they cry,
Little Joey's here.

But when he goes behind the stage
And he didn't do a trick right,
His nasty trainer beats him
And Joey cries all night.

TERESA LANE

Circus Lion

Lumbering haunches, pussyfoot tread, a pride of
Lions under the arcs
Walk in, leap up, sit pedestalled there and glum
As a row of Dickensian clerks.

Their eyes are slag. Only a muscle flickering,
A bored, theatrical roar
Witness now to the furnaces that drove them
Exultant along the spoor.

In preyward, elastic leap they are sent through
    paper
Hoops at another's will
And a whip's crack: afterwards, in their cages,
They tear the provided kill.

Caught young, can this public animal ever dream
    of
Stars, distances and thunders?
Does he twitch in sleep for ticks, dried water-
    holes,
Rogue elephants, or hunters?

Sawdust, not burning desert, is the ground
Of his to-fro, to-fro pacing,

Barred with the zebra shadows that imply
Sun's free wheel, man's coercing.

See this abdicated beast, once king
Of them all, nibble his claws:
Not anger enough left – no, nor despair –
To break his teeth on the bars.

C. DAY LEWIS

Elephants

Tonnage of instinctive
Wisdom in tinsel,
Trunks like questions
And legs like tree trunks.

On each forehead
A buxom blonde,
And round each leg
A jangle of bells,

Deep in each brain
A chart of tropic
Swamp and twilight
Of creepered curtains,

Shamble in shoddy
Finery forward
And make their salaams
To the tiers of people –

Dummies with a reflex
Muscle of laughter
When they see the mountains
Come to Mahomet ...

Efficacy of engines,
Obstinacy of darkness.

LOUIS MACNEICE

126

Street-Markets

It is difficult to say which came first – fairs or markets. Certainly, street-markets have some of the excitement associated with fairs – there are the various stalls, the crowds of people and the stall-owners shouting their wares. Some of you may be more familiar with street-markets than with fairs. There may be one in your area on a Saturday morning or on an early-closing-day. If there is, think about it and the kind of atmosphere there is there as you read this account by Henry Mayhew of a London street-market a hundred years ago.

The scene in these parts has more the character of a fair than a market. There are hundreds of stalls, and every stall has its one or two lights; either it is illuminated by the intense white light of the new self-generating gas-lamp, or else it is brightened up by the red smoky flame of the old-fashioned grease lamp. One man shows off his yellow haddock with a candle stuck in a bundle of firewood; his neighbour makes a candlestick of a huge turnip, and the tallow gutters over its sides; whilst the boy shouting 'Eight a penny, stunning pears!' has rolled his dip in a thick coat of brown paper, that flares away with the candle. Some stalls are crimson with the fire shining through the holes beneath the baked chestnut stove; others have handsome octahedral lamps, while a few have a candle shining through a sieve: these with the sparkling ground-glass globes of the tea-dealers' shops, and the butchers' gaslights streaming and fluttering in the wind, like flags of flame, pour forth such a flood of light, that at a distance the atmosphere immediately above the spot is as lurid as if the street were on fire.

The pavement and the road are crowded with purchasers and street-sellers. The housewife in her thick shawl, with the market-basket on her arm, walks slowly on, stopping now to look at the stall of caps, and now to cheapen a bunch of greens. Little boys, holding three or four onions in their hand, creep between the people, wriggling their way through every interstice, and asking for custom in whining tones, as if seeking charity. Then the tumult of the thousand different cries of the eager dealers, all shouting at the top of their voices, at one and the same time, is almost bewildering. 'So-old again,' roars one. 'Chestnuts all 'ot, a penny a score,' bawls another. 'An 'aypenny a skin, blacking,' squeaks a boy. 'Buy, buy, buy, buy, buy, bu-u-uy!' cries the butcher. 'Half-quire of paper for a penny,' bellows the street stationer. 'An 'aypenny a lot ing-uns.' 'Twopence a pound grapes.' 'Three a penny Yarmouth bloaters.' 'Who'll buy a bonnet for four-pence?' 'Pick 'em out cheap here! three pair for a half-penny, bootlaces.' 'Now's your time! beautiful whelks, a penny a lot.' 'Here's ha'p'orths,' shouts the perambulating confectioner. 'Come and look at 'em! here's toasters!' bellows one with a Yarmouth bloater stuck on a toasting-fork. 'Penny a lot, fine russets,' calls the apple woman; and so the Babel goes on.

One man stands with his red-edged mats hanging over his back and chest, like a herald's coat; and the girl with her basket of walnuts lifts her brown-stained fingers to her mouth, as she screams. 'Fine warnuts! sixteen a penny, fine war-r-nuts.' A boot-maker, to 'ensure custom', has illuminated his shop-front with a line of gas, and in its full glare stands a blind beggar, his eyes turned up so as to show only the whites, and mumbling some beggar rhymes, that are drowned in the shrill notes of the bamboo-flute player next to him. The boy's sharp cry, the woman's cracked voice, the gruff hoarse shout of the man, are all mingled together. Sometimes an Irishman is heard with his 'fine ating apples'; or else the jingling music of an unseen organ breaks out, as the trio of street singers rest between the verses.

Then the sights as you elbow your way through the crowd are equally multifarious. Here is a stall glittering with new tin saucepans; there another, bright with its blue and yellow crockery, and sparkling with white glass. Now you come to a row of old shoes arranged along the pavement; now to a stand of gaudy tea-trays; Then to a shop with red handkerchiefs and blue checked shirts, fluttering backwards and forwards, and a counter built up outside on the kerb, behind which are boys beseeching custom. At the door of a tea-shop, with its hundred white globes of light, stands a man delivering bills, thanking the public for past favours, and 'defying competition'. Here, alongside the road, are some half-dozen headless tailors' dummies, dressed in chesterfields and fustian jackets, each labelled, 'Look at the prices', or 'Observe the quality'. After this is a butcher's shop, crimson and white with meat piled up to the first-floor, in front of which the butcher himself, in his blue coat, walks up and down, sharpening his knife on the steel that hangs to his waist . . .

This stall is green and white with bunches of turnips, that red with apples, the next yellow with onions, and another purple with pickling cabbages.

One minute you pass a man with an umbrella turned inside out and full of prints; the next, you hear one with a peepshow of Mazeppa, and Paul Jones, the pirate, describing the pictures to the boys looking in at the little round windows. Then is heard the sharp snap of the percussion-cap from the crowd of lads firing at the target for nuts; and the moment afterwards, you see either a black man clad in white, and shivering in the cold with tracts in his hands, or else you hear the sounds of music from 'Frazier's Circus', on the other side of the road, and the man outside the door of the penny concert, beseeching you to 'Be in time – be in time!' as Mr Somebody is just about to sing his favourite song of the 'Knife Grinder'. Such, indeed, is the riot, the struggle, and the scramble for a living, that the confusion and uproar of the New-cut on Saturday night have a bewildering and sad-dening effect on the thoughtful mind.

Each salesman tries his utmost to sell his wares, tempting the passers-by with his bargains. The boy with his stock of herbs offers 'a double 'andful of fine parsley for a penny'; the man with the donkey-cart filled with turnips has three lads to shout for him to their utmost, with their 'Ho! ho! hi-i-i! what do you think of this here? A penny a bunch – hurrah for free trade! *Here's* your turnips!' Until it is seen and heard, we have no sense of the scramble that is going on throughout London for a living. The same scene takes place in Tottenham-court-road – the same in Whitecross-street; go to whatever corner of the Metropolis you please, either on a Saturday night or a Sunday morning, and there is the same shouting and the same struggling to get the penny profit out of the poor man's Sunday dinner.

HENRY MAYHEW,
London Labour and the London Poor

Can you comment on any differences between this account and what you would see and hear today?

Sounds of the Street-Market

Here is a poem made up of the various calls you might hear at a street-market. Do you think it creates an impression of what a street-market is really like? Identify the various speakers.

Shouts of Woolwich Market

Sound, solid, salad tomatoes,
Only one and six a pound,
Best in the market.
Four peaches a bob,
Give yourself a treat.
You like to buy nylons,
Half price while stocks last.
Mix the bad uns with the good uns,
Shoot the last box o' coxes up.
Not one, not two, but THREE boxes
Of fine tissues for half a dollar.
'Ere that lady in the red dress wants three –
You've done yourself proud.
Sorry dear we're busy, no time to pick the best for
     you.
Take them as they come.
These beans are the best in the market – you'd be
     surprised.
Order me three quart bags, mate.
God is Love, Wash away your sins in the Blood of
     the Lamb.
Belt up! Wash yourself away.
Honk! Honk! Get that bloody stall out of the way.
Who wants this bag of loose grapes for a bob?
Anybody want to buy a stall?

DAVID

 Assignments

Choose several of the following to write about:

1. If you have visited a local fair, write about what it was like.
2. Write about some of the attractions you might expect to find at a fair.
3. The Circus. Write about a visit to a circus, bringing out especially the feelings of the audience.
4. Imagine you are a performer in a circus. Describe what it feels like to do your act in front of an audience.
5. Do you approve of animal acts in a circus? Give views for and against.
6. Write a poem or a story from the point of view of an animal that performs in a circus.
7. If you have a local street-market, describe what it is like to go shopping there.
8. Write a poem made up of the calls of stall-owners of a street-market.
9. Write a description of a street-market at closing time and after everyone has gone.
10. Write a poem about the experience of going on one of the attractions at a fair.
11. Make out a programme for a circus, including all the acts that you think a proper circus should have. Invent suitable names for the various turns.

Language

A. Prepositions

There is one part of speech we have not yet looked at, and that is the preposition. This is a difficult part of speech to define because prepositions themselves are so hard to explain. For instance, 'to' and 'for' are prepositions. Can you say what these words mean?

The easiest way to define a preposition is as the name given to a word which shows the relationship between one word and another. The relationship is between nouns, pronouns, verbs, adjectives and adverbs on the one hand, and nouns and pronouns (or noun equivalents) on the other. The preposition is a kind of bridge which leads from one of the words in the first group to one of the words in the second. All prepositions lead to a noun or a pronoun or part of the verb which can act as a noun. Here are some examples of prepositions in use:

The price *of* the book was too much. (relating two nouns)
He had no money *with* him. (noun and pronoun)
He walked *over* the hill. (verb and noun)
He was too late *for* breakfast. (adjective and noun)
The dog ran suddenly *into* the road. (adverb and noun)

There are many common prepositions. Here are some of them:

> under, across, through, over, above, to, of, for, with, by, before, after, between, into, without.

Many prepositions can also be used as adverbs or conjunctions. For example:

> He was *after* me in the line. (preposition)
> He came *after*. (adverb)
> *After* the circus was over, we came home. (conjunction)

Make a list of thirty prepositions. Use some of them in sentences.

Say whether the words in italics in these sentences are prepositions, adverbs or conjunctions:

1. The horse jumped *over* the gate.
2. The horse jumped *over*.
3. *After* tea, we all went *down to* the fair.
4. The noise *of* the fair was blaring *out*.
5. Crowds *of* people were moving *to* and *fro*.
6. *After* we had been there an hour, we went *into* the big tent.
7. There were acts *of* every kind *at* the circus.
8. The lion-tamer *with* his long whip was showing *off*.
9. The lion jumped *off* the stool *before* he should have done.
10. No one went *out of* the tent *before* the end.

B.   Question Marks

The question mark (?) is a punctuation mark which you probably already use and which has certainly appeared many times already in this book. **It is simply a punctuation mark that indicates a question.** For example:

> Where have you been?
> Why are you so late?
> Which hat do you prefer?

Sometimes care has to be taken to decide whether a question mark is required or an exclamation mark. Compare these two sentences:

> How could you do such a thing!
> How could you have known?

Complete the punctuation of the following sentences with a question mark, an exclamation mark or a full stop. (Note that alternative punctuation may be possible in some cases. Be ready to justify your choice.)

1. What a long time you are taking.
2. What was that strange noise.
3. What I want to do is see the acrobats.
4. He asked me where I was going.
5. Where are you going.
6. Why did you buy only two tickets.
7. Find out which is the best performance to go to.
8. Which act did you like best.
9. How tiresome.
10. How does the juggler manage it.

Vocabulary

A.   -er/-or

A suffix is an element added to the root or main part of a word in order to indicate the part of speech it is or to modify the meaning of the word. We have already come across some suffixes. There was '-ly' which when added to a word usually indicates that it is an adverb. 'There was '-ess' which when added to a word indicates that the word is feminine. A suffix comes at the end of a word. If something is added at the beginning of a word it is called a prefix.

The suffix '-er' or '-or' added to a word indicates an agent, that is 'a person who does something'. For instance, a juggler is a person who juggles, a lion-tamer is a person who tames lions, a tight-rope walker is a person who walks a tight-rope.

Write down as many words as you can ending in '-er' or '-or' which indicate agents.

B.   The Peppermint Pig

In Unit 1 you were advised to keep using a dictionary to check up on words whose meanings you were unsure of. Have you been doing this? Do you keep a vocabulary notebook in which you write down the words and their meanings?

Look again at the extract from The Peppermint Pig. *Do you know the meanings of the following words?*

guaranteed	meekness
midget	extractions
pursuers	amputated
thrashed	naphtha
hang-dog	lolloping
distorting	crescendo
superior	fondled
barkers	docile
prancing	gruesome
horrendous	squatted

If you are not sure, try to work out the meaning from where the word appears in the passage and use a dictionary to help you. Use each of the words in a sentence of your own.

 Spelling

A. -er/-or

There is no rule to remember whether a word ends in '-er' or '-or', and this can sometimes cause difficulty. The only way is to learn each word separately and remember it. Here are some of the words most easily mis-spelled for you to learn:

adapter	accelerator	editor
admirer	actor	governor
announcer	administrator	narrator
conjurer	auditor	oppressor
eraser	chancellor	orator
gardener	collector	possessor
listener	competitor	professor
observer	conductor	projector
organizer	conqueror	proprietor
practitioner	conspirator	radiator
probationer	contributor	solicitor
smuggler	councillor	sponsor
	debtor	tractor
	demonstrator	traitor
	dictator	visitor
	doctor	

Note also: beggar, burglar, registrar.
Use some of the words in sentences.

What is the difference between 'resister' and 'resistor', 'sailer' and 'sailor'?

B. Plurals

The words 'circus' and 'circuses' can sometimes give rise to difficulty in spelling. When we are talking about one, we use the word 'circus' and this is said to be a singular noun. When we are talking about more than one we use the word 'circuses' and this is a plural noun.

It is as well to know the commonest ways of forming plural nouns as this can help with your spelling.

1. **Most nouns form the plural by adding '-s' to the singular, e.g.**

dog	dogs
stair	stairs
eye	eyes.

2. **Nouns ending in '-ch', '-s', '-sh', '-ss' and '-x' form the plural by adding '-es', e.g.**

bench	benches
circus	circuses
crash	crashes
pass	passes
fox	foxes

3. **Nouns ending in '-y' preceded by a consonant change the 'y' to 'ies' in the plural, e.g.**

lady	ladies
family	families

Nouns ending in '-y' preceded by a vowel form the plural by adding 's', e.g.

valley	valleys
monkey	monkeys

4. **A few nouns ending in '-f' or '-fe' change this to '-ves' in the plural. They are:**

calf	calves
half	halves
knife	knives
life	lives
loaf	loaves
self	selves
yourself	yourselves, etc.
sheaf	sheaves
shelf	shelves
thief	thieves
wife	wives
wolf	wolves

The plural of 'hoof' can be 'hoofs' or 'hooves'; 'scarf' can be 'scarfs' or 'scarves'; 'wharf' can be 'wharfs' or 'wharves'; 'staff' can be 'staffs' or 'staves' (depending on the meaning). All other nouns ending in '-f' or '-fe' just add 's', e.g.

cliff	cliffs
dwarf	dwarfs
roof	roofs

5. A number of nouns form the plural by changing the vowel sound and spelling, e.g.

foot	feet
goose	geese
louse	lice
man	men
mouse	mice
tooth	teeth
woman	women

'Brothers', 'cows' and 'sows' are now more commonly used instead of 'brethren', 'kine' and 'swine'.

6. Nouns ending in 'o' preceded by a vowel form the plural by adding 's', e.g.

cameo	cameos
cuckoo	cuckoos
radio	radios

Nouns ending in 'o' preceded by a consonant tend to form the plural by adding 'es', e.g.

cargo	cargoes
hero	heroes
potato	potatoes

But there are many exceptions, such as:

dynamo	dynamos
grotto	grottos
photo	photos
piano	pianos
solo	solos

7. Most compound nouns form the plural by changing or adding to the most important word, e.g.

brother-in-law	brothers-in-law
looker-on	lookers-on

But NOTE:

man-servant	men-servants

Words like 'spoonful' add 's' at the end, e.g.

spoonful	spoonfuls
basketful	basketfuls
handful	handfuls

8. Some nouns have the same form in the singular and plural, e.g.

deer
salmon
sheep

9. Some nouns are almost always used in the plural, e.g.

billiards
spectacles
trousers

There is a lot to learn here, but it is worth the effort as it will help you with your spelling.

Find further examples where you can of all these different types.

 Activities

A. 1. Staying in one place, take up a posture or imitate a movement as though you were taking part in a typical fairground activity. It might be on a round-about, at a coconut shy or at a rifle range. Can the rest of the class guess what it is?

2. Using mime, practise the kind of movements made by a circus performer. It could be a juggler, or a strong man or a tight-rope walker. Work out an act as this performer – coming on, doing your piece, and going off again. If you can get some music to accompany it, so much the better. What kind of music would it be?

3. Practise the kind of calls stall-holders at a street-market might use – first singly and then one after another or in a kind of chorus.

B. 1. In groups, work out a typical scene at a street-market. One of you can be the stall-holder. What would he be like? How would he attract buyers? Could you trust him? The others can be customers. Try to make them different types. One might be easily taken in. Another might be argumentative. A third could be suspicious. What would happen if a policeman came along?

2. The circus is advertising its arrival in town. Work out the kind of display it would put on in the town square to encourage people to come.

C. 1. Make a survey of the class to find out what their favourite activity is at a fair or their favourite act at a circus.

2. If you have a local street-market, visit it and make a survey of it. How many stalls are there? What kind? Which are the most popular? When does it take place?

3. Make a bill poster for a fair or a circus, including words and drawings. Remember the idea is to attract people to come.

Reading List

Try to read one of the following which are about fairs and circuses or which include scenes set there:

Nina Bawden, *The Peppermint Pig*
Keith Waterhouse, *There is a Happy Land*
Wolf Mankowitz, *A Kid for Two Farthings*
Noël Streatfeild, *The Circus is Coming*
Ruth Manning-Sanders, *Circus Boy*
Bill Naughton, *The Goalkeeper's Revenge*

UNIT 9

Holidays

 ### Reading and Understanding

A Typical English Holiday

When you think of going on holiday, what do you think of? Do you think of the seaside, of sun and sand, of jellyfish and funfairs? This is the picture Dylan Thomas paints in his account of August Bank Holiday. Read it and see whether it stirs up memories in your own mind.

August Bank Holiday. A tune on an ice-cream cornet. A slap of sea and a tickle of sand. A fanfare of sunshades opening. A wince and whinny of bathers dancing into deceptive water. A tuck of dresses. A rolling of trousers. A compromise of paddlers. A sunburn of girls and a lark of boys. A silent hullabaloo of balloons.

I remember the sea telling lies in a shell held to my ear for a whole harmonious, hollow minute by a small, wet girl in an enormous bathing-suit marked 'Corporation Property'.

I remember sharing the last of my moist buns with a boy and a lion. Tawny and savage, with cruel nails and capacious mouth, the little boy tore and devoured. Wild as seed-cake, ferocious as a hearth-rug, the depressed and verminous lion nibbled like a mouse at his half a bun, and hiccupped in the sad dusk of his cage.

I remember a man like an alderman or a bailiff, bowlered and collarless, with a bag of monkey-nuts in his hand, crying 'Ride 'em, cowboy!' time and again as he whirled in his chairoplane giddily above the upturned laughing faces of the town girls bold as brass and the boys with padded shoulders and shoes sharp as knives; and the monkey-nuts flew through the air like salty hail.

Children all day capered or squealed by the glazed or bashing sea, and the steam-organ wheezed its waltzes in the threadbare playground and the waste lot, where the dodgems dodged, behind the pickle factory.

And mothers loudly warned their proud pink daughters or sons to put that jellyfish down; and fathers spread newspapers over their faces; and sand-fleas hopped on the picnic lettuce; and someone had forgotten the salt.

In those always radiant, rainless, lazily rowdy and sky-blue summers departed, I remember August Monday from the rising of the sun over the stained and royal town to the husky hushing of the roundabout music and the drowsing of the naphtha jets in the seaside fair: from bubble-and-squeak to the last of the sandy sandwiches.

There was no need, that holiday morning, for the sluggardly boys to be shouted down to breakfast; out of their jumbled beds they tumbled, scrambled into their rumpled clothes; quickly at the bath-room basin they catlicked their hands and faces, but never forgot to run the water loud and long as though they washed like colliers; in front of the cracked looking-glass bordered with cigarette-cards, in their treasure-trove bedrooms, they whisked a gap-tooth comb through their surly hair; and with shining cheeks and noses and tide-marked necks, they took the stairs three at a time.

But for all their scramble and scamper, clamour on the landing, catlick and toothbrush flick, hair-whisk and stair-jump, their sisters were always there before them. Up with the lady lark, they had prinked and frizzed and hot-ironed; and smug in their blossoming dresses, ribboned for the sun, in gym-shoes white as the blanco'd snow, neat and silly with doilies and tomatoes they helped in the higgledy kitchen. They were calm; they were virtuous; they had washed their necks; they did not romp, or fidget; and only the smallest sister put out her tongue at the noisy boys.

DYLAN THOMAS, *Holiday Memory*

134

Dylan Thomas was a poet and liked playing with words — the sound of them, the sense of them. Look carefully at the first paragraph and say what you think he means by each sentence.

What is surprising about the way the boy and the lion eat the narrator's last bun?

What is surprising about the way the man like 'an alderman or a bailiff' behaves?

What two moods of the sea are described in paragraph five?

Why are the daughters and sons of paragraph six 'proud' and 'pink'?

Contrast the reaction of boys as opposed to that of girls on holiday according to the writer. Do you agree?

Can you find other clues in the passage that Dylan Thomas was a poet? Look at his use of rhyming words, his fondness for using a number of words beginning with the same letter, his playing with the meaning of words. Find examples of each of these.

What impression do you get of the kind of holiday Dylan Thomas is remembering?

How does it compare with the kind of holidays you can remember?

Unwillingly on Holiday

Not all holidays are seen as pleasurable occasions. Sometimes going on holiday can be something to be dreaded. Partly it could be the change from the known routine, going somewhere where you are uncertain of what is expected or what you will find. Some people find this an exciting new experience; others face it with dread. Read the following account. What would your feelings be about going somewhere new on holiday?

If, standing alone on the back doorstep, Tom allowed himself to weep tears, they were tears of anger. He looked his good-bye at the garden, and raged that he had to leave it — leave it and Peter. They had planned to spend their time here so joyously these holidays.

Town gardens are small, as a rule, and the Longs' garden was no exception to the rule; there was a vegetable plot and a grass plot and one flower-bed and a rough patch by the back fence. In this last the apple-tree grew: it was large, but bore very little fruit, and accordingly the two boys had always been allowed to climb freely over it. These holidays they

would have built a tree-house among its branches.

Tom gazed, and then turned back into the house. As he passed the foot of the stairs, he called up, 'Good-bye, Peter!' There was a croaking answer.

He went out on to the front doorstep, where his mother was waiting with his suitcase. He put his hand out for it, but Mrs Long clung to the case for a moment, claiming his attention first. 'You know, Tom,' she said, 'it's not nice for you to be rushed away like this to avoid the measles, but it's not nice for us either. Your father and I will miss you, and so will Peter. Peter's not having a nice time, anyway, with measles.'

'I didn't say you'd all be having a nice time without me,' said Tom. 'All I said was—'

'Hush!' whispered his mother, looking past him to the road and the car that waited there and the man at the driving-wheel. She gave Tom the case, and then bent over him, pushing his tie up to cover his collar-button and letting her lips come to within an inch of his ear. 'Tom, dear Tom—' she murmured, trying to prepare him for the weeks ahead, 'remember that you will be a visitor, and do try – oh, what can I say? – try to be *good.*'

She kissed him, gave him a dismissive push towards the car and then followed him to it. As Tom got in, Mrs Long looked past him to the driver. 'Give my love to Gwen,' she said, 'and tell her, Alan, how grateful we are to you both for taking Tom off at such a short notice. It's very kind of you, isn't it, Tom?'

'Very kind,' Tom repeated bitterly.

'There's so little room in the house,' said Mrs Long, 'when there's illness.'

'We're glad to help out,' Alan said. He started the engine.

Tom wound down the window next to his mother. 'Good-bye then!'

'Oh, Tom!' Her lips trembled. 'I am sorry – spoiling the beginning of your summer holidays like this!'

The car was moving; he had to shout back: 'I'd rather have had measles with Peter – much rather!'

Tom waved good-bye angrily to his mother, and then, careless even of the cost to others, waved to an inflamed face pressed against a bedroom window. Mrs Long looked upwards to see what was there, raised her hands in a gesture of despair – Peter was supposed to keep strictly to his bed – and hurried indoors.

Tom closed the car window and sat back in his seat, in hostile silence. His uncle cleared his throat and said: 'Well, I hope we get on reasonably well.'

This was not a question, so Tom did not answer it.

He knew he was being rude, but he made excuses for himself: he did not much like Uncle Alan, and he did not want to like him at all. Indeed, he would have preferred him to be a brutal uncle. 'If only he'd beat me,' thought Tom, 'then I could run away home, and Mother and Father would say I did right, in spite of the quarantine for measles. But he'll never even try to beat me, I know; and Aunt Gwen – she's worse, because she's a child-lover, and she's kind. Cooped up for weeks with Uncle Alan and Aunt Gwen in a poky flat ...' He had never visited them before, but he knew that they lived in a flat, with no garden.

PHILIPPA PEARCE, *Tom's Midnight Garden*

Why was Tom so angry at having to stay with his uncle and aunt?

Tom claims he didn't say that the family would all be having a nice time without him. What do you think he did say?

What does Tom's mother seem to be worried about concerning Tom while he is on holiday?

Do you think Tom's mother is aware of his real feelings? How can you tell?

Pick out examples of Tom's behaviour that show that he is determined not to enjoy his holiday.

Why was Aunt Gwen worse than Uncle Alan?

What is it particularly that annoys Tom about the place he is going to?

Try to read the whole novel. You will find that Tom's holiday is not as dull as he expected.

Writing

Views and Memories

Here are some comments on holidays written by people of your own age to set you thinking and talking.

I like holidays because they give me a break from school so when I come back I'm ready to get working. During school holidays I have time to pursue my hobbies and play sports like fishing, tennis, football, etc. but during a school week I spend nearly all my time doing homework.

DARREN BORRITT

The only thing I don't like about school holidays is that you have to come back to school. Another thing is that on holiday you can wear what you want to wear, and when you come back to school you have to wear some terrible clothes called school uniform.

BRIAN COPPIN

I myself don't like holidays because I get bored staying home during the holidays. Even if I do go out during the holidays, I don't go out everyday visiting places, because I have already visited so many places while I have been staying in London during the last four years. The best holiday I would like to go on is to India to visit my own country because I have been in Britain for nearly six years and I have not seen India since then. Also I would like to go there because now whoever comes from there says that it has changed but only in some places. I would like to go to India because I have not seen my grandmother or grandfather for nearly six years.

HARSHUDAN PATEL

Sometimes holidays can be really good if you plan something or you're going away somewhere. But otherwise they can get very boring. If you play football one day and you've got nothing to do the next day, then you just sit around indoors all the time. But most of the time I enjoy my holidays, mostly because I plan what I'm going to do day after day. If I don't go anywhere I can go down my friend's house and most probably go out from there. But there's one thing a holiday gives you, and that's freedom from school.

STEPHEN HARDING

I went to Jamaica once and had a lovely time there. It was hot and sunny. I spent most of my time up in the country with my Grandma. There was a river nearby and I went swimming a lot. When I was in town I went swimming a lot on the beaches. I couldn't open my eyes under water because there was salt under the water. I lived in a funny house which did not have any upstairs. It was so hot that when we went to sleep, I slept with no covers on at all. I wore shorts because long trousers stuck to our legs. I rarely wore a shirt and I wore sandals on my feet. I ate different things too – fruit for example. I ate mangoes, guavas and ackee.

DONOVAN THOMPSON

I would like to go to a hot country like Guyana in South America because my mum and dad come from there and they are always talking about it and how lucky we are because we may be going there this year and be able to climb palm trees, banana trees, etc. We will be able to eat lots of water melons because my dad's dad grows his own. We will go to the market and help sell some yams, cassava and milk. When the sun gets so hot you cannot stand it you are able to go under the houses. In this country when you want a house you have to buy one, but in Guyana you have to make your own on your own piece of land.

IAN ROSS

When I last went to Spain, we stayed in a villa right by the sea. Once every day we used to get 50 pesetas and my mum and dad took me and my brother into the town. Every time I got any money I went into this kind of a fish shop and got these long things like chop-sticks and you put sugar on them. There were only about two fish and chip shops in the part of Spain I was in. The time before we went into a rocky area where there were lots of man-made holes everywhere and there was a pile of wood, so me and my brother started jumping on it, and a piece of the wood cracked and a lizard came running out from underneath. My brother and I tried to catch it. We chased it under another pile of wood, so we left it.

MARK NEWMAN

Talk about the various views presented.
Do you think school holidays are boring?
Are you glad to get back to school?
What kind of things do you do during the holidays?
Describe some interesting places you have been to or unusual things you have seen or done or tasted.
If you had a choice of going anywhere in the world, where would you go? Why?
What things would you need for a perfect holiday? Think about climate, surroundings, food, company.

Problems

Holidays can bring with them problems. All your friends might have gone away and you have no one to play with. You may be taken by your family to a place you don't like. Getting ready for a holiday is usually an exciting experience, but that too has its problems. Will you catch the plane or train in time? Have you remembered to leave a note for the milkman or arranged for the cat to be fed? Here is an extract describing how to pack when going on holiday.

I rather pride myself on my packing. Packing is one of those many things that I feel I know more about than any other person living. (It surprises me myself, sometimes, how many of these subjects there are.) I impressed the fact upon George and Harris and told them that they had better leave the whole matter entirely to me. They fell into the suggestion with a readiness that had something uncanny about it. George put on a pipe and spread himself over the easy-chair, and Harris cocked his legs on the table and lit a cigar.

This was hardly what I intended. What I had meant, of course, was, that I should boss the job, and that Harris and George should potter about under my directions, I pushing them aside every now and then with 'Oh, you—!' 'Here, let me do it.' 'There you are, simple enough!' – really teaching them, as you might say. Their taking it in the way they did irritated me. There is nothing does irritate me more than seeing other people sitting about doing nothing when I'm working.

I lived with a man once who used to make me mad that way. He would loll on the sofa and watch me doing things by the hour together, following me round the room with his eyes, wherever I went. He said it did him real good to look on at me, messing about. He said it made him feel that life was not an idle dream to be gaped and yawned through, but a noble task, full of duty and stern work. He said he often wondered now how he could have gone on before he met me, never having anybody to look at while they worked.

Now, I'm not like that. I can't sit still and see another man slaving and working. I want to get up and superintend, and walk round with my hands in my pockets, and tell him what to do. It is my energetic nature. I can't help it.

However, I did not say anything, but started the packing. It seemed a longer job than I thought it was going to be; but I got the bag finished at last, and I sat on it and strapped it.

'Ain't you going to put the boots in?' said Harris.

And I looked round, and found I had forgotten them. That's just like Harris. He couldn't have said a word until I'd got the bag shut and strapped, of course. And George laughed – one of those irritating, senseless, chuckle-headed, crack-jawed laughs of his. They do make me so wild.

I opened the bag and packed the boots in; and then, just as I was going to close it, a horrible idea occurred to me. Had I packed my tooth-brush? I don't know how it is, but I never do know whether I've packed my tooth-brush.

My tooth-brush is a thing that haunts me when I'm travelling, and makes my life a misery. I dream that I haven't packed it, and wake up in a cold perspiration, and get out of bed and hunt for it. And, in the morning, I pack it before I have used it, and have to unpack again to get it; and it is always the last thing I turn out of the bag; and then I repack and forget it, and have to rush upstairs for it at the last moment and carry it to the railway station, wrapped up in my pocket-handkerchief.

Of course I had to turn every mortal thing out now, and, of course, I could not find it. I rummaged the things up into much the same state that they must have been before the world was created, and when chaos reigned. Of course, I found George's and Harris's eighteen times over, but I couldn't find my own. I put the things back one by one, and held everything up and shook it. Then I found it inside a boot. I repacked once more.

When I had finished, George asked if the soap was in. I said I didn't care a hang whether the soap was in or whether it wasn't; and I slammed the bag to and strapped it, and found that I had packed my tobacco-pouch in it, and had to re-open it. It got shut up finally at 10.5 p.m., and then there remained the hampers to do. Harris said that we should be wanting to start in less than twelve hours' time and thought that he and George had better do the rest; and I agreed and sat down, and they had a go.

They began in a light-hearted spirit, evidently intending to show me how to do it. I made no comment; I only waited. When George is hanged Harris will be the worst packer in this world; and I looked at the piles of plates and cups, and kettles, and bottles, and jars, and pies, and stoves, and cakes, and tomatoes, etc. and felt that the thing would soon become exciting.

It did. They started with breaking a cup. That was the first thing they did. They did that just to show you what they *could* do, and to get you interested.

Then Harris packed the strawberry jam on top of a tomato and squashed it, and they had to pick out the tomato with a teaspoon.

And then it was George's turn, and he trod on the butter. I didn't say anything, but I came over and sat on the edge of the table and watched them. It irritated them more than anything I could have said. I felt that. It made them nervous and excited, and they stepped on things, and put things behind them, and then couldn't find them when they wanted them; and they packed the pies at the bottom, and put

heavy things on top, and smashed the pies in.

They upset salt over everything, and as for the butter! I never saw two men do more with one-and-twopence worth of butter in my whole life than they did. After George had got it off his slipper, they tried to put it in the kettle. It wouldn't go in, and what *was* in wouldn't come out. They did scrape it out at last, and put it down on a chair, and Harris sat on it, and it stuck to him, and they went looking for it all over the room.

'I'll take my oath I put it down on that chair,' said George, staring at the empty seat.

'I saw you do it myself, not a minute ago,' said Harris.

Then they started round the room again looking for it; and then they met again in the centre and stared at one another.

'Most extraordinary thing I ever heard of,' said George.

'So mysterious!' said Harris.

Then George got round at the back of Harris and saw it.

'Why, here it is all the time,' he exclaimed, indignantly.

'Where?' cried Harris, spinning round.

'Stand still, can't you!' roared George, flying at him.

And they got it off, and packed it in the teapot.

JEROME K. JEROME, *Three Men in a Boat*

Choosing a Holiday

Look at these advertisements for holidays. Say which is presented in the most appealing way and give reasons for your views. Which of these holidays would you like to go on? Why?

Disappointments

Holidays don't always turn out as pleasant as we expect. We look forward to them with excited anticipation, but the reality can sometimes be a sad disappointment. The weather can be a very important aspect of a holiday – it can make it or break it. Here is one person's view of a disappointing holiday.

I sit by the sea in the pouring rain.
Oh how I wish I were back again.

The noise is so loud, the weather bad,
And when I reach home, I'll be terribly glad.

Canal Cruising

Although southern France is best known for its coastal resorts, the unspoilt inland waterways of the Canal du M... and the Canal Latéral à la Garonne are quiet and uncrowded. There can be f... more relaxing ways to see th... real France than a canal cru... From Castelnaudary, wher... you board your boat, you c... cruise either north west... through the rich country... towards Bordeaux or sou... eastwards along the beau... Canal du Midi to the Mediterranean.

You can choose between... types of boat: the 7 ber... Caribbean or the 5 ber... Bermuda.

Blue Caribbean

The Blue Caribbean c... cruiser offers luxury accommodation for ... people. The forward... includes a fold-dow... berth and a single-b... and there are two o... separate cabins eac... single berths. In a... is room for one ex... a fold-down uppe... centre cabin. Th...

Corsica - near to France, close to Paradise

A mountain island rising from the deep blue Mediterranean, its green slopes fragrant with herbs, Corsica is truly a holiday paradise of warm breezes, crystal waters and the kind of individual atmosphere only the French seem able to create.

Camping on a budget, self–catering apartments or inclusive holidays, Corsica has something for everyone. In spring and autumn the island is at its loveliest, local produce is at its best, prices are lower for car hire and ferries, there is a wider choice of villas, and temperatures are comfortably warm. Fly direct or drive and take one of the Mediterranean ferries.

Just once in your life try Corsica—even though it will spoil you for anything else.

FRANCE
the all-inclusive holiday

5day holidays all year round

A long weekend or short second holiday – four nights in Paris; the real answer to that spring or autumn "must get away" feeling. Paris is so close – so easy to book – so reliable. Paris never changes – there's always something exciting and interesting to do. High up views from the top of the Arc de Triomphe or leisurely sightseeing from the Bateaux Mouches on the Seine, under those beautiful bridges. Paris is fascinating – something to suit everyone. The pavement café in Montmartre or the Latin Quarter, the high fashion shops in the boulevard St. Honore or the legendary Mona Lisa in the Louvre. Included in the price of these holidays is a British Rail ticket from wherever you live in the UK to the London departure point – that's a saving of around £15 from the Midlands or over £20 from Scotland. Compare that value with any other holiday! You must visit Paris this year. And at prices like these – can you really resist the temptation?

ITINERARY
Departures all year round*

SEALINK
Depart London, Victoria morning or afternoon by rail for Dover or Folkestone. Comfortable cross channel boats to Calais then by train into Paris, Gare du Nord arriving during the evening. Departures any day of the week (or with our main group on Sunday).

SEASPEED
Depart London, Charing Cross midday (morning or afternoon service also available) by rail for Dover. Thirty minutes channel crossing by hovercraft. Rail into Paris arriving early evening. Departures any day of the week (or with our main group on Sunday).

DAN-AIR
Depart London, Victoria morning or midday (later flights also available) by coach for Lydd, Avro 748 or Viscount prop jet to Beauvais and on by coach to Paris arriving during the afternoon. Departures any day of the week (or with our main group on Sunday).

BIA SILVER A...
Depart London, ...
evening also ava...
Flight by Dart H...
by train to Paris...
Departures We...
Saturday only.

BCAL GOLD...
Depart London...
(afternoon fl...
1-11 to Paris...
into central...
afternoon. ...
Friday or S...

BRITISH...
Depart L...
morning...
available...
(or 727/...
airport...
(pay lo...
Wedne...
only....
N.B. ...
servic...

No one need be alone on an HF Holiday

Maybe you're a natural loner. So, if you prefer the companionship of nature to that of man, HF provides the ideal base for your holiday and leaves the rest to you. But if you wish to be one of a friendly party, an HF Guest House Holiday ensures congenial companionship, whether you are with your family or on your own, plus perfect facilities for a walking holiday with a wide variety of outdoor pursuits and an exciting programme of optional excursions.

This year you can take your pick of the 35 HF Centres situated amidst some of the most beautiful scenery in the British Isles. Write today for HOLIDAYS THAT ARE DIFFERENT '77 which tells you all about HF Guest House Holidays, Special Activity Holidays, Young World Holidays for the 17-30's and Holidays Abroad.

HOLIDAY FELLOWSHIP (Dept 353)
142 Great North Way, London NW4 1EG
(01-203 3381)

Why the best equipment

Because only a... equipment fro... special items o...

Write today fo... Campers and ... packed with in...

YHA where re...

Please send me fre...
the 40 page catalo...

NAME

ADDRESS

YHA S...
29 John Adam...
14 Cannon Str...
Also in Manch...

The clouds drift along the sky's edge,
Down to the horizon, a thick black wedge.

For once in my life, I feel alone.
How I wish I'd never been born.

At last the time has come to go.
I gather my bags, look round me and though

While I was here it rained all day,
Now I am going, I wish I could stay.

SUSAN DAVIS

Why do you think the writer wishes she could stay at the end?

How important do you think the weather is for a holiday?

Staying at Home

Sometimes people boast about the exciting places they are going to on holiday, and this may make other people who are not going away envious or discontented. What are the feelings of Jane in this poem?

Last Day of the Summer Term

We sit around in the classroom
Exchanging holiday plans;
The many familiar faces—
Kate's and Maud's and Anne's!

Kate's spending a month in Brighton;
Joan is for Paris; Maud's
Going to an aunt in Scotland,
And Anne to the Norfolk Broads.

I listen, envious and silent,
Or do the jobs of the day:
Tidy up; stack books; or I read
In a half-hearted sort of way.

We gather for the last Assembly—
The prayers and the final hymn;
'If you girls go on being fidgety
I shall keep the whole school in.'

But it's over at last, all over;
And I walk along home with Sue,
And stand at her door, while she chatters
About what they're going to do:

They've hired a holiday-caravan
Down on the Isle of Wight:
'We shall set out by car this evening—
We'll be travelling all night . . .

'Ah, well! Good-bye till September!'
I go on to my house alone;
I find my key, and enter
My holiday-home.

The house is close and quiet;
A few dead roses spill
Their petals one by one
On the hot window-sill.

A tap drips in the kitchen;
Two flies buzz on the pane;
There's a note on the breakfast-table:
Two lines from Mother. 'Dear Jane,

'Make yourself a cup of tea, dear;
I'll be working late at the shop.'
And I turn with hardly a sigh
To the uncleared washing-up;

Or wander vaguely upstairs,
To stare awhile at the tall
Unanswering photo of father
That hangs on my bedroom wall.

JOHN WALSH

What do you think is the significance of the 'unanswering photo of father'?

Should you necessarily feel disappointed at spending your holiday at home?

Playing with Friends

Of course, things can go wrong when you spend your holidays at home as well. The weather might be wrong or you might quarrel with your friends and have no one to play with. Read the following which is a complete short story. It is set in Trinidad, but it could be about children anywhere.

Cricket in the Road

In the rainy season we got few chances to play cricket in the road. For whenever we were at the game, the rains came down, chasing us into the yard again. That was the way it was in Mayaro in the rainy season. The skies were always overcast, and over the sea the rain-clouds hung low and grey and scowling, and the winds blew in and whipped angrily through the palms. And when the winds were strongest and raging, the low-hanging clouds would become dense and black, and the sea would roar, and the torrents of rain would come sweeping with all their tumult upon us.

We had just run in from the rain. Amy and Vern from next door were in good spirits, and laughing, for oddly enough they seemed to enjoy the downpours as much as playing cricket in the road. Amy was in our yard, giggling and pretending to drink the falling rain, with her face all wet and her clothes drenched, and Vern, who was sheltering under the eaves, excitedly jumped out to join her. 'Rain, rain, go to Spain,' they shouted. And presently their mother, who must have heard the noise and knew, appeared from next door, and Vern and Amy vanished through the hedge.

I stood there, depressed about the rain, and then I put Vern's bat and ball underneath the house, and went indoors. 'Stupes!' I said to myself. I had been batting when the rains came down. It was only when I was batting that the rains came down! I wiped my feet so I wouldn't soil the sheets, and went up to the bed. I was sitting, sad, and wishing that the rain would really go away – go to Spain, as Vern said – when my heart seemed to jump out of me. A deafening peal of thunder struck across the sky. Quickly I closed the window. The rain hammered awfully on the roof-top, and I kept tense for the thunder which I knew would break again and for the unearthly flashes of lightning.

Secretly I was afraid of the violent weather. I was afraid of the rain, and of the thunder and the lightning that came with them, and of the sea beating against the headlands, and of the storm-winds, and of everything being so death-like when the rains were gone. I stared again at another flash of lightning and before I had recovered from this, yet another terrifying peal of thunder hit the air. I screamed. I heard my mother running into the room. Thunder struck again and I dashed under the bed.

'Selo! Selo! First bat!' Vern shouted from the road. The rains had ceased and the sun had come out, but I had not quite recovered yet. I brought myself reluctantly to look out from the front door, and there was Vern, grinning and impatient and beckoning me.

'First bat,' he said. And as if noticing my indifference he looked towards Amy who was just coming out to play. 'Who second bat?' he said.

'Me!' I said.

'Me!' shouted Amy almost at the same time.

'Amy second bat,' Vern said.

'No, I said "me" first,' I protested.

Vern grew impatient while Amy and I argued. Then an idea seemed to strike him. He took out a penny from his pocket. 'Toss for it,' he said. 'What you want?'

'Heads,' I called.

'Tail,' cried Amy, 'tail bound to come!'

The coin went up in the air, fell down and over- turned, showing tails.

'I'm not playing!' I cried, stung. And as that did not seem to disturb them enough, I ran towards where I had put Vern's bat and ball and disappeared with them behind our house. Then I flung them with all my strength into the bushes.

When I came back to the front of the house, Vern was standing there dumbfounded. 'Selo, where's the bat and ball?'

I was fuming. 'I don't know about any bat and ball!'

'Tell on him,' Amy cried. 'He throw them away.'

Vern's mouth twisted into a forced smile. 'What's an old bat and ball,' he said.

But as he walked out of the yard I saw tears glinting from the corners of his eyes.

For the rest of that rainy season we never played cricket in the road again. Sometimes the rains ceased and the sun came out brightly, and I heard the voices of Amy and Vern on the other side of the fence. At such times I would go out into the road and whistle to myself, hoping they would hear me and come out, but they never did, and I knew they were still very angry and would never forgive me.

And so the rainy season went on. And it was as fearful as ever with the thunder and lightning and waves roaring in the bay, and the strong winds. But the people who talked of all this said that was the way Mayaro was, and they laughed about it. And sometimes when through the rain and even thunder I heard Vern's voice on the other side of the fence, shouting 'Rain, rain, go to Spain', it puzzled me how it could be so. For often I had made up my mind I would be brave, but when the thunder cracked I always dashed under the bed.

It was the beginning of the new year when I saw Vern and Amy again. The rainy season was, happily, long past, and the day was hot and bright, and as I walked towards home I saw that I was walking toward Vern and Amy just about to start cricket in the road. My heart thumped violently. They looked strange and new as if they had gone away, far, and did not want to come back any more. They did not notice me until I came up quite near, and then I saw Amy start, her face all lit up.

'Vern . . .' she cried, 'Vern look – look Selo!'

Embarrassed, I looked at the ground and at the trees, and at the orange sky, and I was so happy I did not know what to say. Vern stared at me, a strange grin on his face. He was ripping the cellophane paper off a brand new bat.

'Selo, here – *you* is first bat,' he said gleefully.

And I cried as though it were raining and I was afraid.

MICHAEL ANTHONY

What do you think about Selo throwing Vern's bat and ball away?

Why does Selo cry at the end?

Can you remember any quarrels you had with friends while on holiday? How did you become friends again?

 # Assignments

Choose several of the following to write about:

1. What I Like and Dislike about Holidays.
2. The Best Holiday I Have Ever Had.
3. A Wet Day on Holiday.
4. My Ideal Holiday.
5. Setting Out. Write about the disorder and chaos and rush of getting packed and ready to go on holiday in time.
6. The Day Out. Describe a day's outing you have had with your family or write a story about such an outing.
7. The First Time I Saw the Sea. This could be real or imaginary.
8. The Pleasures of Spending Holidays at Home. Write about all the discomforts and inconveniences you avoid by staying at home.
9. Write about the things you enjoy while on holiday from school.
10. One of the things that often happens during holidays is that relations come to stay. Write about real or imaginary visitors.

11. Write about the pleasures and attractions of the seaside for a holiday.
12. Write a poem about swimming in the sea or playing with sand or going out in a boat or any other seaside activity.

Language

A. Alliteration

Look at some of the phrases Dylan Thomas uses in 'Holiday Memory':

> a slap of sea and a tickle of sand
> a wince and whinny of bathers dancing into deceptive water
> a silent hullabaloo of balloons
> with cruel nails and capacious mouth
> the town girls bold as brass
> to run the water loud and long.

Dylan Thomas was interested in sounds and the kind of effects words and particular associations of words have. 'Hullabaloo of balloons,' for instance, suggests somehow by the sound it makes the kind of thing it is describing. In other words, it is an example of onomatopoeia. Try saying the phrase aloud. In fact, choose almost any phrase from this piece of writing and say it aloud and you will find that it fits into the mouth and runs off the lips with great effect.

Looking at the phrases quoted above again, you will see that many of them are made effective because the same sound or the same letter is used in a number of the words. Pick out the letter or sound in each phrase.

The technical name given to this kind of figure of speech is alliteration. This is the repetition of the same letter or sound to produce a particular effect. The device is common in ordinary speech. Expressions like 'rant and rave', 'toss and turn' are examples of alliteration. A more sustained example is this from a poem by Tennyson where the poet is trying to create the sleepy soothing effect of a summer afternoon:

> The moan of doves in immemorial elms,
> And murmuring of innumerable bees.

As can be seen, onomatopoeia and alliteration often go together. Comment on their use in the example given above.

The point of alliteration is to give emphasis to particular words by beginning with the same letter (as in 'with cruel nails and capacious mouth') or to create a particular effect by the repetition of an appropriate sound (as in the example by Tennyson).

Write five sentences each containing an example of alliteration.

B. Sentences

Look again at the opening of Dylan Thomas's 'Holiday Memory':

August Bank Holiday. A tune on an ice-cream cornet. A slap of sea and a tickle of sand. A fanfare of sunshades opening. A wince and whinny of bathers dancing into deceptive water. A tuck of dresses. A rolling of trousers. A compromise of paddlers. A sunburn of girls and a lark of boys. A silent hullabaloo of balloons.

Are these sentences?
What is a sentence?
What effect is Dylan Thomas trying to create?
Rewrite a couple of the phrases as 'more complete' sentences.
What do they lose or gain compared with the original?

Remember that Dylan Thomas was a very accomplished writer, and he could make his way of writing work in a way that a less experienced and less talented writer can't. It is normally safer to keep to writing which uses the more common kinds of sentences containing verbs. *For practice though, write a paragraph on one of the following imitating the kind of sentences and the kind of playing with words that Dylan Thomas uses in the opening paragraph of 'Holiday Memory':*

> a busy high street
> a supermarket
> the playground at break
> the circus
> the fair.

Vocabulary

A. What is the difference between 'a holy day' and 'a holiday'?

B. Collective Nouns

Again in the opening paragraph of 'Holiday Memory', Dylan Thomas uses a number of words he has invented to suggest a collection of things in the manner of a *flock* of sheep or a *herd* of cows. For example,

a *fanfare* of sunshades
a *tuck* of dresses
a *hullabaloo* of balloons

The name given to a word that speaks of several persons or things of the same kind regarded as one group is a collective noun. Here are some more examples:

a *school* of whales
a *company* of soldiers
a *pack* of wolves
a *swarm* of bees

See how many more collective nouns you can think of and write them down.

Dylan Thomas invented some fanciful collective nouns. Can you invent some more? Here are a couple to get you going:

a *haunting* of ghosts
a *splash* of fountains

A collective noun is normally regarded as being singular, and it should therefore have a singular verb. For example,

The flock was grazing in the field.
The herd of cows gives a good yield of milk.

Choose ten of the collective nouns you wrote down earlier and put each of them into a sentence using a singular verb.

 ## Spelling

A. Geographical Places

Names of towns and places are sometimes spelled very distinctively and you have to learn their peculiarities in order to spell them correctly. Here are some names with which you might have difficulty. Learn them. Not all of them are places you might go to on holiday!

Antarctic	Lincoln
Arctic	Mediterranean
Australia	Mississippi
Britain	Missouri
Brittany	Morocco
Caribbean	Philippines
Carlisle	Rhodesia
Edinburgh	Riviera
English Channel	Saskatchewan
Ghana	Skye
Gibraltar	Southampton
Gloucester	Torquay
Guinea	Worcester
Guyana	Yugoslavia
Leicester	Yukon

Can you think of any other names that should be added to the list?

B. Earnest/Ernest

Here are some more words which can give the wrong meaning if they are spelled incorrectly. Make sure you know the difference between them.

earnest	Ernest	
envelop	envelope	
faint	feint	
fair	fare	
feat	feet	
flair	flare	
flu	flue	
fogy	foggy	
forego	forgo	
forth	fourth	
gaol	jail	goal
geezer	geyser	
genteel	Gentile	gentle
gild	guild	

gilt	guilt	
grate	great	
groan	grown	
hail	hale	
hangar	hanger	
heal	heel	
hear	here	
heard	herd	
hew	hue	
hoard	horde	
hole	whole	
holly	holy	wholly

Use some of these words in sentences.

Activities

A. 1. Walk as you would on the beach. Decide whether you are walking on loose sand, wet sand, in the water, over rocks. Then change from one to another.

2. You are gazing into a rock pool watching tiny fish swimming about. You put your hand in the water and try to catch one of the fish.

3. In mime, demonstrate how you would put up a deck-chair.

4. In mime, change out of your wet bathing-costume into your ordinary clothes.

B. 1. You are on holiday at the seaside with a group of friends. You are exploring the rocks when you come upon the opening of a cave. It is just big enough for you to get inside. What do you find?

2. You and your friends are at home bored with nothing to do. Various ideas are put forward, but none of them is greeted with any enthusiasm. Then one of you has a brilliant suggestion.

3. You are on the beach with your friends when one of you cuts his foot on a piece of glass from a broken bottle. Work out how you cope with the situation.

4. You have arrived with your family at a hotel. It is a rather grand hotel. Work out how you would respond to the rather superior receptionist and the rather haughty porter. To complicate matters one of your suitcases is missing . . .

C. 1. Make a survey of the class to find out where people have been on holiday. See how many different places are included.

2. Visit a travel agent's and get some holiday brochures. Choose a holiday from one of them and say why you picked that particular one.

3. Again using holiday brochures, find out as much as you can about the holiday attractions of a particular country. Write about it and illustrate your writing with pictures from the brochure.

4. Make an advertisement for a hotel, a holiday camp, a seaside resort or an activity holiday, using words and pictures. Try to make it as attractive as possible.

5. Write two postcards from two different people having a holiday in the same place at the same time – one of them enjoying it and the other disliking it.

Reading List

Many novels written for young readers tell of the kind of adventures they can have while on holiday. Try to read one or more of the following and see whether you enjoy them.

Marjorie Lloyd, *Fell Farm Campers*
   Fell Farm Holiday
   Fell Farm for Christmas
Peter Dickinson, *Emma Tupper's Diary*
Eve Garnett, *Holiday at the Dew Drop Inn*
M. K. Harris, *Emily and the Headmistress*
Noël Streatfeild, *The Growing Summer*
Jill Paton Walsh, *Goldengrove*
Arthur Ransome, *Swallows and Amazons*
Stephen Fennimore, *Bush Holiday*
Philippa Pearce, *Minnow on the Say*
   Tom's Midnight Garden
Jerome K. Jerome, *Three Men in a Boat*
Dylan Thomas, *Quite Early One Morning*

CONSOLIDATION 3

A. Parts of Speech

We have now looked at all the parts of speech.

Here is a chance to revise them and make sure you can distinguish between them.

PART OF SPEECH	DESCRIPTION	EXAMPLES
noun	the name of something	cat, Margaret, river, shop
pronoun	a word that can take the place of a noun	she, they, we, me
adjective	a word that describes a noun or pronoun	red, soft, long, stupid
adverb	a word that modifies a verb, an adjective or another adverb	usually, very, happily, truly
verb	a word that tells us the action someone or something is performing; the state he or it is in; the process of change he or it is going through	look, run, watch, walk be, appear become, grow
conjunction	a word that joins other words or statements	and, but, for, although, after, while
interjection	a word that expresses an exclamation	pooh, phew, ah, oh
preposition	a word that shows the relationship between one word and another	to, for, by, with

B. Figures of Speech

What is a figure of speech?

Here is a summary of all the figures of speech we have looked at in this book.

FIGURE OF SPEECH	DESCRIPTION	EXAMPLES
simile	a comparison in which we say one thing is *like* another	The thief was as wily as a fox. The evening sun was like an orange.
metaphor	a comparison in which we say one thing *is* another (which it literally cannot be)	My heart leaped into my mouth. The river snaked through the fields.
personification	a metaphor in which an inanimate object or animal is given the qualities of a human being	The daffodils were dancing in the breeze. The rooks were speculating on the weather.
onomatopoeia	the use of a word or words whose sound suggests the sense	chirrup; jingle-jangle; melodious murmur
alliteration	the use of the same letter or sound in a number of words to produce a particular effect	Buy British; spick-and-span; bright and breezy

C. Punctuation Marks

Revise these punctuation marks and make sure you know how to use them.

PUNCTUATION MARK	DESCRIPTION	EXAMPLES
full stop	(i) used to show the end of a sentence (ii) used to show an abbreviation	The clock stopped chiming. B.A., viz., Esq.
comma	(i) used to separate different statements in a sentence (ii) used to separate the different items of a list (iii) used before and after words or phrases added to a sentence	When you reach the station, turn right. The shop sold sweets, newspapers, magazines and cigarettes. It is, of course, shut on Sundays.
exclamation mark	used to indicate strong feeling	Fire! How could you!
question mark	used to indicate a question	Where are you going?

D. Mood

What is the mood of a verb?

We have now looked at the four moods which a verb can have. Here is your chance to check that you have understood the difference between them.

MOOD	DESCRIPTION	EXAMPLES
indicative	used for factual statements and questions	It is raining heavily. Will you be going out?
imperative	used for orders, commands, requests and entreaties	Search for it. Please help me.
subjunctive	used to express a wish or uncertainty, hesitation or possibility	*May* you come home safely. If I *were* old, I should sit in the sun all day.
conditional	used to express actions which are conditional (that is, depend) on something else	It *would be* pleasant if all the family were here. I *should go* if I were you.

E. Language

1. What is a paragraph?
2. Why should a piece of writing be divided up into paragraphs?
3. Write a sentence containing a verb in the subjunctive mood.
4. Write a sentence containing a verb in the conditional mood.
5. Name the moods of the verbs in this sentence: 'If I *were* the headmaster, I *should give* the school a half-holiday.'
6. Name the moods of the verbs in this sentence: '*Speak* the truth if he *should ask* you.'
7. Write down twenty prepositions.
8. What part of speech is the word 'off' in this sentence? – 'Get off that table.'
9. Write two sentences, one containing the word 'down' as a preposition and the other as an adverb.
10. When do we use an exclamation mark and when do we use a question mark?
11. Give an example of a sentence containing an exclamation mark and another containing a question mark.
12. Give an example of alliteration.
13. What are the two main effects of alliteration?
14. What is a sentence?
15. What does it begin with and what does it end with?

F. Vocabulary

1. What was the original meaning of 'epic'?
2. Give three examples of words whose original strong meaning has been weakened by constant use.
3. What is the feminine equivalent of the word 'comedian'?
4. What is the masculine equivalent of a countess?
5. What is a suffix?
6. What is a prefix?
7. What suffix usually denotes feminine gender?
8. What gender is 'kitten'?
9. What gender is 'the sun'?
10. What suffix usually denotes an agent?
11. Give two words which mean 'one who listens'.

12. Give two words which mean 'one who tells a story'.
13. What is a crescendo?
14. What does 'gruesome' mean?
15. What is a collective noun?
16. Does a collective noun normally take a singular or a plural verb?
17. What is the collective noun for a group of schoolchildren?
18. What is the collective noun for a group of ships?
19. 'A covey' is the collective noun for a group of . . . . .?
20. 'A gaggle' is the collective noun for a group of . . . . .?

23. What is the plural of 'basketful'?
24. Name five nouns which are the same in the singular and the plural.
25. Name five nouns which are nearly always found in the plural.
26. Spell the name of the sea which borders Spain, Italy and Greece.
27. Spell the name of the sea in which the West Indies lie.
28. The United Kingdom is also known as Great . . . . . .
29. Distinguish between 'flair' and 'flare'.
30. Distinguish between 'hoard' and 'horde'.

G. Spelling

1. Spell the two words which mean 'inspiring fear and wonder'.
2. What is the rule for 'i' before 'e'?
3. Give ten examples which follow this rule.
4. Give four exceptions.
5. Give five words which are spelled 'e' before 'i' when the sound is not 'ee'.
6. How do you spell the word meaning 'one who observes'?
7. How do you spell the word meaning 'one who gardens'?
8. How do you spell the word meaning 'one who edits'?
9. How do you spell the word meaning 'one who acts'?
10. What is the plural of 'gas'?
11. What is the plural of 'donkey'?
12. What is the rule for forming the plural by adding '-es'?
13. What is the rule for forming the plural of words ending in 'y'?
14. What is the plural of 'shelf'?
15. What is the plural of 'thief'?
16. What is the plural of 'dwarf'?
17. What is the plural of 'roof'?
18. What is the singular of 'dice'?
19. What is the rule for forming the plural of words ending in 'o'?
20. Give six examples of this rule.
21. Give six exceptions to this rule.
22. What is the plural of 'passer-by'?

Index of Authors and Titles

Index of Topics

(The main references only are given)

150